Seeking Allah's Hierarchy

SEEKING ALLAH'S HIERARCHY

Caste, Labor, and Islam in India

P. C. Saidalavi

PENN

UNIVERSITY OF PENNSYLVANIA PRESS

PHILADELPHIA

Published by
University of Pennsylvania Press
Philadelphia, Pennsylvania 19104–4112 USA
www.pennpress.org

EU Authorized Representative: Easy Access
System Europe—Mustamäe tee 50, 10621 Tallinn,
Estonia, gpsr.requests@easproject.com

Printed in the United States of America on acid-free paper
10 9 8 7 6 5 4 3 2 1

A Cataloging-in-Publication record is
available from the Library of Congress

Hardcover ISBN 978-1-5128-2848-1
Paperback ISBN 978-1-5128-2849-8
eBook ISBN 978-1-5128-2850-4

To the spirit and passion of relentless fighters for antassu *and egalitarianism, the late P. K. Abu Nilambur and the late M. K. Muhammad Valanchery*

CONTENTS

GLOSSARY

Adutthōn	barber caste among Ezhavas
Angādikkār	townspeople
Antassu	dignity
Baradari	brotherhood
Dars	mosque-based religious institution
Fiqh	Islamic jurisprudence
Hadith	sayings and deeds of the prophet Muhammad
Halal	what is allowed by law in Islam
Halalkhor	one who eats halal food
Harām	what is forbidden by law in Islam
Janmis	hereditary landlords
Jāti	caste or subcaste
Jonaka	a derivation of Sonagam, meaning Arab
Jutha-Mappila	a Jew on the Malabar coast
Kadappurattukār	beach-people
Kāfir	nonbeliever
Kāranavar	senior male member of the family
Kufuv	compatibility
Mahallu	a community attached to a Friday prayer mosque
Makrooh	actions accruing reward if avoided, and unpunishable if committed
Mukkuvar	Hindu fisher caste
Mundu	unstitched, wraparound cloth, worn like a sarong
Murid	disciple, in Sufi terminology
Najas	impure
Nasab	Arabic word meaning clan or tribe, usually translated as taravād by Muslims in Malabar
OBC	other backward classes
Ossān	a male Muslim barber

Ossāthi	a female Muslim barber
Otthān	an unpolished form of ossān
Otthōn	an agreeable person to everyone
Otthavan	an agreeable person to everyone
Pir	teacher in Sufi terminology
Pūsalān	a Muslim fisher
Pūzhi	sand
Puthiya	new
Sonaga	another term for *jonaka*, see above
Sonagam	Arabia
Taravād	originally meaning a matrilineal joint household but now commonly used to signify an ancestral house
Thangal	a descendant of the prophet Muhammad
Thwahāra	purity

A NOTE ON TRANSLATION AND TRANSLITERATION

For both Malayalam and Arabic words, the Library of Congress system of transliteration has been adopted. For the proper names in Malayalam, I have retained the spelling the Library adopted. I have italicized both Malayalam and Arabic words in the first instance, providing approximate English translation on my own in parentheses.

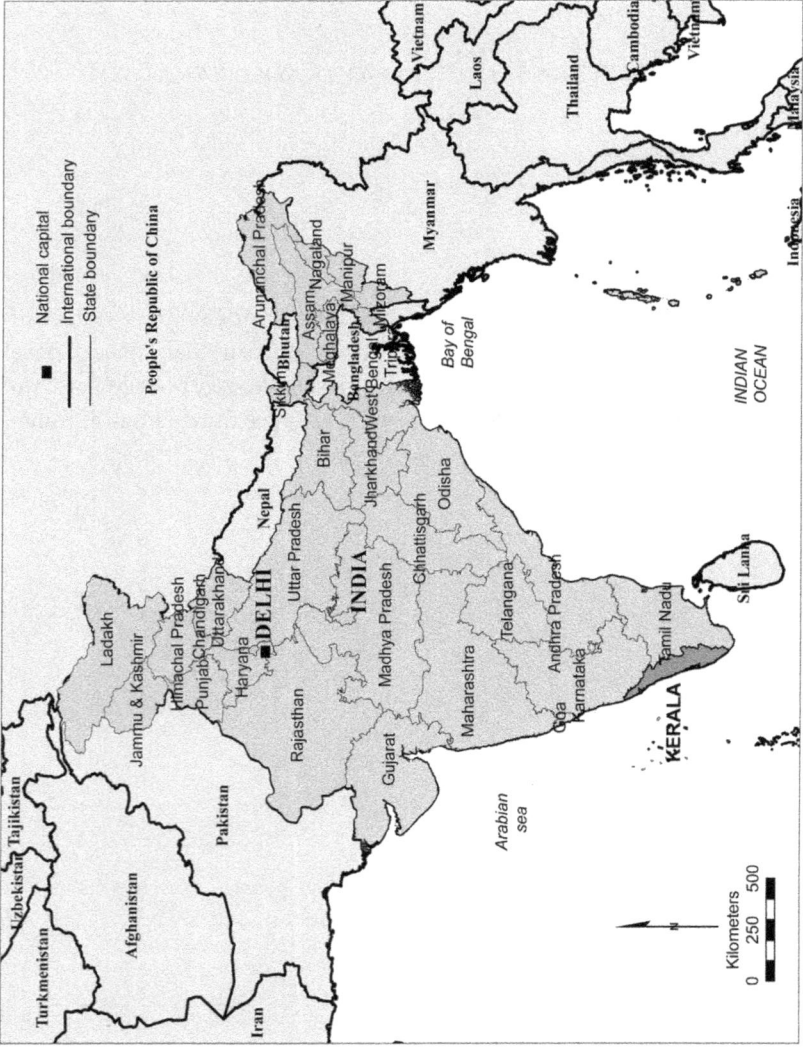

Figure 1. Map of India © Sharath Raj B.

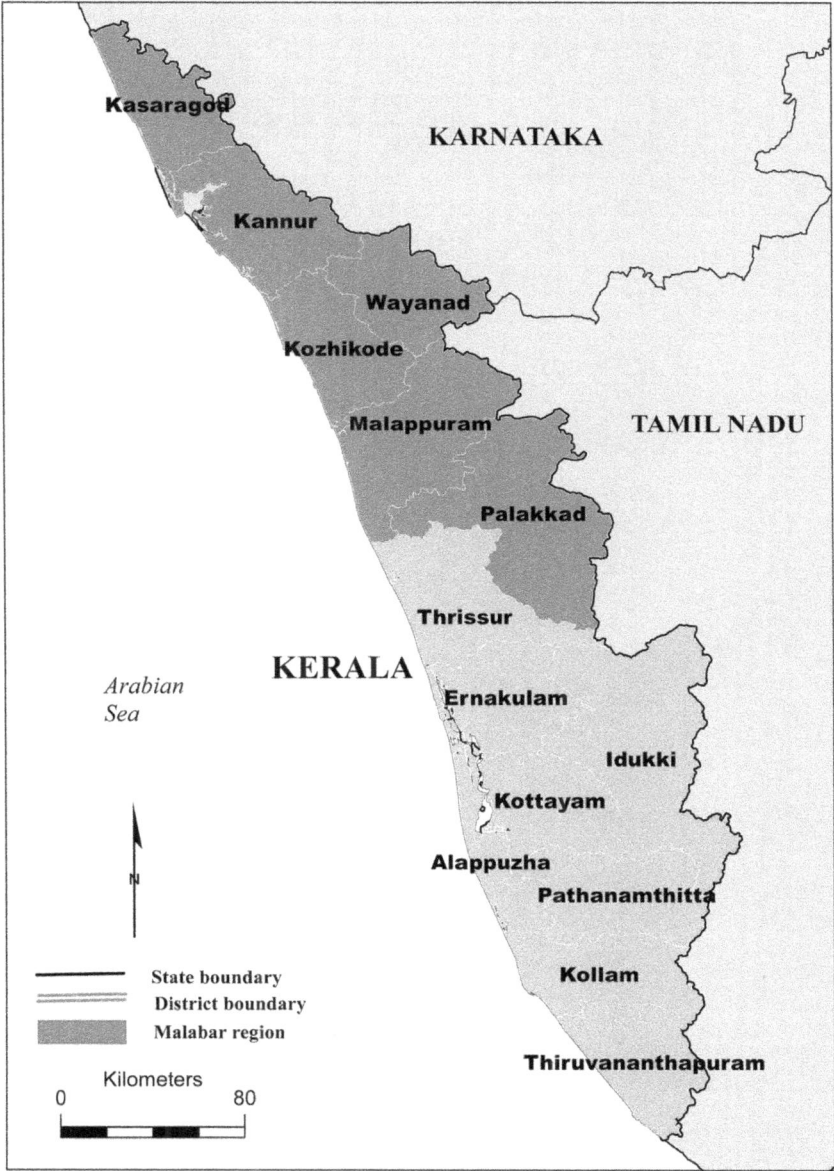

Figure 2. Map of Kerala © Sharath Raj B.

This book investigates the existence of "caste" among Muslims in India. Before diving into the material, however, it is critical to introduce the origins of this project to underscore its political valence and academic importance. As an Indian Muslim myself, I viewed the category of caste as the foundation of Hindu social life. I had never thought about the idea of "caste" as even a remote possibility for social organization among Muslims in India until 2013, far into the middle of my Master of Philosophy (MPhil) program at Jawaharlal Nehru University (JNU), New Delhi. That, too, occurred not as an active choice. My original MPhil proposal submitted to JNU was on Indian Muslim identity in a world-system perspective. My supervisor, Arshad Alam insisted that I should ideally begin my sociology career by conducting an ethnographic study rather than researching an abstract theory. Though I reluctantly agreed to formulate an ethnographic problem, I was not convinced until much later. I burned a lot of midnight oil thinking about various projects, but none impressed him. The difficulty was that I was trained until then in English literature and cultural studies and I could not formulate a sociological problem. Seeing my difficulty, he asked me one day whether there is "caste" among Muslims in Malabar. "No, it is a Hindu institution," I quickly replied. Then he asked, "Why don't you find that out through your MPhil?" I was perplexed. He added, "That is your topic for MPhil dissertation." That is how my curiosity, perplexity, agony, and challenge began: Can we talk about "caste" among Muslims? Is it a suitable category for understanding Muslim social life in the Indian subcontinent? This book will argue that caste does exist, by postulating "caste" as a regime of hierarchical inequality based on birth structuring social relations on the Indian subcontinent. It maintains that Muslims in India do imbibe some features and properties we commonly associate with the Hindu caste system—even if with some modification. More important, it shows how Muslims negotiate with hierarchy, Islam, and Hindu social structure in the region of Malabar, South India.

One of the most influential forays into the caste labyrinth in the Muslim context was Imtiaz Ahmad's pioneering volume *Caste and Social Stratification Among Muslims in India*. Reading it, I realized that there are "real" social divisions among Muslims that often affect how certain groups of people conduct themselves in the world, undertake certain kinds of jobs, express and maintain sociality, and nurture long-standing relationships through marriages. I was also curious to see an article in that volume, written by Victor D'Souza, on Muslims in Malabar. The categorization of social groups and the descriptive details provided by D'Souza, all were quite familiar to me. I began to wonder aloud with my interlocutors whether there is in fact "caste" among Muslims.

As I talked to people belonging to various social groups in Malabar, some were confused and perplexed by my query, others opposed the very conceptual category of "caste." A few others concurred with the existence of "caste" among Muslims but proclaimed that it is a "Hindu" influence among Muslims. Overall, people were clearly reluctant to accept any insinuation of deep relationships between caste and Islam. The characteristic way in which this was aired was like this, "There is caste among Muslims in India, but there is no caste in Islam." This book tussles with such a claim, adopting an anthropological vantage point, interrogating meanings, values, and practices, rather than focusing purely on scripture, theology, or textbook accounts.

The clear distinctions my interlocutors tried to posit between a metaphysical and an existential viewpoint seem untenable. Such a position tries to wrest and abstract religion from its social locations and cultural rootedness and limits its contours to the theological. If the realm of religion can be delimited to the theological, the social world—where human beings try to access and practice religion—in turn, becomes a site of imperfect operationalization, a realm of incompleteness, and a space of infatuation. This definitely is a legitimate way in which Muslims look at the world, and recent anthropological scholarship has correctly conceptualized this division into the binary of the normative and everyday (Fadil and Fernando 2015). To be fair, I should also add that the domain of the everyday is also understood in other ways, as a location where the normative plays out and also as a category that challenges the very conception of the normative. In this sense, a Muslim could be viewed as attempting to embody and practice the normative Islam, but, because the subject is always already located in the everyday, she has to struggle and aspire to realize the normative. This kind of method does justice to how Muslims view the world. However, such a position precludes the complexity of subjectivity. Muslim subjectivity cannot be exhausted either in the realm of the normative where, to follow Saba Mahmood's (2005) key anthropological proposition, Muslims modulate themselves to be pious or in the realm of the everyday where Muslims attempt to become subjects of various persuasions and values and, as a result, haggle with a singular identity of the normative pious subject.

However, the practice of social hierarchy, if one attends to it, presents a different picture. The normative cannot definitely be straitjacketed and limited to the theological. It needs also to be understood in terms of how it manifests itself in the world. This is important because Muslims claim that they are "living" Islam, as the very noun "Muslim" denotes with respect to Islam. If "living" is also the domain of various practices, we need to understand the connections between living and the ideal. I suggest that there is a peculiar way in which both the living and the ideal, or the metaphysical and the existential, or the normative and the everyday are co-produced, formulated, embodied, and practiced. If Muslims accept that there is social hierarchy among them, there are characteristic ways in which it also connects with Islam. The title of this book, *Seeking Allah's Hierarchy*, precisely tries to locate those relationships as they manifest through values, practices, meanings, and forms of reasoning in Muslims' lives.

A book on caste among Muslims will be odd to some readers, particularly on the Indian subcontinent where caste is immediately identified with Hindu social structure. It becomes even more intriguing as Muslims also largely subscribe to such a view and insist that there is no caste in Islam. The confusions and particularities of the hierarchical phenomenon became evident to me as I reflected on my own identity as a "Mappila Muslim," a Muslim whose primary identity is shaped by the term *Mappila*. Mappila connotes both conversion from Hindu castes as well as the communion between Arab men and Indian local women through marriages. I felt that both of these elements that constitute my identity were already embedded in hierarchical relations. Like most Mappilas in Malabar, I believed that "caste" was a Hindu institution, and that Muslims did not have anything to do with it. The question of caste among Muslims began to appear more starkly during my studies at JNU in New Delhi in 2015. While the interest in caste remained an academic endeavor initially, the everyday realities of it began to appear more clearly. In my own life, I encountered it more forcefully when I actively started looking for marital alliances in 2017. Knowing me and my research and political leanings well, a friend suggested I meet and converse with a potential marriage partner who came from the coastal belt of Malabar. Before doing that, I presented the case to my mother over the phone, and her immediate response was, "We don't want that. Is it because there are no girls here?" Her statements were clear; as a Mappila family, she did not want to have a marital alliance with a family from the coastal belt. Because Muslim fishers live along the coast, the inland Mappilas look at the coast with derision and project it as an enclave of ignorance and danger. Hearing this response from my mother, I did not pursue the matter further, telling my friend that his proposal would not work out within my family. I realized then that it is one thing to conduct research on caste relations and quite another to be able to translate my own research and political commitments to restructuring social relations through a marital alliance with a woman belonging to the lower rung of social hierarchy among Muslims.

My mother is a devout Muslim—the embodiment of piety emphasized throughout The Book. She conducts all the obligatory prayers and recites the Quran, hagiographic songs of Sufis and holy men, and prayer manuals for accruing reward from Allah. While following the normative precepts of Islam, she did not have any qualms about segregating Muslim communities by status-based (geographically mapped) marital compatibility. She took it as a natural response, one that is shaped by her own familial networks, neighborhood relations, and understandings of Islam; they all followed marital compatibility as a criterion for distinguishing between "different types" of Muslims. I, too, was shaped by these ideas and shades of hierarchy, and I was socialized into them from childhood through stories, educational institutions, and friendship circles, among other things (what Pierre Bourdieu might call a Habitus).[1] Invisible lines and more clearly contoured ones mark ("other") Muslim communities in Malabar so that arranged marriages between various social groups remain rare.

Further reflections on my position in the field led me to focus on my identity as a person who identifies as a Muslim. I have studied in madrassas and other higher forms of religious institutions in Malabar. There is indeed a hierarchy in these spaces between those who are offering instruction and those who are pursuing knowledge, and between those who possess religious knowledge and the laity. These are all forms of hierarchies recognized by religious traditions as virtuous and beneficial, where reciprocal exchanges between student/layperson and teacher reflect the values, institutions, and aspirations of the religious endeavor. My confusion has been that if hierarchical relationships are evaluated as natural, desirable, and valuable in religious institutions and interactions, won't that also affect the social interactions of everyday life? Can the everyday social be dissected as separate and distinct from the religious plane? I find that hierarchies curtail opportunities and relationships in ways that are discriminatory and unequal as and when they are used as a scale of inherent social worth. My own experiences of hierarchies in daily interactions and the institutional settings of madrassas, schools, and marriages compelled me to investigate these sites more closely through the medium of ethnography. It is within this double-bind—as a Mappila and a Muslim, socialized and still partly enmeshed in these hierarchical relations— that I am offering an ethnographic analysis.

While I do not place myself as a key actor in this book, others felt my own positionality as much as it informed my own research questions. To this end, it is also an auto-critique, by which I mean it is also a set of reflections that emerge out of my own identity and interactions in the "field": as a Muslim, a Mappila, a male, and a researcher. These have direct bearing on how I conducted my fieldwork; the kind of questions I asked, and I could ask; and the nature of events I could attend and others to which I was not privy. My hope is that my work can help to build an understanding of caste among Muslims and reveal some of the mechanisms by which it operates and endures. I hope, too, that research that follows will deploy a range of views to probe these issues still further.

Seeking Allah's Hierarchy

CHAPTER 1

Values of Hierarchy

It is value that brings universes into being.

—David Graeber (2013)

On an early morning in June 2019, I walked with my backpack into the lobby of a small hotel in an inland town in Malabar, South India. In my fieldwork journeys, the backpack was a constant companion, holding water bottle, pen, and notebook. Here, it had come with me to a semi-urban town located about 50 kilometers from my home, and I traveled there by hopping on three buses. Muhammad, a retired schoolteacher from southern Kerala who belonged to the Muslim barber community, greeted me in the lobby. While the status of the barber community is often described as analogous to a lower Hindu caste, Muslim barbers in Malabar are better understood as belonging to a lower socioeconomic class. Barbers, about 3 percent of the population of fourteen million Muslims, are both men who perform physical tasks of grooming or circumcision and women who commonly conduct grooming and midwifery; all practices that upper socioeconomic classes eschew. Muhammad was tall, slim, and swarthy. He wore a white *mundu* (an unstitched, wraparound cloth, worn like a sarong) and a white long-sleeved polyester shirt. The cuff of the shirt was folded a bit, showing his silver-colored wristwatch. His hair was black, long, and combed back. He had come to the hotel to participate in a meeting convened by various Muslim barber organizations in Kerala. He represented the Muslim Socialist Association (MSA)—a barber organization working among barbers in southern Kerala. I had called him a few days back, and we planned to meet close on the heels of their meeting. I was led to a conference room where around thirty men, representing various organizations active among

Muslim barbers in Kerala, had gathered. They had assembled to discuss the long-standing humiliation faced by the community from Muslims, particularly religious scholars, and to brainstorm ideas to counter their own enduring predicament.

As I learned from Muhammad, what triggered this present meeting was an incident that had occurred a few weeks earlier at a mosque in a prominent inland town. It was 2019, and Ramadan, the Arabic month of fasting, fell in May. Ramadan is seen as a month of exceptional piety in which Muslims intensify their pious activities, such as prayer, recitation of the Quran, and charity. During this period, there is also a special prayer (*tarāvīh*) conducted every night at mosques after the fast is broken. At the mosque in the town, about six hundred people congregated for the special prayer every day. The religious scholar leading the prayer conducted a question-and-answer session after the prayers, responding to questions directed at him by the believers. Most Muslims sought answers for their pressing moral and religious dilemmas and resolved their doubts regarding proper religious conduct, correct ways of prayer, and any other questions related to the Islamic way of living. During one such session, a participant asked whether children born of adultery can be allowed to lead the prayer for Muslims. The religious scholar responded that they could not. He further reasoned that, much like Muslim barbers, children born of adultery are not suitable to lead a prayer and, if conducted, such prayers will be deemed invalid.

One of the people in the congregation was a barber. He was mortified to hear the scholar equating children born of adultery with barbers. He reported the incident to the community following which a meeting was called to discuss the urgent incident and plan a detailed course of action. As a researcher on Muslim barbers, I was invited by Muhammad to attend the meeting, and he introduced me to the organizers at the hotel. I was offered a seat in the conference hall, and I talked to a few people who sat on chairs nearby. But, before the meeting formally started, Muhammad summoned me outside the hall and said that the organizing committee members decided not to allow me—a non-barber—to attend their community deliberations. While Muhammad believed that researchers like me can make various interventions and generate discussions in the community on issues faced by barbers, the organizers believed that internal discussions within the community should not go public. As I belong to the Mappila[1]—a majority-Muslim social group from whom barbers face subordination and humiliation—it has often been difficult to access some of the programs and discussions conducted by barbers and, while I have been honored to be invited into these spaces on occasion, such access is not guaranteed or expected.

Questions of Hierarchy

While barbers felt restive about caste practices and values that operate among Muslims in Malabar, they were dead set against using piety as a legitimate criterion for constructing the social worth of themselves as low. This incident of humiliation appalled barbers because it challenged their claim to piety as a universal capability that Allah has endowed in every individual. Whether one realized this capability in one's life was an altogether different matter because, as Muhammad told me, Allah professes in the Quran that piety (*taqwa*) is the only value He looks for among his subjects and this is the sole criterion for distinction in front of Him. Barbers accepted this religious hierarchy based on piety but believed that the status of achieving piety was open to all Muslims irrespective of birth, genealogy, wealth, and occupation. Barbers looked at the "piety-based social strata" in a positive light and considered piety as a paramount value in one's life. Barbers accepted that social worth and status should be achieved qualities through religious devotion and not fixed from birth. They vehemently challenge the ways in which piety itself is often used to categorize and subordinate social groups.

Hierarchy is accepted as a legitimate value for organizing social relations not only among Muslims but also among other people in various parts of the world (Marlow 1997; Dilley 2004; Ku and Gibson 2019; Rio 2014; Rio and Smedal 2009; Haynes and Hickel 2016; Bell and Pei 2020). In their study on social hierarchy in China, Bell and Pei (2020) note that it is often accepted in the Shandong province of China for people to be treated unequally in social gatherings. But that behavior is not based on any kind of discriminatory principle. Rather, it is considered desirable and a just form of hierarchy. A hierarchy becomes just when there is a possibility of role reversal, and it also is not based on any ascriptive characteristics such as race, gender, and caste. Similarly, while Muslim barbers accept hierarchy in terms of piety as just, they contest other hierarchical practices and sensibilities existing among Muslims.

Muslims order, negotiate, justify, and contest hierarchical relations in their communities through a range of values, such as piety, genealogy, and wealth. Yet, piety remains a primary value and an ideal in Muslim social lives. These values are sometimes mediated through Islamic notions and at other times augmented by the cultural repertoire of the broader social milieu of caste and Hindu social structure. It is important to emphasize what I mean by caste here. I consider caste as a regime of hierarchical inequality based on birth, which is operative on the Indian subcontinent, expressed in various modes of social spheres.[2] My aim is to showcase the negotiations and conflicts that take place among Muslims over the interpretation of caste, Islam, and Hindu social structure. I show that Muslim caste works on its own terms on the Indian subcontinent, drawing on a rich set of values, practices, and discourses. This is not to say that caste as it gets articulated among Hindus has not been influential in the shaping of hierarchical relations, not least when many Muslims are former converts. Rather, I argue that those who seek to understand Muslim life as based on a Hindu blueprint rob Muslims of agency (Islam as a derivative discourse), as such views are historically inaccurate and anthropologically misleading.

My aim in presenting Malabar as a case study is not to suggest that it is a synecdoche of Muslims across the Indian subcontinent. That would be defeating the ethnographic purpose altogether. Rather, with its unique history and social formations, Malabar acts as an excellent case study to engage with and question how caste and intercommunity relations on the Indian subcontinent have been understood. Key reasons furnished for the perpetuation of hierarchical practices among Muslims, which is often termed as caste or caste-like in South Asian scholarship, have been all too often culturally driven by the ideas of diffusionism. In these narratives, beginning with Dumont (1980), Islam's arrival and its subsequent flourishing is viewed as a political project, furthered by the aggression and invasion of several Muslim rulers to various parts of India. Since these new rulers had to assimilate to the alien environment of the ruled population, it is claimed that they accommodated various cultural features and practices of the subordinated population, including caste practices. Such a rationale for understanding caste among Muslims in South Asia does not hold water if we turn the analytical lens to Malabar in South India.

Islam arrived in Malabar, probably at the time of the prophet Muhammad himself, in the seventh century AD, following the rhythms of the sea and monsoon winds. Islam flourished in Malabar under the patronage and support of the local Hindu rulers. Despite the absence of acculturative pressures and political hegemony, Muslims have still generated and perpetuated caste sensibilities and practices to distinguish between groups and to order social relations. In short, political expediency and theories of acculturation or diffusionism do not seem to be the underlying reasons for the preservation and persistence of caste practices among Muslims. The reasons for and the mechanisms of that need to be located elsewhere. I also suggest that there are multifarious values by which Muslims operationalize caste in their everyday lives, which may not be similar to the ones we find in Hinduism. Rather than overemphasizing behavioral similarities between Hindus and Muslims, we need to focus more on the values on which Muslim hierarchical relationships are lodged. In what follows, I explain how I use the idea of caste and values here and then go on to consider the relevance of these ideas for understanding Muslim social life today.

Valences of Caste

Caste has been signified as the quintessential social structure of Hinduism in the Indian subcontinent. Yet, a survey of studies on social organization of non-Hindu communities also reveals that "caste" is the principle of social organization. Most scholars have followed the rationale for the same in the Dumontian proposition of acculturation and diffusionism (Ahmad 1978; Fuller 1976; Jodhka 2004; Mosse 2012; Silva 2017). However, while Dumont ([1980] 1998) devoted much energy to investigating the values of hierarchical relations among Hindus, he dedicates only a few pages to reflecting on hierarchy among other religious communities. What is quite striking in those reflections, however, is that he glosses over the values of these communities as hardly relevant in structuring social relations. Rather, he focuses on how Hindu hierarchy has "influenced" other communities, such as Christians and Muslims. This approach echoes diffusionism insofar as it privileged Hindu cultural values and their distribution from one society to another. This theoretical slippage in Dumont is important to us only because most scholars working on Muslim communities sought to find caste by adding adjectives that signify similarity or correspondence between two social structures. Beginning with Gaus Ansari (1960) and Imtiaz Ahmad (1978), many scholars have posited that, although the social stratification among Muslims is certainly comparable to the Hindu caste system, an exact replica cannot be found to exist (Madan 2001; Jairath 2011; Levesque 2021; Lee 2018a). Yet, caste as a category of analysis has enjoyed much attention in scholarship on Muslims in India (Ansari 2009; Levesque 2023; Ahmad 2023; Azam 2023). This is because scholars are increasingly thinking about caste as a category of the state where

marginalized sections among Muslims can make a political claim to alleviate their social suffering and gain dignity and recognition. Yet, caste as an
analytical category still defies definition. While scholars have enumerated
various features of caste among Muslims, such as endogamy, occupational
specialization, and hierarchy, pinning down the religious and ideological basis
of caste among Muslims becomes problematic. Most Muslims across India
hold Islam to be an egalitarian religion, despite rampant hierarchical practices
existing among them. A few scholars have even emphasized how Muslims use
the Koranic injunctions and formal religious values to denigrate rigid ethnic
and social divisions, while, at the same time, perpetuating hierarchical sensibilities and practices in their everyday lives (Uddin 2023; Bellamy 2021). I
believe that beginning with a presupposition of Dumontian ideas of Hindu
caste and seeking to map its influence or translation onto Muslims is the first
theoretical problem we should do away with. I suggest that the categories of
caste and Islam need to be rethought by paying close attention to how Muslims are engaging with these ideas in their everyday lives. We must consider
how these categories come into being to be able to help Muslims organize,
understand their lives, and configure social relations.

While I have reservations about Dumont for his template of caste-
imposed non-Hindu communities, he remains a key figure to think with for
understanding the importance of values. His book *Homo Hierarchicus* not
only advances a value-centered approach for comparative anthropology[3] but
also delineates how value in various arenas is related to each other. Dumont
emphasized that caste in India is a system of values, and this could be reduced
to a single principle: the opposition of the pure and the impure. As is clear
here, Dumont's hierarchy works with a fundamental conception of ontologi-
cal difference between elements in the system. As he ([1980] 1998, 43) wrote,
"This opposition underlies hierarchy, which is the superiority of the pure to
the impure, underlies separation because the pure and the impure must be
kept separate, and underlies the division of labor because pure and impure
occupations must likewise be kept separate. *The whole is founded on the necessary and hierarchical coexistence of the two opposites*" (italics in original).
Dumont argued that at the two extremes of the caste system are placed the
Brahmin and the untouchable. At the religious and spiritual level, which is
considered the highest level, the Brahmins are placed and represent humanity
as a whole. The operative principle here is purity and all the castes are accordingly ranked. As Jonathan Parry (1974, 98) puts it, "The jurisdiction of the
king is confined to the politico-economic domain of *artha*, while the priest

presides over the whole as the representative of the cosmic order, the realm of *dharma*." Dumont emphasized that this system of values cannot be dealt with as the extension of economic and political relations. Rather, it is a system bearing an autonomous existence, and one that overrides political considerations. In the subordinate political sphere where humans relate only to other humans, the dominant value was power. In Hindu society, however, status as a principle of social organization was considered superior to the principle of power. Though the kings were superior to Brahmins at the political level, they were ultimately charged with upholding the values of caste hierarchy. Brahmins were thus seen as central to any successful political entity because the spiritual realm in which they arbitrated was cosmically privileged and most encompassing.

It is important to note that Dumont juxtaposes hierarchy (which is synonymous with varna) as a value in India, along with equality in the modern, western societies. It was claimed that the modern west foregrounded equality as the paramount value for organizing social relations. At its heart lay the conception of individualism, which means that "every man is, in principle, an embodiment of humanity at large, and as such he is equal to every other man, and free" (Dumont 1977, 4). It is a "free association of men, an association without subordination or mediation, where the whole will not transcend its parts but only be immanent in them" (128). In India, however, Dumont averred, the idea of individual did not exist. A person was always already a social being, conceived in terms of his belonging to the group into which he was born.[4]

At the same time, there are also instances when Dumont (1977, 5) perceptively notes that in any social system, equality and hierarchy should combine, "as the ranking of social groups entails equality within each of them." So, it is possible that equality is valued, to some extent, without being a part and parcel of individualism. If we follow this line of argument, we might think that Dumont should have analyzed how Indians, for example, negotiated and struggled with the idea of individualism during colonial modernity. Instead, Dumont's analysis has been limited to scriptural understanding of a society of hierarchy in the Indian context. While this study's attempt is not to engage with the colonial encounters of ideas of individualism, it should be emphasized that many aspects of individualism, such as dignity, equality, and rights, as theorized by Dumont (1986), not only came to the imaginaries of the elites and middle classes who directly negotiated with colonial power but also structured the imaginaries of the subaltern populations through the

activities of Christian missionaries and colonial encounters. This has been
well illustrated by Sanal Mohan (2015) in his study of how former agrestic slave castes in Kerala, such as Parayars and Pulayars, creatively used the
scripts of modernity inaugurated by Christian missionaries in their attempts
to claim and construct an idea of the individual. Such examples abound in
studies across India from across religious traditions (Aloysius 1998; Khare
1984). Scholars have also suggested that both hierarchical and egalitarian
tendencies have existed in Indian society for a long time and these egalitarian tendencies have not been related to modern ideas of individualism
(Béteille 1979; Parry 1974). In my own case, we see Muslim barbers in Malabar adapting in the latter half of the twentieth century both modern ideas of
individualism as well as egalitarian impulses of Islam to remake their social
relations with other Muslims.

Dumontian relationships among all the elements of such an "ideological
system" have been thoroughly examined and challenged in subsequent scholarship (Fuller 1996; Gupta 2000; Khare 2009; Jodhka 2015; Raheja 1988). Yet,
they all have emphasized power and status as fundamental concepts by which
social worth of individuals and groups are measured. Contemporary anthropological scholarship in South Asia can be enriched by analyzing how status
and power are reorganized and reformulated across non-Hindu communities
in India. I suggest that contemporary analysis of caste should begin by noting
how status and power have been organized in a locality and how changes
have occurred to their relationships historically. In positing such a framework, I am inspired by E. P. Thompson's (1967) arguments in the context of
changes in the apprehension of time in the social lives of working classes in
England. He notes that in task-oriented societies, there was least demarcation
between "work" and "life" and the lives of working people were organized
according to observed necessities. But with the onset of industrial capitalism, a greater synchronization of labor takes place that aligns with a specific
and well-defined abstract category of time. Such an imposition of time was
calibrated toward a capitalist mode of production and commodification of
labor. According to Thompson, to evaluate such a tremendous transformation, it is not enough to analyze a single process, such as the changes in the
notation of the time through the "clock." Rather, the transformation must be
considered within the wider historical and social structures that underpin
such changes, such as changing systems of power, property-relations, religious institutions, and cultural mores. Following Thompson's analysis, I pro-
pose that social hierarchy, and its transformations are informed by a range

of practices, events, and ideologies and cannot be straitjacketed merely into changes in ideological systems.

Various aspects of Dumont's theory of caste have been criticized.[5] Many studies have argued that the pan-Indian, single-axis notions of caste forma-tions in India do not correspond to empirical realities and question if they ever did. Drawing on these critiques, I suggest that three key concerns are critical to understanding Muslim social hierarchy today. First, it has been noted that political power, rather than the religious ideology, determined the status of a group in a locality (Hocart ([1950] 1968); Fuller 1996; Dirks 2001). These scholars have also noted that Dumont and his followers have based their analysis on the injunctions of Hindu sacred texts without attending to ethnographically examining the validity of the claims embedded in such sacred texts and their application in everyday life. Dirks (1987) has shown, in the context of Pudukkottai, which was the only princely state in the Tamil-speaking region during the British colonial era, that political power shaped the hierarchical relations and status of a caste group within the territory of the kingdom. While he emphasizes political power as encompassing the reli-gious domain in the case of the caste system among Hindus at least in South India, what is also evident in his analysis is the centrality of material resources such as land, titles, honors, and emblems as key to maintaining the intercaste relations in Pudukkottai. The close relationships between material resources and ritual participation were central to organizing the status of a group in the locality and it was amenable to change from time to time owing to political pressures, internecine wars, and military pressures from the outside.

Second, scholars like Bernard Cohn (1987) and Nicholas Dirks (2001) have shown that colonial state apparatuses had a crucial role in consolidating a Brahmin-centric framework of understanding Indian society and rigidify-ing the hitherto flexible and nebulous social categories and groupings into a single system of caste. For better or worse, Dumont builds his theoretical scaffold on colonial interpretations of Hindu sacred texts. He does not reflect upon the modern inflections of caste. While caste had a social life of its own in precolonial India, it becomes imbricated in governance structures of the nation-state through colonial power and thereafter (Lee 2021b). This is evi-dent if we attend to how colonial officials tried to enumerate, tabulate, and categorize the entire population of the subcontinent through categories of caste and tribe. We will see how colonial tabulations and categorization efforts worked in the case of Muslims in Malabar, through the example of the fishers. At the same time, colonial efforts were not simply directed at categorizing social groups but also in constructing homogenous ideas of community. This is well illustrated in the formation of the identity of Mappilas in colonial Malabar. I describe both these tendencies in Chapter 2.

Third, the idea of a pan-Indian caste system was also questioned by Susan Bayly (1989), who has shown in the context of Tamil Nadu that it was the "warrior" kingdoms that determined the political affairs of the region and that they also controlled the sacred spaces through aggression, benefaction, and munificence. She also notes that it was certain family lineages (rather than castes) that claimed these kingdoms and other forms of authority in these regions until well into the eighteenth century when they became recognized as belonging to corporate social groups such as castes or communities. In the case of various Muslim rulers who sprang up in many Tamil-speaking regions, she argues, the controlling of shrines and Sufi pirs have been key to organizing and legitimizing their authority and power. Sumit Guha (2016, 56) has recently infused another specification into Bayly's argument. He notes that it was not the "warrior kingdoms" that were the organizing unit of hierarchical organization in South Asia, but it was a "village cluster" often referred to as *nādu* in the South and *pargāna* in the North. The social unit has, therefore, been more elastic than simply a rigidly hemmed one by caste. I consider these arguments as key to understanding Muslim hierarchy today because they illustrate the elasticity of hierarchy, dynamism of power structures, and place-bound understanding of social relations.

Building on these arguments, I suggest that we should understand caste as a regime of hierarchical inequality based on birth operating on the Indian subcontinent. And, yet, if this is a necessary basis to understand caste as an ascribed category, it is also insufficient. Caste is dynamic and operates in various domains of social life and has distinctive characteristics in social, economic, political, and religious spheres. Following Dumont, the best method to capture the vicissitudes of caste is to pay close attention to values as they operate in various social spheres. For maintaining and reproducing control over various forms of capital available, social groups can stake claims drawing upon the available values. However, ultimately, these values get mediated through hierarchical inequalities based on birth. These hierarchical inequalities are expressed and experienced through specific bodily attitudes, behaviors, and deference structures among the members based on descent. When I describe caste as a regime, it is also to refer to these modes of controlling and regulating the body and bodily behavior. However, caste does not simply remain a site of domination and exploitation. As Foucault (1982) writes, power also works as a site of creative opposition, resistance, accommodation, and innovation.

Rather than proposing "caste" as the conceptual foundation of hierarchy among Muslims, my idea is to tussle with this concept by attending to various sorts of hierarchical practices among Muslims and the values structuring them. By the end of the book, it should be clear that "caste," if at all we must define Muslim hierarchy by this term, works differently among Muslims. The difference, however, can also be mapped into how caste is looked at, whether it is conceived as a cultural phenomenon unique to Hindus or a structural principle at work across communities in the Indian subcontinent. I side with the latter proposition and posit that there are unique values structuring caste relations across the communities.

Significance of Values

In calling attention to values to understand social relations, I join a long-standing conversation in anthropology that has sought to overcome the agency or structure impasse as a way to understand social relations (Eiss and Pedersen 2002; Graeber 2001, 2013; Robbins 2013). In using values throughout the book, I follow David Graeber who observes that values can be seen as the "way in which actions become meaningful to the actors by being incorporated in some larger, social totality—even if in many cases the totality in question exists primarily in the actor's imagination" (Graeber 2001, 3). The social totality need not be comprehended by actors in order to modulate one's actions in the world. They usually go about doing whatever they do without rationalizing every choice. At the same time, one can locate values in the way certain actions and choices and modes of behavior are considered suitable and appropriate for certain social occasions and practices. Values can, therefore, be designated, to use an apt phrase from Graeber (2001, 3) as "conceptions of the desirable." In social relations, people attempt to realize various values based on their own desires and interpretations of what is important. Many scholars have explored the value forms by focusing on how those values are realized and related to each other in different societies (Poyer 1993; Robbins 2015; Robbins and Siikala 2014; Strathern 1988). Robbins (2013, 100) notes that there are primarily two philosophical viewpoints on value relations in society: monist and pluralist. Those who subscribe to monist positions suggest that there could be many values in society, but they may all work together to help people to realize a supervalue. Those who hold pluralist positions suggest that more than one worthy value exist and some of these values may conflict with each other with the result that pursuing some may lead to failing in others. The focus of any study on values should be to unpack the working mechanisms and structure of value relations empirically.

We can consider values as collective representations of what is good or important in ordering one's lifeworld. Individuals strive to realize these values in their personal lives; they organize their fears and desires around them through following correct moral behavior. The values become compelling to social actors through collective experiences, mythical and lineage narratives, and political and economic arrangements. Since all cultures contain more than one value, people often face a dilemma when confronted with which to prioritize and when, and this can be difficult to reconcile. Others seek to pursue them all at once, but they often fall short. In his study of Muslim youth in Egypt playing soccer during the month of Ramadan, which is considered a time of exceptional piety, Samuli Schielke (2009) argues that people are often motivated by various registers of action, such as piety, fun, secularism, fashion, and so on. Which course of action and subjectivity one chooses to embody will be decided by context and individual life choices. People work out their relations and accommodate them to the requirements of everyday life (Robbins and Sommerschuh 2016, 8). Values, as they are sought to be realized by individuals and groups, necessarily create hierarchy because of the distinctions between those who are said to possess the values and those who do not. How such value-based determinations are decided, and by which authority, can be subject to contention and interpretation. In this context, the concept of hierarchy serves as a prism through which we can examine the social fabric of not just Muslim communities but also of societies at large. Here, hierarchy isn't just about power or status; rather, it's a reflection of how closely individuals or groups align with the values deemed important by their community. This creates a vertical structure, informed by adherence to these values. Such hierarchies, however, are not static; they're shaped by contentious debates and interpretations, often influenced by various authorities within the community. Therefore, while the concept of hierarchy is universal, its manifestations and implications can be highly specific and culturally anchored.

I use the term *hierarchy* in a specific sense here to refer to relative standing between individuals and groups. This relative standing operates within the system of a religious whole among Muslims, by virtue of belonging to the faith of Islam. Hierarchy is based on the idea that people are differently positioned (vertically) with relation to values espoused and embraced by the community. Hierarchy is a general model of social organization not only in Muslim societies but across the world (Dilley 2004; Piliavsky 2021). In hierarchical modes of social organization, there will be a range of values that structure social relations. Piliavsky (2021, 25) notes that values can be either possessive, located at the level of individual (purity, wealth, and strength), or transitive, located and realized only through social relations (care, loyalty, and generosity). Even the possessive values become meaningful only if they are brought to bear on social relations. Social relations are therefore shaped on the basis of those differences in access to and association with those values, which also grants them a range of opportunities (Keeler 2017, 11). It imposes obligations on all parties involved; just as much as subordinates have obligations toward the superordinates, the reverse is also true. In many cases, it is the relative position in the hierarchy that makes the system appear, on the face of it, unjust and indeed unacceptable to many people, particularly as it affects people in subordinate positions. The subordinates can contest the hierarchical arrangements using whatever ideas, practices, discourses, and tools they have at their disposal. This book is focused on Muslim social relations, arguing that everyday life is capacious enough to accommodate a range of values across both religious and secular domains. These values are sometimes aligned with each other; at other times, in direct conflict with each other, giving the social agents a plethora of subjectivities to position themselves. In the next section, I will outline the range of values that shape, sustain, and contest caste among Muslims in Malabar.

Islam and Values Among Muslims in Malabar

In a much-cited article titled "The Idea of an Anthropology of Islam," Talal Asad (2009, 20) has posited that Islam should be understood as a discursive tradition, meaning "a tradition of Muslim discourse that addresses itself to conceptions of the Islamic past and future, with reference to a particular practice in the present." I want to pick two key elements from this conceptualization: practice and present. About practice, Asad has this to say: The proper theoretical beginning for an anthropologist of Islam is the "instituted practice (set in a particular context and having a particular history) into which Muslims are inducted as Muslims." The practice becomes Islamic and the doers become Muslims because "it is authorized by the discursive traditions of Islam, and is taught to Muslims" (21). The problem with this position is that often the point of conflict and debate among Muslims is not simply about the proper conduct of practices but also about the legitimacy of certain practices and whether they can be deemed "Islamic" by any means. It is true that Asad recognizes power as an important element in designating the truth of a practice and its claim to being Islamic. Yet, the idea of power is a very complex affair in societies like India where Muslims are a minority, and often the state meddles in deciding whether a practice is truly "Islamic" through secular judicial processes. While practice should be the theoretical starting point for an anthropology of Islam, it must unearth the value relations structuring practices and the powers in which they are implicated in. Now, let us look at how Asad conceives of the present. At the beginning of the same article, he asserts the following: "Narratives about culturally distinctive actors must try to translate and represent the historically situated discourses of such actors as responses to the discourse of others, instead of schematizing and de-historicizing their actions" (10). This suggestion to closely attend to the context in which the actors operate is a valid one for any anthropological project and is repeated a few times in different ways. He goes to say that "it is clear that there has never been any Muslim society in which the religious law of Islam has governed more than a fragment of social life" (19). It is implied that Muslim lives are complex now and Muslims are not motivated and regulated by Islam alone. As he proceeds to conceptualize discursive tradition, Asad's capacious idea of the context becomes limited and narrow. It becomes about how orthodoxy defines certain practices as Islamic.

Seeking Allah's Hierarchy characterizes Islam as a lived tradition. By lived tradition, I mean both the discursive tradition as well as how Muslims engage with and employ Islam to order and make sense of their everyday lives. I borrow the term "lived" from the conceptualizations of "lived religion" proposed by scholars like Meredith McGuire (2008) and Nancy Ammerman (2021). They consider "lived" as a specific configuration of contemporary life where individuals have a range of competing registers of moral action from which to choose. For instance, some of the characters described by McGuire (2008, 3–16) are combining Catholicism, Buddhism, and Zen meditation in creative ways to organize their religious lives. While they may claim to belong to either Catholic or Protestant faiths, their lives are not regulated by a rational coherence of a singular doctrine. Rather, as McGuire, puts it, their religious lives are modulated by a practical coherence—that is, what works for them. My point is that in understanding Muslim lives today, we need to attend to the complexities of the social context of Muslims' lives rather than reducing it to simply a background frame where Islamic practice is being played out. This book, as a whole, illuminates this context as a key register for thinking about what Islam is. In a context where the category of practice is a challenging idea, I find values to be a useful analytical entry to understanding Muslim everyday life. The realm of values is not homogeneous, and Islam is not the only frame that is providing a strong motivational setup for the actors. In conceiving Islam as a lived tradition, I follow and extend Shahab Ahmed's idea of con-Text, which he uses to refer to a diverse range of contexts in which the Quran and *hadith* have been interpreted and used by Muslims. He argues that in conceiving Islam as a historical and human phenomenon, we cannot be limited by an understanding of Islam as "discursive tradition" as proposed by Talal Asad, which emphasizes established practice and establishing authority and power as the domain of understanding Islam. My point is that the con-Text should also be complemented by the idea of a "context" in which interpretations and engagements of Islam develop. The context throws up a range of normative schemas originating from various social spheres, and Muslims often engage with them using a con-Text. This does not mean that all aspects of their lives will be punctuated by normative aspects of Islam. Rather, even while engaging in seemingly non-Islamic practices, Islam can be called upon to justify, negotiate, challenge, and discard practices. To reiterate a point made by Asad, what is designated as Islamic at a time is an effect of power.

Muslims order their lifeworld using a range of values, such as piety, wealth, lineage, morality, *antassu*, and egalitarianism, that are often framed and reconfigured by their associations with sacred scriptures and prophetic traditions, as well as being shaped by secular orientations. Some values are taken to be normative, in the sense that they are held to be an ideal to be realized by the aspiring believer. Since there is a range of values from which to choose, each individual may prefer one value over another, and this may be informed by the person's class, gender, caste, and religious orientation. In a sense, we can say that different values may be related to each other in a hierarchical manner. Muslims in Malabar, by way of their common faith in Islam, assert that their religion provides the blueprint for ordering their lifeworld (Kiliyamannil 2023; Osella and Soares 2020; Visakh, Santhosh, and Roshan 2021). Islam provides, to use a felicitous phrase from Geertz (1993, 93) both "a model of and a model for" organizing one's actions in the world. At the same time, what this ideal consists of is always contested. There are many different sects and groups among Muslims who contest what is entailed in Islam, and, therefore, the projects of self-cultivation are varied (Kasim 2025; Osella 2015). Yet, Muslims largely agree that a key value for ordering their lifeworld is piety. Piety is taken to mean closeness to Allah and is socialized to the community through family, instructions in religious institutions, and sermons, and it is made visible through the life-course and actions of individuals. Pious believers are regarded as the most respectful and the most distinguished in an Islamic society. This is proclaimed through various verses in the Quran by Allah. For instance, Allah declares it unequivocally: "Certainly, the noblest of you, in the sight of Allah, is the most pious" (49:13). In recent times, piety and ethics have become the tropes around which anthropological studies of Islam have converged (Mahmood 2005; Masquelier 2009; Deeb and Harb 2014; Smith-Hefner 2019). Studying the women's mosque movements in Egypt, Saba Mahmood (2005) describes how her subjects view and define piety. It is a manner of being and acting in the world with the conviction that Allah is close to you. Such a disposition "suffuses all of one's acts, both religious and worldly in character" (Mahmood 2005, 122–123). While achieving such a disposition or a pious comportment involves a complex disciplinary program, at a basic level it requires that a Muslim perform those acts of worship that have been made incumbent upon him by Allah (*al-farā'iḍ*), as well as Islamic virtues (*faḍā'il*) and acts of munificence that secure Allah's pleasure (*al-a'māl al-ṣāliha*). The attitude with which these acts are performed is as important as their prescribed form.

When barbers envision piety as the only legitimate criterion for hierarchy, they conceive Muslims not as "owners" and "masters" of goods, lineages, and objects, but of actions and dispositions of piety. If actions and dispositions are the key markers of one's social identity, occupying such positions is open to everyone. It is useful to reflect on this value of piety using Naomi Haynes and Jason Hickel's (2016) conception of "egalitarian hierarchy," by which they refer to hierarchical social systems where positions are open to everyone. One's ascribed rank or status does not predetermine the opportunities for occupying social positions. Similarly, barbers use the idea of egalitarianism espoused in the Quran by Allah as an "egalitarian hierarchy" by which Muslims should be gauged on the basis of capabilities and virtues to personify piety—the marker of distinction set by Allah. Virtuous fear, humility, sincerity, and awe are all emotions through which virtuosity and excellence in piety are cultivated, marked, and measured among Muslims. Accordingly, each person is assumed to have unique individuality, and no one can be treated intrinsically superior to another. The only axis of distinction between individuals is piety, which, in principle, can be acquired by anyone. One's birth or genealogy are deemed irrelevant in acquiring piety and finding proximity to Allah. In Malabar, Muslims keep this value as an all-important axis of social relations. Religious scholars, owing to their knowledge in Islamic textual traditions, are looked upon by lay Muslims as embodying piety. Muslims claim that every aspect of one's life needs to be mediated by the prescriptions and proscriptions of piety. While piety is the divine scale of evaluating a Muslim, on the social plane, one's piety is difficult to evaluate because it is an internal acquisition. At the same time, there are many characteristics outlined above through which Muslims can identify and evaluate actions of others that may potentially reveal someone's piety. Such evaluations are often deployed by lay Muslims to both assess an individual and his family status in a locality. Religious authorities and officials in a *mahallu* (a mosque-based community) may often make such judgments on the basis of an individual's attendance in the mosque and participation in other religious activities.

While piety is a divine criterion, Muslims also resort to various values in their everyday lives while ordering their social relations. Two more ideas are held to be key by Muslims in Malabar in general: *taravād* (family lineage) and *mutal* (wealth). The term taravād was originally used to refer to the matrilineal household of Nairs, a Hindu-dominant caste in Malabar (Fuller 1976; Schneider and Gough 1961). In Kathleen Gough's (Gough 1961, 323) words, "'Taravād' is derived from 'tara,' meaning 'mound,' in this case the raised foundation on which a Nayar house was built. Its members derived a sense of unity from the belief that their matrilineal forebears sprang from the same ancestral house, and if the site of this house still existed, they retained a sentimental attachment to it." Muslims in Malabar generally use this term to refer to their ancestral household, though they mostly follow a patrilineal form of inheritance. Among Muslims, this term is understood as a Malayalam translation of the Islamic juristic category of *nasab*, which is used as a determinant for estimating suitability between two potential marriage partners. The idea was initially used in the Islamic world to distinguish Quraysh, the tribe of the prophet Muhammad from other Arab tribes, and later to distinguish between Arabs and non-Arabs. The "concept of tribe in Arab genealogy relates to a concern with tracing blood descent to either a real or legendary ancestor of the distant past" (Varisco 2004, 141). Muslims in Malabar consider that if they can trace their lineage to a taravād that has been Muslim for more than three or four generations, it accrues much prestige and status to their family in the locality. The concept of taravād is used among Muslims to create distinctions between social groups. Sayyids, owing to their descent from the prophet Muhammad are held in high esteem. Next come Mappilas among whom those who can trace their family lineage to the past are held high in status. Fishers and barbers are placed at the lower rung of hierarchy among Muslims. Muslim fishers are derogatorily called *pūsalān* and are spatially segregated from the coastal Mappilas. I describe them in detail in Chapter 2. Barbers, owing to their obscure genealogy and the undignified nature of their work are seen as low in taravād status. Yet, as I show in Chapter 2, barbers contest this dominant narrative about themselves by tracing their lineage back to an Arab Muslim who came to the Malabar coast at the time of the prophet Muhammad—that is, in the seventh century AD. Barbers deploy the discourse and practice of taravād itself to reposition themselves in the social hierarchy and, in this way, to claim dignified status among Muslims.

Closely tied to the idea of taravād in Malabar is the concept of wealth. Wealth is looked at as an allurement in this world provided by Allah (Quran, 18:46). Since human beings are deputies of Allah on earth, the wealth provided by Him should be spent in ways that are agreeable and pleasing to Allah. Of course, such textbook ideas are somewhat different in practice, and, for many generations, wealth was associated with land. In Malabar, one's wealth was estimated in the past by the land one owned. At that time, it was the taravāds of both Nairs and a few Muslims who owned land wielded authority in a locality. The majority of the population was agricultural labor or was attached ritually to the taravāds to provide services and to receive recurring compensation. The landowners controlled the rest of the population either by providing avenues of livelihood or by being the patron of the ritual economy of the locality. Barbers were dependent on all other Muslims who acted as their patrons and provided rewards in kind for the services provided by the barbers, such as hair and nail cutting, bodily hair removal, tonsure, circumcision, and midwifery. Barbers did not generally own any agricultural land and were settled by the landlords at their property freely. Inequalities such as this created a propertied class and further cemented the hierarchical distinctions among Muslims in Malabar. Yet, one cannot simply portray barbers as submissive subjects, as I describe in Chapter 3.

The above-mentioned three concepts—piety, taravād, and wealth—constructed a hierarchy in which barbers were placed at the lower end. Barbers were often characterized as unsuitable to acquire and embody piety because of their social origins. Hence, their individual capacities were already viewed as constrained by their collective ones, as members of a poor taravād or a

denigrated occupation. I showcase many instances and aspects of such discrimination and humiliation in Chapter 4. My argument is that, in most social
spheres, wealth and taravād have often subordinated piety as the medium
of social relations. Power has often subordinated status among Muslims.
This began to change in the 1970s when the domain and locus of piety—the
mosque-based communities—became democratic with the emergence of new
classes and egalitarian assertions.

While society was hierarchically structured for generations, as evidenced
in the oral narratives of barbers, we cannot pinpoint a date at which such
relations emerged. However, as we will see in Chapter 2, barbers imagine
their identity as a separate social group, taking shape from the seventh century onward in Malabar. The hankering after origins becomes a particularly
thorny issue in the case of subordinated populations whose only archive is
orality and memory. While no community and social relations remain static
for centuries, it is difficult to provide a chronology of social change for Muslim
barbers beyond the twentieth century. In stories and narratives that populate
this book, one can, however, see the contours of a social transformation that
spanned more than a century.

From the 1970s, barbers in Kerala started unionizing themselves and
establishing shops with a view to ending the patronage system of their work
and gaining social dignity in Kerala society. Considering social dignity as
"the universal human need for and pursuit of positive self-worth," drawing
on the works of Doron Shultziner and Itai Rabinovici (2012), I illustrate how
Muslim barbers extricated themselves from a patronage system to that of a
profession anchored in market transactions. Muslim barbers also joined the
union movement with a view to reorganizing the mode of their attachment to
Muslim groups, considered their patrons. Barbers set up shops, fixed rates for
each task, refused to engage in the demeaning work of bodily hair removal,
and decided the daily working hours of their shops. The opening of the
shops and other actions brought far-reaching changes in the social relations
between barbers and other Muslim groups. Their work became detached
from the patronage system and organized along monetary relations. The new
work arrangements they constructed had implications for labor relations and
for understandings of the body and personhood, coupled with wider notions
of public and private space.

Such far-reaching changes also led to barbers calling out the established
hierarchical practices among Muslims. They often drew upon Islamic history and prophetic traditions to contest the hierarchy. Three tendencies were

visible in the contestations between barbers and other Muslims. A few barbers sought to acquire secular education and employment and thereby gain marriage alliances from forward-thinking Mappila families. Others tried to attain religious scholarship, which was earlier denied to them through various measures as I will explain in Chapter 4. They hoped that discarding the traditional profession of barbering would enable them to extricate themselves from the stigma. Yet, their identity remained; for example, a barber who became a religious scholar came to be identified as a "barber religious scholar." While barbers have attained economic mobility, they have largely failed to garner social status. The majority of barbers persisted with their traditional occupation while, at the same time, striving to realize the potential of egalitarianism, which they believed to be inherent in Islam. By harping on such narratives, barbers challenged the religious scholars whenever they sought to belittle and malign the barber community and barbers actively engaged in organizing family gatherings, demonstrations, and other activities that highlighted their distinguished heritage as worthy Muslims. In short, Islam has now become a central ground for the renegotiation of caste among Muslims.

To understand the negotiations and conflict over the legitimate hierarchical frames of Muslims, one needs to look more closely into Islam, rather than beyond. In fact, the whole conflict between values and the legitimate criterion of hierarchy among Muslims in Malabar can be usefully framed by anchoring these discourses into two conceptual categories available in the Quran. What barbers denote as piety is referred to as *taqwa* in the Quran. One who personifies this quality is known as *muttaqi*. Barbers would like the hierarchy to be fixed on this category and this positionality is theoretically available for every Muslim to occupy. This category is also more than what jurisprudence can entail, and it is beyond what can be measured empirically.[6] There are also two other positionalities for believers in Quran; namely, Muslim and Mu'min. Both these categories are often used interchangeably. They must follow the mandatory requirements of a believer in Islam. While a Muslim or Mu'min can aspire to and work toward attaining the station of a muttaqi, the latter term always already encompasses both the former categories. I also contend that the personified category of Muslim or Mu'min are so capacious that they can contain a whole range of practices in the world, including hierarchical relations. But if you are a muttaqi, Allah is the sole criterion for not only organizing your social relations but also for marshaling your perceptions, behavior, and thought. Barbers call upon other Muslims to realize this idea of taqwa to reorganize everyday life in Malabar.

To elucidate my argument further, I find Shahab Ahmed's concept of con-Text very useful. By con-Text, Ahmed refers to how the revelatory text of the Quran was understood, used, and interpreted in each historical context and it is as important for thinking about Islam as we understand the Quran as a text in itself. This con-Text is not just limited to interpretations and commentaries of the Quran, it also includes hadith, jurisprudential texts, and even literary and fictional writings that sought to explain, make sense of, and interpret what is contained and even possibly promised in the Quran. If we conceive the Text (divine revelation) in such a holistic manner, it cannot be wrested away from the context in which it was read, understood, and interpreted. Following the Ahmedian line of reasoning, we can conceive hierarchy itself as precisely an instance of what Ahmed refers to as con-Text—it is the social institutional context in which the Text is lived, interpreted, and enacted. This is why the religious scholars can, without reference to any texts, so easily suggest that adulterers are the equivalent of barbers—because "Islam" here isn't found in a text, but in a con-Text. Interestingly, the barbers' appeal to the Text, in the form of the Quran, also undoubtedly includes hadith studies as well, but in order to buttress the reenvisioning of this same con-Text; namely, a hierarchy that in their reading can allow one to realize egalitarianism through piety. In short, I have argued that Muslim barbers in Malabar imagine social relations in a hierarchical frame of piety. It isn't that they want to do away with hierarchy, or even climb it; instead, they want to be recognized as equals to others in the hierarchy in terms of the category of piety. Indeed, piety alone should permeate it because piety is, in part, about playing one's role within the hierarchy, and playing it well. Thus, Muslim barbers get upset about the implications that they cannot serve as imams not because they find the hierarchy itself offensive but because they understand the role of imam to be designated for the most pious of men, a quality or position they understand themselves as capable of achieving because it is universally promised by Allah.

Plan of the Book

Seeking Allah's Hierarchy unravels intergroup negotiations, contestations, and living with hierarchy. Hierarchy is not a fixed category among Muslims. Whether it implied rigidified notions and attendant categorizations of groups or whether it was a terrain of possibilities, including that of becoming a muttaqi, mattered a lot to my interlocutors. While contesting the possibility of any

hierarchy in terms of fixed, endogamous, and occupational identities (sometimes signified by caste), Muslim barbers looked for reorienting hierarchy in
Islamic terms. The terms of negotiation and the terrain of contestation were
largely Islamic. Ideas of piety, genealogy, and morality became categories that
militated against any of the entrenched notions of status. The very idea of
hierarchy was accepted, negotiated, or challenged based on whether the hierarchical relations were just; the idea of "just" being thought in such terms that
if there were opportunities and possibilities for everyone in hierarchy to pursue and attain the valued social dimensions (Bell and Pei 2020). The moral
horizons were defined in terms of both Islam and the broader categories of
dignity and respect. The unravelling of Islam as a lived tradition complicates
and challenges the attempts to subsume Muslim hierarchy in India within the
terminology of caste and rooting it predominantly under the sign of the state
through calls for extending and expanding the benefits of the reservation to
the lower classes among Muslims.

   This book consists of seven chapters and an Afterword. Chapter 2 investigates the origin stories among various Muslim groups in Malabar. These stories, except those narrated by the Sayyids, are related to the arrival of Islam on
the Malabar coast through Mālik-ibn-Dīnār and his companions from Arabia at the time of the prophet Muhammad in the seventh century AD.[7] These
missionaries were well received by the local kings, and they supported the
dissemination of Islam along the coast. Unlike Islam in North India where it
is usually thought to be connected with military aggression and invasion, I
note that Islam in Malabar has a unique history as a result of a longstanding
trade relations and interactions with the Arab countries, and Islam settled
into the local milieu of iniquitous social relations by following the political-
economic structures of patronage relations in the region. Muslim barbers
were integrated into such a structure of patronage system among Muslims
with the moral underpinnings provided by Islam. Yet, they reconfigure the
myth of the arrival of Islam in Malabar to claim that their original ancestor
was one of the members who came to Malabar for the dissemination of Islam.
Their historical subordination is deemed a mistake and a damage to their
community.[8] By unravelling the origin myths, I argue that various Muslim
groups in Malabar weave unique genealogies for themselves with reference to
the myth. The idiosyncratic claims each group makes to the myth also reveal
the structure of caste relations among Muslims.

   Chapter 3 looks at how Muslims in Malabar operationalize caste with a
particular focus on barbers and their relationships with other Muslim groups.

Since barbers were engaged in a patronage network to provide barbering services in each locality with other Muslims, they received their return more in
kind rather than in cash. During ritual ceremonies such as tonsure and circumcision, they received some amount of cash. Delineating the mechanisms
of the patronage system in Malabar and how barbers were placed in it, I argue
that wealth and power shaped the hierarchical relations among Muslims.
These two categories were inflected in Malabar in terms of Islamic jurisprudential claims and narratives, making it difficult for an easy juxtaposition with
the broader socioeconomic arrangements in the region.

Chapter 4 probes the way barbers were subjected to ongoing humiliation in all aspects of their lives because of their social identity, their hereditary occupation, and the indignity associated with their work. Unearthing
the experiences of barbers and other Muslim groups in Malabar, I illustrate
how such experiences contribute to rationalizing the caste relations among
the groups. I note that the material inequalities in society are often sustained
by discourses that naturalize them. This is done by constructing a barber as
embodying low social worth. I also emphasize how barbers use such experiences to make a moral claim against humiliation by asserting their individual
worth and dignity.

Chapter 5 digs into why Muslims in Malabar ardently claim that there is no
"caste" in Islam. This claim is advanced by Muslims in general on the Indian
subcontinent, but scholars usually brush it aside as irrelevant to their analysis
because, in Muslim social practices, one can find many hierarchical actions
that seem similar to the practices seen among Hindus. I challenge this easy
correspondence by analyzing the practice of endogamy—marriages restricted
within a group—among Muslims where the Islamic idea of nasab (genealogy,
but this is locally reframed as taravād, or family lineage) is used to evaluate
potential marriage alliances among Muslims. I suggest that rather than considering endogamy as a common practice among both Muslims and Hindus,
one needs to look at the values underlying the hierarchical actions among
Muslims to conceive the full meaning of Muslims' claim that "there is no caste
in Islam."

Chapter 6 analyzes how barbers sought collectively to create *antassu* (which
can be roughly translated as dignity) by reorganizing their work into dignified
labor through political mobilizations. They sought to establish labor as the
touchstone of their social relations among Muslims, in contrast to the earlier
value of "moral duty" as the basis of their work in patronage relationships.
Since the 1970s, barbers started organizing themselves through unionizing

and by establishing barbershops. This began to put an end to the patronage mechanism and resulted in more egalitarian forms of labor relations. Barbers also started challenging the hierarchical relations based on wealth and power and started calling upon Muslims to live the ideals of Islam and recognize piety as the worth of Muslims.

The final chapter looks at how the value of egalitarianism is being played out in Malabar, sometimes challenging or reproducing hierarchy. Through unionization, Gulf migration, secular education, and employment, few barbers challenged hierarchical relations. In contrast, those who still pursued the community occupation sought to reimagine the history of the barber community by organizing family gatherings and producing calendars. These latter methods creatively draw on existing cultural scripts of genealogy production among Muslims in Malabar. As a result, the barbers tended to reinforce the values of taravād (family lineage) along with their attempts to realize piety as the touchstone of hierarchy among Muslims.

I end by reiterating the argument that Muslims bring a set of values to bear upon caste practices, informed by local schemas of social power arising from both Islamic notions of lineage, wealth, morality, and piety as well as larger cultural context including that of Hinduism. I aim to avoid the trap of reducing Muslim hierarchical practices to the schema of Hindu caste on the Indian subcontinent. Rather, I argue that the story of Islam, its dissemination and its engagements in the region of Malabar, has produced a distinctive modality of constructing, operationalizing, and justifying hierarchical relations among Muslims. Any theory of caste in non-Hindu communities should be able to capture the complexity and dynamics of such reformulations. These relations are negotiated, contested, and challenged in recent decades through secularization, political action, and socioeconomic improvements in the region.

CHAPTER 2

═══════

Fashioning Origins

Whenever I imagined the beginning of this book, I pressured myself to think about a particular interlocutor or an incident or even a scene to invite you to read it. I could choose from many characters who populate this book. I could land you at a barbershop in a small town in Malabar on the southwest coast of India where a forty-five-year-old man explains that his barber identity does not relate to caste but to the volition his ancestors expressed to the original Arab Muslim. We could visit a seventy-five-year-old Mappila who claims direct descent from a family who was presumably converted by an Arab missionary in the eighth or ninth century. Or I might introduce Bāva, a sixty-two-year-old Muslim fisher from the Malabar coast who proclaims that his ancestors were the first ones to embrace Islam. I was drawn to all these options also because they shared a story that frames the arrival of Islam in Malabar to an Arab group of Muslims. I had heard the story countless times, so many that it had become a cliché. Any seminar or workshop in Malabar on Muslim history invariably referred to this origin story and I immediately thought "Not again." I thought I did not want to recount the much-repeated story and bore you. Yet, in the course of researching and writing this book, it dawned on me that such a story among Muslims in Malabar remains valuable only because of its multiple iterations and how far each social group among Muslims uses it to construct its own identity and social history. So, there is no escape. As far as I can, I will seek to enliven the story, with a version drawn from the ethnographic vantage point. By outlining the story of the arrival of Islam on the Malabar coast, I go on to detail key groups among Muslims here—barbers, Mappilas, Sayyids, and fishers—and how they use the story. I illustrate how the narratives of Muslim social groups help us think about Hindu-Muslim relations in the region as embedded and mutually implicated in the economic, political, and cultural structures and practices.

The story, shortened in oral traditions to a simple phrase, "Mālik-ibn-Dīnār and twelve companions," is the common inheritance of Muslims in Malabar. I do not remember exactly when I first heard this story; but it could have been either from a teacher in our local madrassa or from my own grandmother or mother. The important point is that a Muslim child gets to hear this phrase whenever the history of Islam in Malabar is referred to, recounted, or read about. While specific details may vary in each rendition, the skeleton of the story remains the same. It describes the arrival and spread of Islam on the Malabar coast at the time of the prophet Muhammad in the seventh century AD at the behest of a local king, said to be a Hindu[1] who went to Mecca and accepted Islam. The king subsequently arranged for the propagation of the faith on the Malabar coast.

As in an Arabic text, *Qissat Shakarwatī Farmād*, there are four pieces in the story that unfurl at different localities and during different historical periods. I have heard all these episodes of the story from many of my interlocutors. They are usually narrated without pinpointing precise dates or years. The following narrative is based on the Arabic text. First, there was a miracle of splitting the moon performed by the prophet Muhammad in Mecca as evidence of his prophethood in front of the infidels. This particular spectacle is observed by a Malayali king at that time, and he records the nature and the time of the incident in his annals. Upon inquiry by the king, his astrologers and wise men are unable to explain the incident. The king is subsequently visited during a dream by the prophet Muhammad who corroborates the miracle.[2] Though the king is convinced of Muhammad's prophethood, he cannot reveal his true faith to his subjects. The second piece of the story occurs after a few years. A group of travelers chanced upon the territory of the king and, during private consultation with the leader of the group, the king checks the details and time of the incident and becomes convinced of his own vision. These travelers were headed for Adam's peak in Sri Lanka and the king makes a pact with them that he and a few of his servants would accompany the travelers on their return journey toward Arabia to meet the prophet Muhammad and embrace Islam. The departure of the king is the third segment of the story. Before departing, the king divides his kingdom equally among his lords and secretly accompanies the travelers on their return journey. He reaches Jeddah and meets the prophet Muhammad and embraces Islam, reiterating the vow of belief uttered by the prophet. This all takes place when the prophet is said to be in his fifty-seventh year. He is renamed by the prophet as Thājuddīn and he lives in Mecca for a few years. The attempted return of the Malayali king to the Malabar coast is the final element in the story. While the Malayali king was staying in Mecca, a king in Medina, named Muhammad-ibn-Mālik, hears about him and comes to meet him in all grandeur. He offers to accompany the Malayali king to the Malabar coast to spread Islam and they set about their journey to Malabar. As they reach Shahr, a port city in Yemen, the Malayali king falls ill, but he encourages his companions to continue their onward journey. He offers them a letter detailing the dominions of his kingdom and requests his lords to offer all the help and support for his friends to propagate Islam on the Malabar coast. The Malayali king subsequently dies and is buried in Shahr. While the group was still waiting to make their onward journey, they hear about the prophet's death and decide to return to Medina to join in the mourning. After a few years, a group of travelers, at the behest of Muhammad-ibn-Mālik, ventures toward the Malabar coast. The group was led by Mālik-ibn-Dīnār and, according to the Arabic text, they were more than twenty people at least. They arrived on the Malabar coast and, with the support of the local kings, constructed ten mosques in various places across the Malabar coast.

To refer to the origin story and its life, I use the term "myth" throughout this chapter. Here *myth* refers to the status of a story whose immediate social connections and direct linkages with contemporary realities have been lost. The term does not imply the fanciful, improbable, and untrue renditions of the past, but rather a way in which the past corresponds with the present. For an anthropologist, the phrase "Mālik-ibn-Dīnār and twelve companions" alluding to the story becomes relevant only if her interlocutors use it in their everyday life. In many of my encounters, whenever I asked about the origin of a Muslim social group, as to how the group was initially formed and its historical trajectory, my respondents invariably found refuge in this much-told story, but they emphasized multifarious scenes, actors, and interpretations of it. As Lévi-Strauss (2001, 17) has emphasized in his study of myths, "By using the same material, because it is a common inheritance patrimony of all, all social groups can succeed in building up an original account for each of them." In each rendition, the story belongs to a given group and the group aims to explain its own fate with it. This can be either successful or disastrous, intended to account for privileges and rights that they enjoy or tailored to validate a group's claims for rights that they consider for themselves denied. The story is recounted, contested, and interpreted in multiple ways each time there is a change in the stakeholder.

This story can also set the scene for a discussion of connections and relationships between Muslims and Hindus in India, which is a key reference point of any discussion of Muslim caste in South Asia. In the case of North India, the primary connections between the two communities are portrayed as conflictual and confrontational in both colonial and nationalist historiography, where Muslims are commonly portrayed as an invading army subjugating local rulers, said to be Hindu. This characterization has been challenged by much recent scholarship in India (Eaton 2000; Gilmartin and Lawrence 2000; Metcalf and Metcalf 2001). For example, it has been contended that it is misleading to speak of the Turko-Afghan rulers as Muslims and they were motivated by political imperatives rather than dissemination of the faith. Successive Turko-Afghan regimes, together called Delhi Sultanate, dominated political life in North India since the late twelfth to the eighteenth century. Their kingdoms had much in common with Indic polities of the times. Like these other states, the Turks and Afghans sought military success to get access to the agricultural surplus of the countryside (Metcalf and Metcalf 2001, 4). They offered scope for individual advancement irrespective of one's religious orientation, above all through military prowess. While the contemporary Ottoman Empire necessitated those non-Muslim recruits to the military convert to Islam as part of their assimilation to the ruling class, the Turko-Afghan rulers in India allowed non-Muslims into the ruling classes as non-Muslims (Eaton 2000, 255). Most important, the core military, economic, and political institutions of these dynasties were not specifically "Islamic" (Metcalf and Metcalf 2001, 4). The sultans themselves were not religious scholars, nor were they interested in Islamizing their dominions. They gained their authority and legitimacy for rule through military prowess and governing skills, not through their holiness or the sacredness of their learning.

In the context of Bengal, Richard Eaton (2000) observes that, although the Mughals ruled the region since the early thirteenth century, it was only from the sixteenth century onward that the local population started becoming the major carriers of Islamic civilization. Until then, Islam had remained predominantly as a religion of the ruling class, associated with the Turko-Persian civilization. This major shift in Bengal coincided with the Mughals' changing their capital to Dhaka, the heartland of eastern Bengal. Concerned with bringing stability to the new capital and constructing a loyal community for the kingdom, the Mughals granted favorable or even tax-free lands to individuals who were prepared to clear and bring into cultivation untouched forest tracts. One of the conditions for obtaining such a land grant was to build on the land a temple or a mosque, to be supported in perpetuity from the wealth produced on the site. Grants made to Hindu institutions ultimately became integrated into a Hindu-cultural universe and grants authorizing mosques or shrines eventually integrated the local communities into an Islamic-ordered cultural universe. "Since most pioneers were Muslims, . . . the dominant mode of piety that evolved on East Bengal's economic frontier was Islamic" (Eaton 2000, 264). The institutions thus built became, even long after the death of the originators, sources for disseminating Islamic ideas to the local population. This was also because readers of the Quran, callers to prayer, and preachers were supported in perpetuity in such places, according to the terms of the grants made by the Mughals. In Bengal, Islam came to be ultimately understood as a religion not only of the plow and axe but also of the book.

Unlike the north Indian context, in Malabar, Islam was introduced in the wake of long-standing relations between Arabs and local rulers. A Muslim community developed there through peaceful and gainful trade and commerce (Panakkal and Islam 2024; Prange 2024). Apart from approaching this story from various angles, this book, more broadly, suggests that the destiny of both Hindus and Muslims here also intertwined and overlapped through socioeconomic arrangements, cultural practices, and activities of everyday life. As an anthropologist, my interest is to think about how the myth is used by various Muslim social groups in Malabar to forge an identity and to stake a claim to an elevated social status. This myth has been described at least since the sixteenth century and, later, reported by colonial travelers, administrators, and ethnographers since the eighteenth century. So, we could assume the myth to have a long history of oral transmission in Malabar and it is still recounted today. As we shall see, it says something about how various Muslim social groups view themselves and their place in the world.

Origin of Islam in Malabar

One of the famous, anonymous Arabic texts that recounts the myth is titled *Qissat Shakarwatī Farmād*, which can be translated as *Story of Chakravarti Perumāl*. Though the text is anonymous, we can surmise its existence before the sixteenth century because it is used by a sixteenth-century author as a source for his own text.[3] The same myth is also recounted by Ibn Batuta who visited the Malabar coast in the fourteenth century. I have drawn the kernel of the story from the scholarly works done by Friedmann (1975) and Kugle and Margariti (2017) on the Arabic text. All of them have emphasized the importance of Arabic as the language of this text, as it implies the cosmopolitan nature of the Muslim community along the Malabar coast at the time of its compilation. Arabic, both as a divine tongue of the Quran and language of the mercantile class, was the bearer and transmitter of new stories, beliefs, ideas, and scripts, as well as linguistic and literary forms. Muslims from across the south and southeast Asian coasts came to share "inscribed texts as well as oral sources, poetics, and genres derived from or inspired by Arabic models" constituting what Ricci (2011, 3) calls an Arabic cosmopolis. I am interested here to analyze how Muslims in contemporary Malabar make use of the myth narrated in the text.

While the Arabic text in discussion relates the myth to the time of the prophet Muhammad, various scholars have questioned the veracity of such claims based on various intertextual references that locate the incident and the text at a later period in history (Anchillath 2015; Makhdum 2006). My interest here is to think about two aspects of this myth that have a direct bearing on my own work. First, the myth intertwines Muslim and Hindu fate in a single narrative, as if it is an unbreakable bond where the precedence is given to the local as it responds to the global. The global is already present in this context through the Indian Ocean network, which has been bringing goods, people, and ideas for centuries (Prange 2018). It is the local king, a Hindu, who takes the initiative to choose, learn, and verify from the ideas that became available on the Malabar littoral. He subsequently accepts Islam as the ultimate faith and arranges for the propagation of it among his people. The promotion and dissemination of the Islamic faith along the coast was facilitated by local Hindu rulers. Such an easy rendering was possible within the context of long periods of peaceful exchanges between the local kings and Arab traders and scholars. This whole process also has implications for thinking about the links between Muslim and Hindu social organizations advanced throughout this book.

The myth also highlights how Muslims were implicated in the local structures of authority. The fact that local rulers saw Islam as a distinct faith seeking avenues for its flourishing is quite clear from the story. It was a common phenomenon across the subcontinent for the rulers to offer endowments in the form of land, titles, emblems, and honors to the religious institutions, which in turn legitimized their authority and beneficence as a ruler (Bayly 1989). Maybe Arab Muslims were thus offered lands and all other amenities in the same manner. In later times, as many scholars have noted, the local rulers appointed Muslim religious scholars as important legal authorities among Muslims, and prominent Arabs were offered honorary positions within the kingdom, such as the position of port manager (Ayyar 1999; Haridas 2016). Most important, it was Muslims who constituted the naval force of the local rulers. While the myth does not dwell on all these details, how various Muslim groups use it certainly points to the nature of exchanges that might have existed between Muslims and Hindus in the region. My own ethnography suggests that Muslims and Hindus were knit into a single fabric of political-economic structures and practices in the region, but each used, in turn, vocabularies and meanings from their own religious traditions to add ideological underpinnings to certain practices.

Based on the myth, various Muslim social groups in Malabar imagine and construct not only their origins and intra-religious interactions but also the distinct ways in which intercommunity relations developed here. We cannot pinpoint exactly which historical moment gave rise to these narratives. Still, it seems certain that the exchanges between the two communities were inevitable. The connections between Hindus and Muslims in the region were based on the common sociocultural and economic practices in the region, which tied various groups to a single political-economic structure in Malabar. This cultural exchange was not predicated upon domination by one group over the other but was organized through a process of mediation. As a result, Muslims sought to understand the persistence of socioeconomic inequalities experienced by them using various Islamic registers, at the same time challenging the caste inequalities existing among Hindus. It is the dual aspect of this latter process—redefinition of hierarchy using Islamic ideas and challenging Hindu caste—that contributed to a sense of obliteration of caste among Muslims. While many Hindu lower castes were attracted to Islam because of its challenge of the Hindu caste system and the exemplary ethical behavior of Muslims, Muslims continued to reconstruct a different hierarchy defined by moral personhood, impure occupations, and socioeconomic differences. These are important points I take up for analysis in Chapters 3, 4, and 5. The origin stories of social groups provide a key window into understanding how Muslims conceive their past and frame their social identities using the history and cultural mores of Islam in the region.

Analysis of origin stories among Muslims provides an opportunity both to think about the relevance of the past for contemporary claims and to see the connections between Hindus and Muslims as they existed in everyday life. These stories offer records of origin in the past, although their preservation, invention, or even spread can derive from the social institutions of the present. Even if they may not be faithful records of past reality, they are memories of probable social relations of a constructed past. Drawing on these stories, my intention here is to suggest that Muslim social formation along the Malabar coast worked with a set of strategies and practices that were quite distinct from those of the surrounding communities of the region. However, one cannot overlook the fact that the axis of social formation bears a resemblance to the arrangements of castes among Hindus. The identities were sometimes formed along the lines of caste, without necessarily subscribing to the same sets of ideological underpinnings, and, at other times, the identity formations were clearly marked as distinct from the Hindu caste identities. Let me now describe the four main Muslim groups in Malabar, particularly focusing on their origin stories and identity formations in Malabar.

Barbers

Barbers constitute roughly 3 percent of Muslims in Malabar. They live among other Muslim groups. They have been locally known by the term *ossān*, which most now consider derogatory and demeaning (Amir 2019; Saidalavi 2017). My interlocutors repeatedly told me that they now prefer to be addressed by the English term "barber" and I try to use this throughout the book. When I asked, most barbers did not know what the term ossān meant and how it originated. This word does not appear in Malayalam or in any other language in the surrounding regions such as Tamil or Kannada, but it has a longer history in the region. For instance, Hermann Gundert (1872) lists this word in his Malayalam-English dictionary—the first of its kind in the Malayalam language; the fact that it was published in 1872 means that the word was in common usage even at that time. A few barbers offered a possible etymology and meaning for the term. Muhammad, a seventy-year-old barber professed that the term ossān comes from the Malayalam word *otthōn* or *otthavan*, which means a suitable person. He remarked that a barber was an indispensable part of the Muslim community in each locality. A barber developed a relationship with everyone in the locality through the patronage network. Every family needed a barber at some time and barbers cultivated their patrons and had a reputation for being agreeable, reliable people who could be admitted close to (if not within) the homes of their patrons on a regular basis. They were also admitted inside the house during ritual ceremonies. The epithet otthavan referred to this agreeable nature of barbers in a locality. It is important to note that Muslim barbers are referred to as ossān, otthān, and *ostha* in various places in Kerala even today. This term is also comparable to the name *adut-thōn*, meaning a close person, and is used to refer to the barber subcaste among the largest Hindu service caste in Malabar—namely, Thiyya, also known as the Ezhava. This Hindu subcaste acted as barbers and have been involved in various life-cycle rituals, including death, and the term might have also indicated their intimate relations with their clients. This congruence is hard to prove but, in any case, that is beside the point. In both cases, the terms signify the hierarchical and intimate relations barbers fostered with their clients.

Another story, narrated by Muhammad, relates the origin of the term ossān to the arrival of Mālik-ibn-Dīnār and his companions on the Malabar coast, outlined at the beginning of this chapter. As he said,

> When they came to the Malabar coast, they built ten mosques along the coast on lands offered by the local kings. Gradually, the Muslim settlements grew around the mosques with the help and support of the local kings. There soon arose a crisis in the community because Muslims were unable to procure barbering services from Hindu caste barbers. Among Hindus, barbers were only allowed to provide their services to fellow caste members. Transgression of the caste rules resulted in punishment including penalty fee and banishment from the caste. To resolve the issue, Mālik-ibn-Dīnār assembled his companions and sought their suggestions. One of his companions volunteered and said, "I can serve the community, provided a *vilakkatthala*[4] Nair gives me the tools and teaches me the trade." Mālik-ibn-Dīnār replied to the volunteer, "you are agreeable and suitable for all of us." The Malayalam term for the expression was *otthōn*, meaning "suitable person." The Muslim barbers are therefore descendants of this Arab Muslim.

This commonly told story among barbers is interesting here for three reasons. First, it supports their claims of origin from an Arab Muslim, a lofty claim most Muslims in Malabar cannot make. Muslims in Malabar are said to be formed initially through the communion of Arab traders and local women and later augmented through conversion from various Hindu castes, predominantly from those placed at the lower rungs of hierarchy. So, most Muslims cannot put forth a claim to genealogy as barbers do, that too, from the Arabs. Second, there is an element of duty and obligation the Arab volunteer embodies, one that foregrounds service to the community of Muslims to fashion their bodily comportment according to the tenets and principles of Islam—shaven head, trimmed beard, and orderly moustache among Muslims in Malabar in the past. Because of the intimacy a barber had with his patrons, rectitude was seen as an essential trait for a barber (or dharma, as Hindus often label it), so his characteristics included commitment, decency, reliability—being an otthōn. Third, the demand that a Nair should teach him the profession is an important one within the strictures of the caste system in Kerala. In the local caste system, Nairs occupied a position just below Brahmins and they controlled the agricultural production in the region. Vilakkatthala Nairs, a barber caste among them, served his own caste and Brahmans. The Arab volunteer's demand that a Nair should both give him the tools (e.g., knife and touchstone) and teach him the trade is a meaningful request as it demonstrates a relationship of equivalence sought in the local caste structure. Barbers were positioning themselves along with the dominant caste of Nairs in Kerala, in contrast to other barbering castes among Hindus. The Arab's willingness to become the disciple of a Nair and seek his blessings to undertake the barbering services should be understood as a proclamation of a distinct status for barbers among Muslims. This claim makes sense if we attend to the status and distinction accorded to Nairs in Muslim social imagination. Many prominent Muslim families in Malabar contend that they belonged to the Nair caste prior to their conversion; therefore, they seek distinction among Muslims on the basis of this descent. So, the barber story sought to reproduce the same cultural notions and memories of caste domination in the region. We see that even the occupational origin of lower classes in a different community other than Hindus still valorize caste social structure, even if they do not directly partake in exchange relations. It is the valorization of Hindu-caste social structure that provides the legitimacy to hierarchy among Muslims. In contrast, if the Arab had learned the profession from a lower-caste barber among Hindus, his profession may have been looked down upon, and Muslim converts from higher castes might even have objected to receiving services from the Arab Muslim. By embedding their occupation within the strictures of Hindu hierarchical relationships of the region, barbers' origin story also implicitly endorses the hierarchical mentalities of Muslim social groups.

The story clearly articulates that barbers in Malabar are descendants of a prudent Muslim, originally from Arabia, who was a companion of Mālik-ibn-Dīnār. Because the term ossān has not been used to refer to any of the barber subcastes among the Hindus, one should understand that the term does not have a Hindu cultural origin. Moreover, the two tasks that Muslim barbers undertook, bloodletting and circumcision, were until that time neither common nor institutionalized across India. Both these tasks were, however, well-known in the Muslim world. Circumcision was understood to be a key initiation ceremony for Muslims, a practice nonexistent in other communities on the Malabar coast. Muslim barbers were thus charged with new responsibilities directly related to Islam, which many barbers argue are further evidence that they originally came from the Muslim world. Adding further to this claim of elevated status, many barbers also narrated incidents of various Prophets and their companions involving themselves in the services of circumcision and midwifery. Hamza, a forty-year-old barber I met many times, showed me a clip of his talk at their fourth family gathering where he talked about the barber community's past. He said that there is a hadith, records of sayings and actions of the prophet Muhammad, in *Saheeh-al-Bukhari* that described how the prophet Ibrahim conducted circumcision even after turning eighty years old. He also narrated an incident about Umar Khathab, the second caliph in Mecca, after the death of the prophet Muhammad. When he was the ruler, he would disguise himself and roam around at night in his dominion to gauge the condition of his subjects. One night, he heard a scream coming from a house; when he approached the house, he realized that a woman was undergoing birth pain, and she was having a lot of difficulty. Then Umar went back to his home and brought his wife to the house to look after the delivery. Barbers narrate such events from recorded Islamic history to support their affirmation of the value and dignity attached to their occupation. A few barbers and Mappilas claimed that the term ossān is a derivative of some Arabic words. Hamza, a fifty-year-old barber posited that "the term ossān comes from the Arabic term *muzayyin*," which means one who beautifies others. He was unable to provide any kind of rationale for the transfiguration of this Arabic word to ossān. When I inquired further, he said that the information was shared with him by a religious scholar. Recently, a Mappila religious scholar named Shuaibul Haithami (2023) has suggested that "the term ossān comes from the Arabic word *oʾsn*, meaning horn. Ossān was originally used to refer to those who undertook cupping using animal horn. But our barbers [in Malabar] are not doing that activity." According to Haithami, "in the past, the same people who did cupping, also did barbering work. That is why they came to be referred to as ossān." This claim doesn't stand scrutiny because, as he claims, if barbers in Malabar did not do cupping, why should they be called by the term ossān at all, particularly when there is another, specific Arabic word *hallāq*, to refer to a barber. Despite their claims to truth, what these narratives suggest is that there have been attempts to define and constitute barbering work using Arabic terms and Islamic jurisprudential categories. This is important because these attempts also signify and imagine a relationship for the epithet beyond the cultural boundary of Malabar.

The same Mālik-ibn-Dīnār myth was narrated by Mappilas slightly differently. As the patrons of barbers, they harbored a sense of social superiority. Even if a majority of them were converts from low-caste Hindus, as we shall see shortly, their sense of superiority was augmented because of the power they could exercise in their everyday interactions with barbers. Yousuf, a seventy-five-year-old Mappila, who maintained that he had converted from a high-caste Hindu Nair family, offered the following version of the myth. He did not question the veracity of claims advanced by the Muslim barbers. He recalled that he had heard the myth of barber origin from his grandfather, and he did not have any doubts about the prevalence of this myth among Muslims. Yousuf, however, interpreted the whole incident in a different way. According to him, "When Mālik-ibn-Dīnār assembled his companions, they chose a person among themselves who was lazy and uninterested in the works of religious propagation. The assembly compelled this person to learn the barbering services and serve the community of Muslims." The version of the myth advanced by Mappilas assigns a socially inferior position to the barber. Accordingly, the key activity during the initial stages of Islam along the coast was the propagation of the faith and practices. As such, those people who are unqualified to carry out lofty and sacred tasks were charged with performing menial and mundane activities, such as barbering. This version basically suggests that a barber is not suitable for the fundamental activity of Islam and therefore he or she should be pursuing the barbering profession. This interpretation could be seen as a reading back to the myth so that barbers' current social positioning could be justified as the outcome of a natural process of selection based on merit. By signifying barbers' occupation on the idea of merit rather than as an ascriptive positionality, Mappila narrative obliterates any possibility of thinking about hierarchical inequality. Merit, as a modern category of individual achievement and ability transcodes caste in other terms in India. In her study of engineering education in India, Ajantha Subramanian (2019) has observed that the idea of merit, apparently an achieved quality, has been operationalized as a mechanism of reproducing inherent caste inequalities. Barbers themselves do not subscribe to this version of the myth. According to their telling, barbers are descendants of an original Muslim who took it upon himself to serve an Islamic community and to fulfill a vital obligation. Therefore, as far as barbers are concerned, it is a dignified and respectable means of livelihood and profession. To understand the nature of hierarchy and meanings attributed across social groups, we need to look at other communities, including the Mappilas to whom I turn next.

Mappilas

The term *Mappila*[5] is used to refer to the majority of Muslims in Kerala. They constitute more than 80 percent of Muslims in Malabar. The term was originally used as an honorific title to refer to the progeny of Indian Ocean traders.[6] The communities that originated in the coastal settlements through marital or temporary exchanges with the traders were designated using the term. There is no evidence in either literary or epigraphic sources that the term Mappila was ever used to designate Muslims of Malabar before the sixteenth century (More 2011, 32). To refer to different communities on the Malabar coast, various prefixes were used along with the term Mappila. Muslims were designated as *Jonaka*-Mappilas. J. B. P. More (2011, 32) writes that the term "Jonaka is derived from Sonagam which in Tamil literature signified Arabia." Since Muslims of Malabar owed their origin to the Arabs (*Sonagars*), they were rightly identified as *Sonaga* or *Jonaka* Mappilas. Similarly, the progeny born of Christian traders were called *Nasrāni*-Mappilas (*Nasrāni* derived from Nazareth, the birthplace of Christ) and of Jews as "*Jūtha*-Mappila." These titles themselves originated after the arrival of the Portuguese on the Malabar coast in the late fifteenth century because it was Duarte Barbosa (2009 [1866], 146), the sixteenth-century Portuguese traveler who had first used the term *Mapulers* to designate Malabar-native Muslims. He writes, "There are a great quantity of Moors, who are of the same language and color as the gentiles of the country. They go bare like the Nairs, only they wear, to distinguish themselves from the gentiles, small round caps on their heads and their beards fully grown. So that it appears to me that these people are a fifth part of all the inhabitants that there are in this country. They call these Moors Mapulers, they carry on nearly all the trade of the seaports: and in the interior of the country, they are very well provided with estates and farms." By the eighteenth century, "Mappila" came to be used to refer to the Muslims on the southwest coast in general, which also included local converts. The term was popularized by the British colonial records as a criminal category, and terms like "fanatic" and "jungle Mappilas" were commonly used to refer to the Mappilas who were antagonistic to the British (Abraham 2014; Kasim 2020; M. T. Ansari 2005). What is interesting about this term is the fact that not only the progeny of Arab traders but also the local converts to Islam came to be referred to as Mappilas. While the majority of such converts came from the lower rung of the Hindu-caste social order, they have been enjoined to the group identity of Mappilas to such an extent that their former Hindu-caste demarcations have been practically obliterated. The baggage of conversion remains only with families whose grandparents were Hindus or if local memory still persists of their original Hindu-caste background. Most Mappilas are converts from groups in the lower rungs of hierarchy such as Thiyyas, Cherumars, Pulayans, and Nayadis (some of these groups are referred to as Dalits today). Their conversion to Islam meant that many of their caste-associated menial jobs such as toddy-tapping and scavenging were not allowed to be practiced within the context of Islamic norms. Dissociation from such menial occupations also aided their overcoming social inferiority. For instance, C. A. Innes (1908), the settlement officer in British Malabar from 1904 through 1905 reported that the population of one of the principal Hindu untouchable castes, Cherumars, who converted to Islam in large numbers in Malabar, was estimated to be 187,758 in 1856. Their number was reduced to 99,009 according to the 1871 census, while, by 1881, the population had further decreased to 64,725—a 65 percent decline in just 25 years—and at a time when the general growth of the population in Malabar was 5.71 percent. Many reasons could be behind this erasure of stigmatic caste names among Muslim converts. As I noted above, many lower castes who engaged in lowly occupations involving substances considered *harām* in Islam, such as liquor, may have been forced to disown their hereditary occupation. Another key reason might be the nature of some conversions, which was described to me by many wealthy Mappila family members. Many lower castes employed in wealthy Muslim households were attracted and motivated to enter Islam by having observed the faith and actions of their patrons. In such cases, the newly converted were taken under the wings of these dominant families in the locality and their family lineage was altered to that of their patrons. In addition, the sheer number of conversions occurring from the lower castes, such as the Cherumars, at a time of increasing conflicts and confrontations between Mappilas and their predominantly Hindu landlords and colonial authorities in the nineteenth century provides another clue (Innes 1908). Some members of the lower castes accepted Islam not only as a faith but also as a weapon against oppression, as many untouchables were attached as slaves to the land and sold along with it (Osella 2009; Panikkar 2001). Because agricultural labor did not have any stigma attached to it, their conversion may have aided in effacing their social origins particularly after two or three generations. Accommodating them into the fold of Islam strengthened the community feelings among Mappilas (Aslam 2013) and the social stigma may have been blunted somewhat in such circumstances.

While most converts to Islam came from the lower rungs of the Hindu social order and from the order of agrestic slaves, there have been converts from upper echelons of the Hindu caste as well. Some of them still asseverate to be converts from this or that caste among Hindus and therefore proclaim their higher social worth compared to other Muslims. These assertions are not often contested because the families who make such claims have been wealthy and wielded great authority and power in the locality. Since the resources and social prestige are still possessed by certain groups among Hindus in Malabar, the declarations made by these Muslim families seem to be an indication that they should also be respected for what their worth is. There are also family lineages among Mappilas who avow descent from the companions of Mālik-ibn-Dīnār or from some other Arab or Persian migrants. Some of these lineages have produced religious scholars over several generations and swear to high status among Mappilas because of their religious scholarship and lineage. It would be useful to compare the status claims made by Muslims in North India to understand the uniqueness of the situation in Malabar. It has been noted in the context of North India that many Muslim groups have taken up new names to elevate their statuses. For example, Arshad Alam (2009) observes that Muslim julahas (weavers) in the north Indian state of Uttar Pradesh sought to prove that they were no less Islamic than the upper-caste Muslims who had represented them in matters of faith. They pursued these interests and announcements by engaging in religious activities such as building mosques and madrassas in their localities and changing their caste name to Ansaris. It is an Arabic term meaning "helpers," which the prophet Muhammad used to characterize people in Medina who provided safety, livelihood, and care to the immigrants from Mecca. Whether such a move brings better status to the lower classes is a thorny issue, but what is important is the fact that all these communities are reconfiguring their history within an Islamic idiom through meaningful practices. Such a reconceptualization should be understood as attempts to frame their ancestral backgrounds in an Islamic cultural milieu, as distinct from a Hindu one.[7] While people in the lower classes attempt to erase their former identities and stigma attached to them through such Islam-izing efforts, those at the higher levels of caste can still claim status owing to their presumed origins from Hindu high castes. Even if caste is dismissed as an unproductive way to think about social hierarchy among Muslims, the sta-tus in the local milieu is still mediated through honor and prestige associated with the caste system.

Because Mappilas were constituted of various social groups, both low and high in status prior to conversion from the Hindu hierarchical schema, such mythical origins have come to shape present identities among Muslims. If a family could claim to be converts from Hindu upper castes such as Brahmins or Nairs, it gave them much prestige in a locality. This insistence, however, needed to be corroborated by many other factors, as all the Mappila interloc-utors who ventured such a contention had other material evidence as well. First, the family genealogy should be extended far beyond the local memory of one or two grandfathers. Most of the families in a locality could enumerate one or two grandfathers who were Muslims. Some of these families could have converted sometime in the nineteenth century and their "pre-history" before they converted may be absent from local memory. Second, the statement of a good lineage needed to be accompanied by property in the form of lands that were bequeathed over generations. Here, too, the underlying principle is local memory. If the property was acquired three or four generations ago, it would suffice to elevate the status of a family in the locality. It is possible that a few individuals amassed wealth through maritime trade; others may have converted from high castes among Hindus who held vast lands as family property. Personal wealth of a family may decline over generations, too, but those families will still retain their status in the locality due to memories (and documents) attesting to their past prestige. In fact, marriage alliances may be sought with these families, even if they lost most of their wealth and power. For example, families of the newly rich Mappilas, who acquired wealth and property from the money acquired in the Gulf countries, might seek to ele-vate their status by contracting a marriage alliance with such families.

Sayyids

The Sayyids in Kerala are honorifically called *Thangal*, a Malayalam term sig-nifying respect and honor. The term "thangal" was earlier used as an hon-orific title for Hindu upper castes like Namboodiri Brahmins and Nayars.

Dale (1980: 131) notes that Sayyid Fadl, the prominent crusader of Muslim revolts in Malabar till his deportation in 1852, had instructed Muslims not to address their Hindu landlords using this honorific title. At the same time, a casual observation of local literature, especially Arabimalayalam writings in the nineteenth century, implies that Thangal was used among Muslims, too, as an honorific title, not only for Sayyids, but also for other religious scholars. Probably due to this flexibility of usage in the nineteenth century, the German lexicographer Gundert (1872: 455) noted that the term was used not only as an honorific title for Namboodiri Brahmins, but also for "Muslim high priest[s] at Ponnani," though they were not traditionally Sayyids. Gundert (1872: 455) further added, on the basis of Tellicherry records for 1796–99, that many people consented to the usage of the term for "descendants of high-priests in each mosque." Kareem (1957: 46) also noted this shift in usage when he argued that all Thangals in Malabar are not necessarily Sayyids. It is reasonable to assume that the term was initially used as a respectful title among Muslims in general, but in later transformations came to denote only Sayyids in Kerala. The slippage in the usage refers to the close relations it had with the Hindu terminology of Thangal, which is said to have been used to refer to Brahmin Sanskrit scholars on the southwest coast of India.

Even though they make up only less than 1 percent of Muslims, Sayyids are held in high esteem among Muslims in Malabar. Still, this is not a Malabar-centric phenomenon. Because Sayyids claim that their family genealogy is linked to the prophet, they are held in high esteem across the Muslim world (Anjum 2011; Gautier and Levesque 2020; Niazi 2020). Soheb Niazi (2020, 472) specifically indicates that declaring affiliation to the family of the prophet or Sayyid status, "whether fictitious or otherwise, has been the most widespread way for communities to support their moral and material objectives with genealogical credentials." Sayyids possess the highest taravād status among Muslims in Malabar.

Taravād originally referred to a matrilineal ancestral household, but today it refers to both the patrilineal and matrilineal ancestral house. It is used as a category to assess the marital compatibility of potential marriage partners. Unlike other Muslim social groups, Sayyids do not send their daughters in marriage to non-Sayyids, alleging that the descendants of the daughters would lose their genealogical links to the prophet Muhammad since the descent is traced through the father. Sayyids may marry women from Mappila taravāds who are held in high esteem in a locality. There have been contestations regarding the relative merits of genealogies among Sayyids in Malabar and there seems to be a clear distinction between Bukhari and Yemeni lineages, which trace descent to the prophet through different ancestors. Marriages between these two lineages were fairly rare in the past, though they are more common today. Irrespective of such inter-lineage distinctions, Sayyids are considered superior to other social groups.

In the case of Mappilas and Sayyids, the kinship grouping, based on its history in the locality in terms of its presumed former social identity, wealth, and power, are further used to estimate the worth of its genealogical status. I address these issues in Chapter 3 with reference to the relationships between barbers and other Muslim groups. Perhaps the group most nearly equal to barbers in terms of its low social status is fishers, which I examine below.

Fishers

The fishers make up more than 10 percent of Muslims in Malabar. They are derogatorily referred to as *pūsalān*. But this term, like the term used for barbers among Muslims, is absent in the Malayalam language. For Mappilas, the term signifies not just the fishers but their sociocultural identity and low status (Mathur 1978).[8] But the fishers posit that the term is a transfiguration of two terms, *pūzhi* (sand) and Islam, and they assert that since Islam arrived through the sea, it was the fishers who embraced Islam earlier than those in the inland areas. They believe that their encounter and acceptance of Islam give them precedence and status among Muslims. This is also articulated in the very geography of these encounters, such that the term pūsalān actually refers to Islam that flourished in the coastal sand. While we do not have much evidence about the Islamization process among the fishers, one can see an edict from a Hindu local king in Calicut, eponymously known as the Zamorins, that he instructed the Hindu fisher communities to bring up one of their male children as a Muslim so that he can assist the Muslim traders (Ayyar 1999; Haridas 2016). Along with the derogatory reference to fishers as pūsalān, one also observes spatial differentiation on the coast between them and the Mappilas. My example comes from the coastal town of Tanur in south Malabar, and such spatial differentiations have been common across the Malabar coast where trading communities flourished. The fishermen along the coast in Tanur are, almost entirely, Muslims. At Tanur, there have been two groups along the coast: the Mappilas living along the beach, concentrated at the trading center near the harbor, who were referred to as *angādikkār* (townspeople), and the fishermen living to both the south and the north sides of the trading center were known as *kadappuratthukār* (beach-people).

Unlike other group names among Muslims, the term *pūsalān* can also be related to the process of tabulation and classification undertaken by the British colonial authorities as part of the census operations. Caste enumeration was a key element of British census operations in India until 1931. The caste subdivisions among various religious communities in India were also tabulated in the 1891 census. In its 1891 Madras census report, Malabar Muslims were categorized into various subdivisions, such as Mappilas, Sayyids, Pathans, Ravuthars, and others. There was also a subdivision called *putiya Islam* (*putiya* means new) in which a few members were identified. In the census report, it was used to signify a convert from the fisher caste of Mukkuvars among Hindus (Stuart 1893, 210). A few historians of Malabar Muslims have surmised that the term *pūsalān* originated from the fusion of these two terms (Koya 1983; Kunju 1989; Lakshmi 2012; Miller 1976). But this seems to be a classic case of colonial operation of producing and reconfiguring new categories to enumerate and rigidify social identities, a process well documented by Nicholas Dirks (2001). When I presented the opinion of a few historians, many fishers contested it, asserting that the term pūsalān does not have anything to do with British colonial operations. They argued that it is possible that some newly converted fishers responded to colonial officials as putiya Islam when they were asked to state their caste identities. They were actually following a common custom among Muslim converts in Malabar in identifying themselves. In fact, they were proclaiming that they do not have caste any longer and that their Muslim identity is the one that is more important. Even today, those who have converted recently or a generation ago are still identified by Muslims as belonging to putiya Islam, and sometimes even the caste markers prior to their conversion remain as exemplified below. While I was doing fieldwork at Tanur, a new convert was mentioned as *Kanakkan Aboobakkar*, and the term *Kanakkan* was used by Muslims to refer to the former slave caste of Cherumars among Hindus. Even after the conversion and assuming the name of the intimate companion of the prophet Muhammad, Aboobakkar's former caste marker was used as a prefix and as an identifying marker for him among Muslims.[9] Such caste or social-identity markers remained with new converts and barbers among Muslims. Whereas fishers were listed as *putiya* Islam in the British census, barbers were recorded in the nineteenth-century British records by using the prefix ossan or otan.[10]

Distinguishing between social groups based on their family origin, status, and occupation continues to be common among Muslims in Malabar.

Although I spent many months doing fieldwork along the coastal settlements in Malabar, I have decided to leave out fishers from the book because the social organization of Muslims along the coast is significantly different from that of the inland areas. As someone originating from the inland area, I had close access to my informants and general knowledge about the social dynamics in the inland areas. To this end, this book focuses on barbers and their social interactions and relationships with Mappilas and Sayyids in inland areas.

Origin Myths Among Non-Muslims

It will be fruitful to compare the origin myths among non-Muslims in India to understand, compare, and contrast the values and methods employed across the communities. It will also help to understand the uniqueness of origin myths among Muslims. Across castes among Hindus, one finds myths that recount the origins of their caste and their contemporary status both in the locality and along the lines of fourfold varna classification of Brahmins, Kshatriyas, Vaisyas, and Sudras. People from various subcastes who make a claim to belong to the highest status group in the varna system, the Brahmins, trace their beginning to Purusa (Sharma 1978), the primal being, and their roles in assisting the various incarnations of the gods. Brahmins in Kerala, who are called Namboodiris, hold that the land of Kerala was created from the sea by Parasurama, the avatar of Vishnu, and they inhabited this land because of him. The myths of upper castes predominantly rope in gods and goddesses as key figures in the origin and formation of their community, enhancing their status and establishing their credentials.

Among the untouchables and lower castes, one finds similarity in the structure of their myths across India (Deliege 1993). Robert Deliege notes that, in the origin myths narrated by Parayars in Tamil Nadu, it is always brothers who are distinguished into untouchables or Brahmins. This occurs as a result of a misunderstanding either in front of God, deities, or parents, or as a result of a conspiracy among brothers. Commonly, these myths attribute the lowly position occupied by untouchables to their involvement with a dead cow. Among the brothers, when asked to remove the dead cow or eat the meat, it is mostly the older brother whose reply or action is misunderstood to mean "my younger brother is a Brahmin." Eventually, the older brother becomes an untouchable, and the younger brother transforms into a Brahmin. This misunderstanding is key to the untouchable myth and is present in many versions, argues Deliege (1993, 536). If untouchables have lost their original relative superiority, it is not because they did something wrong or because there was something inherently bad about them; rather, it is due to a misunderstanding, a pun, a trick, or even because of the conspiracy of their brother. There was nothing inherent in the older brother's condition that made his loss of status inevitable. It is not a result of their deeds in a previous life or because of some congenital defect—both arguments advanced by Brahminical ideology of caste. The poverty and servitude of people in low castes is deemed humanly instituted and is not understood as an inherent attribute of caste. In many versions of this foundational myth, the ancestor of the untouchables behaved in an exemplary way, so, generally speaking, his fall was undeserved and unjust. At worst, the older brother was naïve, but this hardly justifies his consequent downfall. At the same time, these myths accept that cattle scavenging, funeral service, drumming, and beef eating are indeed polluting and despicable activities. The lower castes refuse to admit that these tasks are an inherent characteristic of their own caste but acknowledge that those who engage in them are contemptible. This critical nuance suggests that untouchable myths do not reject the caste system as such but agree with its ideological foundations revolving around the impurity axis. They legitimize untouchability but do not consider that they themselves are degraded and polluting.

One way in which some Hindu lower castes sought to improve their status usually began by adopting a new myth of origin that was consistent with their ambition. This is part of a process that was identified by anthropologist M. N. Srinivas as *Sanskritization* and through which a low caste changes its customs, ideology, ritual, and way of life in keeping with high-caste practices (Srinivas [1972] 2020, 6). Others challenged the entire caste edifice by constructing alternative visions of egalitarian social relations, as is evident in many Buddhist traditions among lower castes across India (Khare 1984, 17). They often reject the "Hindu's idol worship; gods and goddesses; Vedas and law codes; belief in rebirth; Brahminic rites, ceremonies, and sacrifices; and the entire *varna* and *jāti*-engendered hierarchical relations." The nature of the myths narrated by middle castes is radically different from those of the untouchables. Their myths do not contain any elements of degradation. Rather, all elements express their dignity, from their birth to their heroic actions and their refusal to be associated with servile classes. Pan-Hindu beliefs, symbols, and practices continue to figure discursively in their myths. As Assa Doron (2006, 346) puts it, they "play a dominant part within the indigenous framework where local actors employ such symbols and myths to assert their rights in everyday practice, creatively resisting domination and subordination." Among certain castes, associating one's caste with a deity from time immemorial or from a mythical age to elevate its status has been a fairly common practice across India, particularly since the late nineteenth century when the British sought to tabulate and categorize castes on the order of their precedence. A similar phenomenon has been noted in the case of Muslims in North India in the early twentieth century. Muslim weavers tried to relate their community formation to imagined ancestral figures from the Arabian lands (Mehta 1997). To this extent, Muslim and Hindu myths of origin traverse along coalescing lines. To be sure, both groups may seek to attach themselves to charismatic figures, such as the prophet Muhammad or key mythical beings in the Hindu case, to enhance their status. Yet, the cultural anchoring rests upon different discourses, values, and belief systems.

Conclusion

Muslims in Malabar trace their origins from a range of interactions and connections with a group of Arab Muslims who came to the Malabar coast probably in the seventh century AD. Apart from barbers who swear to descend from one of the Arab members, there are many lineages among Mappilas who depose descent from these members. The arrival of Islam on the Malabar coast is a key resource for various groups to imagine and refigure their social identities in Malabar. As I have shown, the myths of origin among Muslims in Malabar are also intertwined with the history of Hindus in the region. The movement toward Islam was not restricted by the political power and authority in the region. On the contrary, the local kings facilitated the dissemination of Islam as long as it contributed to their coffers owing to the increased trade and commerce through the Indian Ocean (Dale 1980; Prange 2018). It is also within the Indian Ocean trade networks and the arrival of Islam through those networks that various Muslim social groups formulate the myths of their origin. These myths are quite distinct from those we find among various Hindu caste groups, both in the region and across India.

The myth helps various Muslim groups fashion a story of their origins. Each group's narration does not alter the structure of the myth; rather, the narrations work as creative interventions that legitimize each group's relative social status and standing among the broader Muslim community. To follow an argument that Edmund Leach (1970, 278) made in the context of highland Burma, myth is a "language of signs in terms of which claims to rights and status are expressed, but is a language of argument, not a chorus of harmony." In the same vein, each social group constructs a version of the story that projects differing and distinctive ideas about what this rank order should be. Precisely, this is what one can observe among Muslims in Malabar. In all versions, respective social groups agree with the general order of the myth. They all agree on the arrival of Mālik-ibn-Dīnār and his companions as the true propagators of Islam along the Malabar coast. The particular versions are built into the story using some historical contingencies. For barbers, the origin lies in the unparalleled need for a barber in the Muslim community; for fishers, the origin lies in the inevitable landing of the Arabian group at the coast and them being inhabitants literally at the seashore and therefore being the first group who originally met and conversed with the newcomers. While the barbers' story is based on the idea of need, the fishers' story is based on the idea of precedence.

Despite the tension over the rank and status between social groups, they all agreed on a single theoretical point: Rank and status among Muslims should somehow be related to making claims with reference to the Arabs who propagated the faith along the Malabar coast. How one relates to these missionaries depended squarely on the membership of the individual within a particular social group. In rendering one's status in the community, Islam and Arab connections were key referents. At the same time, in practical life, as and when social interactions and relationships were to be modulated, various groups constructed status schema like the Hindu social structure in which hereditary descent, occupation, and hierarchical notions were important. One may be tempted to follow Pierre Bourdieu's (1977, 30) point that practice has its own logic and it should not be confused with the logic of the rule. If we confuse the two, we may end up presenting the "objective meaning of objects or works as the subjective purpose of action of the producers of those practices or works." Gyan Prakash (1986) has ethnographically illustrated Bourdieu's point by looking at the social interactions between the lower-caste agricultural laborers and their landlords in Gaya, Bihar. Both groups believed in various forms of spirits and dangers of possession and possibility of harm. While the material world was clearly in control of the landlords and it manifested in the inequalities in landholdings, assumption of local authority, and power, the same could not be said about the spirit world. The lower-caste agricultural laborers were believed to be more powerful in controlling the spirit world. Therefore, upper-caste landlords tried to save their spirit world from having any connection with the lower-caste one through various means. But everything could not be ensured. So, as and when required, the upper-caste landlords also tried to propitiate the lower-caste spirits. However, they did not simply follow and submit to the demands of the lower-caste spirits. They always sanitized and subordinated them through some Brahminical rituals or meanings. The point here is that both theoretical and practical realms may follow distinct logic. They can coexist in everyday life through variegated forms of interactions and compromises.

The coexistence of the theoretical and the practical may take various forms. They need not necessarily follow the logic of the dominating classes. In the case of Muslims, the realm of the theoretical is never in contestation among various groups. They all agree that Islam and Arab connections are the two registers through which rank and status should be claimed. On the practical level, however, we see a multiplicity where various groups tussle with each other using the theoretical registers. The lower classes imagine new social relationships through Islam and the Arab connection. This also takes different forms in the case of barbers and fishers. Barbers imagine new social relationships by connecting themselves to the Arabs genealogically and finding equivalence with the caste of Nayar-barbers among Hindus. The myths among them valorize the Hindu caste social structure. The fishers, however, cannot claim any kind of genealogical connection with the Arabs. Rather, they imagined it through Islam and through precedence. They claimed that Arabs made the first contact with them and accepted them without any barriers of caste as it existed in the locality. Fishers further claim that they accepted Islam in Malabar earlier than everyone else and the treatment shown by the original Arabs is the quintessence of Islam, which is not practiced by local Muslims. The Mappilas, however, vouch for higher status not only through Islam and Arab connections but also by tracing their genealogy through the Hindu caste framework. Although a few Mappila families claim to have been directly converted by Mālik-ibn-Dīnār and his companions, most of them cannot claim a direct relation with the Arabs. Rather, they construct their status by proclaiming their belongingness to some upper-caste Hindu families prior to their conversion. Both theoretical and the practical diverge here, by positioning one's status within the cultural frame of Hindu caste system in Kerala. At the same time, this is not a claim that can be publicly valorized because it locates one's social location in an uncertain past which cannot be elucidated by any mythical narrative. In contrast, Mālik-ibn-Dīnār myth gives you a blueprint for thinking about status. This is so because the theory adhered to by all Muslim groups is singular and it is the push and pull of the practical that shapes how theory can be used for particular purposes.

The origin myths of Muslim social groups provide a useful window into the overall argument of this book and to what comes in the following chapters. The nature of Islam in Malabar was irrevocably intertwined with the political, economic, and cultural repertoire of the region since the beginning. The local rulers initially provided a safe and comfortable abode for the faith and followers to flourish, as in the case of Mālik-ibn-Dīnār and his companions, outlined above. The Muslim community along the coast grew and, by the fifteenth century, Muslims came to dominate the entire Indian Ocean trade and constitute a major naval force for the local Hindu rulers. All Muslim groups share a narrative in this common fate of the region. In addition, in analyzing how Muslim groups weave origin myths, my intention has been to highlight the co-embedding and mutual implication of Muslims and Hindus. They all share in the local structure of the patronage system, its pervasive memories and lore, and the role of family lineages. Even in these generally available repertoires, Muslims also try to compose their fate with a fabric of Islam without necessarily discarding the local cultural practices. They all have a place in these myths to emphasize, corroborate, and sometimes uphold the economy, the political structures, and the cultural beliefs and values in the region.

It is the common inheritance of these values and culturally meaningful structures that become points of negotiation, overlapping, and contestation, which drives barbers in their self-assertion. They seek to redefine, shape, and restructure their social relations with other Muslim groups in Malabar. As a group, barbers are often defined and shaped by reference to their inferior social status vis-à-vis other groups that draw upon ideas and practices of Islam to denigrate them. However, barbers actively contest these claims by drawing upon Islam as a vital ideological force to challenge and negotiate established hierarchies and relationships. The varied threads that make up this understanding of Islam—historical, economic, political, and cultural— thus form a capacious terrain that can accommodate a host of contradictions and assertions, to which multiple groups strategically align themselves.

CHAPTER 3

Hierarchical Intimacy

Sitting on the verandah of our two-story house, I sometimes see Maryam, a bent-over figure enveloped in a black burqa walking either up or down the road in front. From her gait, one could be confused over whether she is just walking briskly or running. She looks frail, her back stooped, yet her steps are agile and quick. Maryam, as the barber woman in our neighborhood, is always in attendance in houses where a woman has delivered a child recently. She visits these houses to provide various services, such as oiling and bathing newborns and their mothers and helping to cook special foods for new mothers. I have seen Maryam in her younger days as well, walking straight-backed in traditional clothing of white mundu, *kuppāyam* (blouse), and *thattam* (dupatta). Nowadays, she wears a burqa over these clothes, removing it once she reaches her client's house. When I asked Maryam's age, my mother estimated that she could be over seventy years old. In spite of her advanced age, Maryam continues to regularly visit homes in our locality for work. My mother laments, "She still has to work, poor woman!" implying that a woman of Maryam's age is not supposed to work for anyone. According to my mother, she needs to be resting at home and preparing for her onward journey to the hereafter. My mother attributes Maryam's plight to the lack of kindness and generosity on her children's part. At the same time, my mother wonders who will succeed Maryam after her death, as her daughter-in-law refuses to offer barbering services.

As I sit on the verandah, if our eyes meet, Maryam will beam a nearly toothless smile and invariably say, without ever being asked, "I am going to that [names the person] house today. Please tell your mother that I will come later." She occasionally visits our house, and my mother, behind her back, always refers to her as "our *ossāthi*," a derogatory term that roughly translates as "barber woman" and which most barbers I know detest. When she visits, my mother often asks me for money. "Give 100 rupees. I want to give to ossāthi Maryam." If I ask why we should give her money, my mother replies: "She is our ossāthi. It is for her happiness." There is no rhyme or reason for this gift, other than the long-standing reciprocity of relationships that can be traced back to the services provided in the past. It is simply a continuation of a custom that existed in other modes in the past.

Each time Maryam drops in, it is not to provide any barbering services. Rather, it is to exchange pleasantries and share local gossip. My mother will give Maryam tea, snacks, and some money when she is about to leave. While sipping her tea, Maryam will tell all the news in the neighborhood, particularly about childbirth: who is pregnant, who has delivered or is about to, which houses have a home nurse to attend to the mother and the newborn. The news will be interspersed with gossip about women in the community; how a particular mother-in-law or daughter-in-law may be behaving with each other, who is getting married, or why someone is getting a divorce. Maybe my mother, apart from continuing a custom, was equally interested in listening to the neighborhood gossip. Once she finishes her cup of tea, Maryam will offer a prayer for our general health and well-being and then rush away, saying she needs to attend a particular house in the next neighborhood.

The monetary gift on the part of my mother and the services provided by Maryam hark back to the reciprocal relationships that existed between barber families and other Muslim groups. These associations were modeled on patron-client relations and the payment was always rewards in kind. Such relationships existed in Malabar until the 1970s at the very least. It was around then that barber men started opening shops and unionizing themselves, despite resistance from their patrons. Stirred by the union movement, barbers sought to restructure their interactions and relationships with their patrons through financial transactions, shifting their work from domestic to public spaces. Barber women, too, began demanding financial remuneration, instead of rewards in kind, for their services.

This chapter details the patron-client relationships that existed in Malabar until the 1970s, highlighting the economic and political structures that sustained these relationships. Using personal and familial stories shared with me by members of the barber community, I want to showcase the hierarchical nature of relationships that barbers cultivated with Mappilas and Sayyids in Malabar. I suggest that the barbers' relationship with other Muslims is better understood by the idea of *hierarchical intimacy*. I develop this concept from the works of Lawrence Babb (1975; 1983b; 1986). Studying the relationships between gurus and devotees in many modern devotional traditions of popular Hinduism in India, he posits that hierarchy and intimacy constitute the modality of their relationships. The devotees sought to partake in the spiritual powers of the guru by offering unflinching service to the guru and through acts of touching, taking, and even consuming materials that emerged out of the guru's body. It may be the remnants of food eaten by the guru or water used by the guru to wash his feet. The devotees believed that the inner spiritual nature of the guru flowed through these mediums, and one could assimilate such powers into one's own body, thus enhancing the devotee's ability to achieve salvation. The result of this physiological engagement is the closest possible intimacy with hierarchical implications. In the context of wider Hindu cultural practices, Babb notes, to submit to each of these physiological engagements is to accept subordination by engaging with what is otherwise considered polluting, crude, and filthy. Yet, the hierarchical implication of such transactions is recognized by religious traditions as of high religious value. As Babb (1983b, 307) observes, "Serving the guru, obeying him in all things, being his slave, and accepting his interiorizing body-flows are all gestures that 'banish egoism' by expressing humility and surrender." Such actions were geared to leading the devotee on a path of self-realization and salvation.

Such practices are common in the wider Hindu culture. For example, Chaitanya (2014) describes a ritual called *made snana* in a temple in the south Indian state of Karnataka. In the ritual, Brahmins eat meals on plantain leaves at designated places in the temple. After they eat, those who want to perform the ritual pick up the banana leaves with leftover food. "The leaves are spread on the floor of the temple and the devotees begin to roll over them, spreading the leftover food all over their bodies." They later bathe in the nearby river. The underlying belief is that the saliva of Brahmins has the power to alleviate and cure the maladies of those from other communities. A vital prerequisite for the self's liberation is the devotee's cultivation of humility, enacted through these practices, among many others. The spiritual transformations associated with the interactions and behavior between a guru and the devotee are not limited to Hinduism alone. It takes different forms, cultural attributes, and meanings in the case of Islam.

In Islam, we can observe the guru-devotee relationships playing out in a slightly different manner between Sufi pirs and their murids. The most common relationship between a Sufi pir and a murid "is established by a pledge of allegiance (*bai'at*) in which a disciple makes vows of obedience and service to a spiritual guide who is the head of a Sufi order" (Pemberton 2006, 62).

Here, too, the self of the murid as an autonomous decision maker is denied in the presence of the pir. He must obey the pir however irrational or absurd his directives may appear on the surface. The killing of the *nafs* (self) is believed to be achieved here by "the disciple merging himself with the saint, and ultimately with the prophet and God" (Werbner 2003, 146). The total submission is articulated by the rejection of even the probability of questioning the decisions made by the pir. While in some Hindu traditions, salvation was seen as the ultimate goal of the guru-shishya relationship, in Islam, it is directed toward the knowledge of Allah facilitated by the spiritual guidance to inculcate piety provided by the pir. In both religious traditions, physical intimacy, submission, and lack of questioning are held as supreme virtues.

Such intimate, hierarchical relationships are not limited to the religious milieu alone. In studies on patronage in India, scholars have noted similar associations structuring the relationships between a patron and a client (Bayly 1989; Breman 1993; Dirks 1987; Piliavsky 2021). In the case of Rajasthan, Piliavsky (2021, 29) emphasizes that clients always look up to the patrons for the flow of materials from them, in terms of money, rewards, care, and protection. It is the active relationships between a client and the patron that construct the full personhood to both parties. She also notes that various moral registers, such as compassion, empathy, and responsibility also factor into the patronage relationships.[1] However, she does not address how these patronage relationships flow from the idioms of larger South Asian devotional forms and traditions. The linkage with the devotional traditions is key to understanding patronage relationships on the Indian subcontinent so that we do not reduce such relationships as characteristic of economic relationships alone.

To my mind, one can draw a comparable analogy in examining the relationships between Muslim barber servants and their Muslim patrons in Malabar, as that of a guru-devotee or pir-murid relationship. Unlike these religious pairings, which are imbued with sacred teachings, practices, and meanings, the barbers' relationships with their patrons are routinized in the mundane, everyday domains. This absence of spiritual element is key, as it means that rather than acceptance and devoted submission, the relationship turns on domination, inequality, and power over the subordinated. At the same time, as we saw in the previous chapter, a moral coloring is provided to barbering services as religious obligation toward the Muslim community. A barber is an indispensable figure in the Muslim community and the barber's identity is intimately tied up in his patrons. While barbers are considered brethren in faith and in offering an essential service to Muslims, their social subordination is activated through various routine and ritual practices. I show that the relationships between barbers and others were shaped by wealth and power, and they appear to be based on a form of exchange that prioritized intimacy, hierarchy, and dependence. It is to refer to the everyday workings of the patronage relationships that I use the term hierarchical intimacy. Hierarchical intimacy means that the patron and client are located within moral relationship of dependence and domination. The intimacy that is brought about through dependency should always be mediated through hierarchy that ensures subordination. It cannot revolve around a mutual understanding of each other, as the term intimacy would usually mean. The knowledge of the other that is acquired through intimacy cannot be repurposed for any other relationships than that of hierarchy.

I describe these relations, following the works of scholars like Dilip Menon (1994a; 1994b) and P. Radhakrishnan (1989), both of whom show how Hindus and Muslims in Malabar participated in a common patronage system without their religious identities getting in the way. Menon further notes that the clearly demarcated and straitjacketed religious identities of Muslims and Hindus and bounded notions of community are products of the late nineteenth and early twentieth century in Malabar. I add to these conversations by suggesting that Muslims not only partook in a common repertoire of patronage relations but also infused these practices with Islamic ideas and meanings, often providing support and justifications for the hierarchical relationships among themselves.

I posit that patronage needs to be understood as a key form of social organization today, however we might feel opposed to such an idea in the modern world. We presuppose that individuals are autonomous, free actors, who then come together to imagine the common good that works for all. As opposed to this idea, we need to reflect on the multiple patronage relationships that structure our everyday behavior, as parents, siblings, teachers, bosses, leaders, and entrepreneurs. Not only is patronage a valued form of relationship in multiple social spheres, I contend that, but it also works as the underlying mechanism of caste in South Asia, structuring relationships of subordination and dependence between the haves and the have-nots. Rather than looking at caste (in the form of varna) as the quintessential South Asian form of social organization,[2] we need to analyze patronage as the South Asian habitus to be able to understand the workings of hierarchy in several contexts. Scholars have usually analyzed patronage as a key terrain of the manifestation of caste. A clear exception has been the work by Piliavsky (2014) in which she and others have looked at how patronage is structuring political relationships in South Asia. As I have already noted, patronage also structures relationships with the sacred in religious traditions. If we analyze social relations through the lens of patronage, we may get better insights into the workings, rationalizations, and contestations structuring hierarchies today.

Mahallu: A Muslim Locality

As I learned through conversations with many barbers and Mappilas, Muslim settlements in Malabar pivot around Friday prayer mosques. Nowadays, each Muslim family is attached to such a mosque through monthly contributions, involvement in Friday prayers, participation in various rituals at the mosque, solemnization of marriages by mosque officials, and the right of each family member to be buried in the mosque graveyard. This socioreligious ecosystem is called *mahallu*, derived from the Arabic term meaning space, locality, or station. This institution is quite distinct from the north Indian *mohallas* or *mohullas*, which means "a place where one makes a halt" (Yanagisawa and Funo 2018, 386). These were administrative tax units established by the Mughals in North India. They were autonomous residential units headed by chiefs, or *mohulladars*, and functioned as organizing units for social activities such as celebrations, festivals, and negotiations with city authorities (Bayly 1983, 2002; Yanagisawa and Funo 2018).[3] In Malabar, mahallu was more of a socioreligious institution without much administrative significance. At the same time, matters such as resolving disputes between husbands and wives, between children and parents, and between member households were overseen and arbitrated by the mahallu authorities. While the solemnization of marriages is conducted by the mosque officials, it needs to be registered at the local panchayat with a letter from the mosque. In one sense, the mahallu acted as a civil-society institution without any legal authority for punishments but with its own forms of control and authority.

The institution of mahallu drew its authority from the religious and managerial officials associated with the mosque, which was in turn accepted by the community associated with the mosque, often through custom and sometimes through democratic participation. Rather than a geographical boundary, its borders were social and therefore shifting due to the movement of people in and out of a locality. Moreover, if we consider the geographical extension of a mahallu, it also consisted of Hindu families, but they did not have any role in a mahallu nor were they subject to its arbitration. In the past, the institution of the mahallu was controlled by wealthy Mappilas. In fact, the land for the mosque and graveyard was gifted by wealthy Mappilas or Sayyids through *waqf*. The term *waqf* denotes an inalienable charitable endowment given for a religious institution or practice. Muslims offered paddy fields, orchards, and even individual coconut trees for the maintenance of mosques, other religious institutions such as madrassas, and for practices like the recitation of the Quran or feeding religious students (Naseef and Santhosh 2022). The mosque and other religious institutions were also sometimes solely built by rich Mappilas and Sayyids. These influential families controlled the affairs in the mahallu, as they were the officials who managed the mosque and maintained the religious officials. As such, they had the power to boycott any family in the mahallu by not only denying the services of the religious officials but also prohibiting all members of the mahallu from mingling with the boycotted. This was easier in the case of barbers who were dependent on their patrons in the locality. As these prosperous families generally controlled the local trade and commerce, facing their wrath could be against the interests of people in the mahallu.

It is within this structure of asymmetrical wealth and power that we should understand the key role played by a barber family. A barber family was an important social and religious functionary in a mahallu, as barbers provided services like hair removal, nail-cutting, tonsuring, circumcision, and midwifery. In the past, under each mahallu there was a barber. As soon as a new mahallu was formed in a locality, breaking from an extended older mahallu because of the increase in population or due to logistical difficulties,[4] a barber family was invited to join the mahallu. I met a few barbers whose grandfathers were relocated in such a manner from the localities of their ancestral households to new mahallus established many kilometers away. It is possible that barbers did not have much say in choosing whether to relocate because their matters were mostly decided by the landed elites and the mahallu committee and the discussions for their relocation also happened between mahallu committees. At the same time, we cannot also say that barbers were uninterested in the whole matter because increase in population generally motivated barber families to relocate from one place to another, if opportunities arose. Muhammad, one among my seventy-year-old barber respondents, recollected that his grandfather was invited and relocated to a new mahallu by a Mappila landlord in the late 1920s or early 1930s, thirty kilometers away from his ancestral household. The landlord gave his grandfather one acre of land on his word. In those days, the land was not measured; rather, the seller would talk about boundaries in each direction, marking them with a specific tree or with topographical features such as rocks or streams, and so on. Muhammad surmised that the land was about an acre. The land was not registered to his grandfather's name. This practice was quite common and most older barbers I talked to attested to this practice as common in those times between a client and a patron. The patron's verbal promise was enough to guarantee a deal. However, when the patron died and the property divisions were afoot later, in the 1960s, his children refused to honor the patron's verbal promise made to Muhammad's grandfather. This is also the time when discussions on land reforms and redistribution of land on the part of the government gathered steam in Kerala. People were trying to register lands in their names or to evict or coerce their tenants and clients to relocate or to be satisfied with the offer made by the landlords. After much bickering and negotiation involving the mahallu committee, Muhammad's grandfather was coerced into being satisfied with forty cents of land (equal to 2/5 of an acre) and he immediately registered the land in his name. His descendants, including Muhammad, continued to live in this plot of land. Similar mechanisms are also observed among Hindus. In his study on potters in a village in central India, Miller (1986, 538) notes that a working potter family was brought to the village by the headman when the village lacked a working potter in the previous generation, and the family was given about three acres of free land and housing. The difference between the patronage systems of Hindus and Muslims seems to be related to the religious justifications and cultural sensibilities attached to them, an issue I will address later.

While the whole mahallu depended on the services provided by the barber, an individual member of the mahallu, often one belonging to a wealthy and landed Mappila or Sayyid family, organized the living arrangements (including land and housing) for the barber family. If the individual owned land adjacent to the mahallu mosque, the barber was offered a plot of land close to the mosque. Or, if the individual was more interested in receiving the services of the barber family, he provided a small plot of land to the barber closer to his ancestral house. In other cases, barbers themselves bought small plots of land in new localities and moved there either because of an increase in members in the household or a resultant lack of work in the locality for barbering services. As far as I know, this was possible only for a few barbers who were experts in conducting circumcision and could receive cash payment for the same. Unlike normal barbering services, circumcision and midwifery always involved money transactions between patrons and the barbers. In most cases, the living arrangements offered to the barbers meant that they were indebted to their wealthy patrons and could not overstep patron's authority. To appreciate the role and significance of barbers in the lives of Muslims, we should understand the materiality of their occupation—in particular, how hair was conceived as a symbolic register of caste and community in Malabar.

Significance of Hair and Other Bodily Waste

As elsewhere, hair—its manipulation, absence/presence, and materiality—had cultural significance in Malabar. There was a correct hair behavior, as it were, for most of the Hindu castes and other religious communities in India. Hair is primarily a public symbol as Gananath Obeyesekere (1981, 15) would call it, as it conveys a public message—the social identity of the individual. The essence of publicly shared symbolic behavior is communication, and, as we will see, such behavior conveys culturally meaningful ideas about self and other, across gender, age, and caste/class divisions. Such meanings are upheld through institutional mechanisms, such as family, kinship, and caste networks.

Muslims and various Hindu castes in Malabar considered hair to be an important marker of social identity and sought to fashion it in particular ways. Across religious communities and groups in Malabar, hair had highly significant connotations with its ritual, symbolic, and hierarchical implications.[5] Many castes among Hindus and religious communities such as Muslims and Christians had unique hairstyles, which denoted their respective identity either as a caste group or as a religious community. In Malabar, many castes, such as Nairs and Ezhavas, had their own barbers. As Edgar Thurston, the British ethnographic surveyor of South India between 1901 and 1908 noted, the Nairs were served by their own caste barbers known as Velakkatthalavan (Thurston 1909, 7:336) and the Ezhavas were served by a group within them called the Kāvuthiyya (Thurston 1909, 3:266). The barbers among Hindu castes also officiated as ritual specialists in the funeral ceremonies. According to my interlocutors, transgression of caste boundaries among Hindus was met with severe sanctions—excommunication—even in matters pertaining to providing and securing services. Thurston (1909, 3:269) notes that if "a high caste barber operates for a man of lower caste, he loses his caste thereby, and has to pay a fine, or in some other way expiate his offence before he gains re-admission into his community." Regarding barbers among Muslims, Thurston (1909, 3:269) further observed that barbers "are employed only by the Muhammadans. Even in their own community, however, they do not live in commensality with other [Muslims] though gradations of caste are not cognized by their religion." Cross-faith services were also forbidden. A Muslim barber never provided services to Hindu castes or other religious communities. Similarly, non-Muslim barbers would refuse services to Muslims. At the same time, unlike Hindu-caste barbers, Muslim barbers served all Muslims irrespective of their social standing.

Such restrictions may have had their origin in caste-based conventions, but they also relate to the materiality of hair itself, with its cultural meanings driving social action. There was a deep link between hair and social relations. Hair was considered a product of systematic ordering, signifying both the moral comportment of a Muslim self and a marker of identity that distinguished Muslims from people belonging to other faiths. The ideal self-fashioning of a Muslim male was that of a clean-shaved head and a trimmed beard and moustache. Since barbering activities were conducted in the domestic sphere, which was controlled by the eldest male member, such organizational structures imposed the "Islamic" style upon every member of the household. I have put "Islamic" in quotes because what the Islamic style has been varied and changed over time, subject to multiple forces, such as migration, changing consumer choices, and social relations, among other things. I will address these issues in Chapter 6.

For now, I want to focus on the living arrangements within a typical Mappila household in Malabar. It was largely dominated by the male head of the family, in part because he also controlled the family's wealth and resources. As soon as some members were able to move out of the restricted milieu of the family because of migration in pursuit of jobs, they took the liberty of sporting long or unruly hair. If they returned to their locality with their new style, they were mocked or even insulted in the community. According to what I was told by a seventy-year-old barber, such wayward Mappilas were even called the respective caste names based on which caste's hair and facial style they apparently imitated. Further, they also suffered pressure from the family and mahallu officials to discard the new style and return to the ways of a "true Muslim." They were also maligned by being called a *kāfir*, a severely degrading term to attribute to a Muslim, as it carried the meaning of a heathen, with all sorts of demeaning connotations. The fashioning of one's hair represented belonging to the Muslim community and carried significant implications for one's own religious values and beliefs, as well as for one's social identity more broadly.

Apart from being a public symbol, hair had other connotations in Muslim communities. It was considered, like other bodily waste, such as saliva, sweat, and blood, as dirt, which calls for specific engagements. These materials take on the form of dirt once they are removed from their natural environment. They are all potential sources of impurity, and water should be used to remove the waste from the body. As Mary Douglas ([1966] 1988, 2) pointed out, dirt is essentially disorder and therefore needs attention to bring order into our lives and environment. Douglas sought to universalize this idea through a structuralist analysis, observing that "matter out of place" cut across cultures to render materials polluted, impure, and ambiguous. As such, the materiality of things expresses the values of a community and mediates the experiences of individual members. Douglas ([1966]1988, 35) further notes that dirt-avoidance is a matter of religion, drawing on the Judeo-Christian world. For Muslims, she maintains, it signifies a set of ordered relations and contravention of that order. Dirt is a by-product of systematic ordering and classification of matter, insofar as ordering involves rejecting inappropriate or ambiguous elements.

Apart from hair, the engagements of barbers with other Muslims also involved encountering strangers and their other bodily waste. It is, therefore, instructive to look at how the engagement with the body of the other is conceived in Islam (Amir 2019, 2024; Frembgen 2008; 2011; Marva 2018). Wasim Frembgen (2008, 4), who studied the profession of Muslim masseurs in Pakistani Punjab, specifically highlights how social inferiority was operationalized through touch and working on other peoples' bodies. He notes that while "there is a clear valorization of massage among Punjabi Muslims, . . . official Islamic morality, which treats the body as a source of shame, condemns an occupation where caste-like menial people . . . work with other people's bodies and remove waste products." Such shame is also traced back to the prophet Muhammad who is said to have never shown his body to strangers, as explained to me by a Mappila religious scholar. To this end, even if the sight of the naked body constituted an act of shame, then physical engagement through touch with foreign bodies carried further restrictions and taboos. Islam had a range of cultural norms and social relations that conceptualized what constituted bodily comportment, dignified action, and taste, which were publicly sanctioned and recognized. Accordingly, contact with sweat, stray hair, and all other waste products coming out of the body were regarded as dirty and ritually polluting (Frembgen, 2008). Muslims in Malabar usually bury the stray hair, nail cuttings, and so forth. While it is a Sunnah (following the tradition of the prophet) in the case of men, for women, it is mandatory to bury these stray materials. They were undesirable stuff, that needed to be discarded in proper manner.

A Muslim barber works intimately with his or her clients by touching, holding, and massaging various body parts. For example, a barber dampens the head of patrons before shaving, by applying water using his hands. While shaving, holding his knife in the right hand, a barber holds the heads of patrons at particular angles to make their job easier. The engagement with bodily secretions and hair, sweat, and odor were considered undesirable and sometimes impure in Islam. When I asked Rasheed Saqafi,[6] a religious scholar, what the legal status of bodily secretions was in Islam, he opened his copy of *Fath-ul Mueen*, a key text used in Malabar in institutions of higher religious learning, such as dars and colleges,[7] and read aloud a few passages. He posited that in Islamic jurisprudence materials like hair, sweat, and odor are considered undesirable and unhygienic, while materials like blood are considered impure. When I asked him what this conception means in practical life, he narrated a hadith from the prophet Muhammad where he advises his companions not to eat onion before appearing in public. Rasheed Saqafi interpreted it, "If you eat onion, whenever you open your mouth, it will emit bad odor, and it may create distress among your brothers." He continued his reasoning, "similarly, stray hair, sweat and odor will create distress among those whom you encounter; so, one should take care of such things. With all these materials on your body, you can pray but it is better avoided. As for blood, it is *najas* (impure) and you cannot pray without cleaning it." The general perception of these materials is that they were undesirable and unhygienic, and engagements with them shaped the perception of barbers' work as undignified.

In various professions, people meet several forms of dirt. For example, in the medical profession, lab technicians, nurses, and doctors engage with various bodily wastes. But the services they provide are not looked down upon as undignified compared to the services barbers provide. While these two professions are considered distinct now, as Sajdi (2013) and Amir (2019, 3) note, barbers also acted as surgeons in most parts of the world. In the case of Britain, as early as 1745, barbers and surgeons parted ways to set apart their own professions as unique and specialized. In the case of Malabar, while barbers continued to perform minor surgical procedures, there were local doctors or *vaidyans*, as they were called, to attend to the physical ills.[8] What

distinguishes the barbers and the vaidyans is the nature of their relationships to the patrons. While barbers were involved in long-standing patronage
relations, vaidyans entertained professional relationships that often revolved
around monetary compensation rather than rewards in kind. The barbering
services remained in the domestic sphere and were only professionalized in
the 1970s, as we will see in Chapter 6. In the next section, I look at how the
barbering services were organized in the domestic sphere in Malabar.

Barbers in a Patronage Network

"My grandfather started early in the morning," Abu, a sixty-eight-year-old
barber said when I asked him about the routine of his grandfather, a Muslim barber in a small village in the 1930s in southeast Malabar. Abu and I
were sitting in his house on a summer morning in 2019, and he was narrating
to me his personal and family history. As a barber, his grandfather ventured
out of the house, walking the length and breadth of the locality to serve his
patrons. Barbers' services were sought for regularly shaving hair and cutting
nails, trimming beards and moustaches, shaving armpits, and participating
in various life-cycle rituals, such as circumcision, tonsure, and ear piercing.
They were required to visit every home sometimes once a week or once a
fortnight as demanded by the patrons. As I learned from a few barber women,
they too were attached to houses in each mahallu. Barber women cut the nails
of women and children, removed the hair of children, shaved the crotch and
armpits of women, and provided midwifery and related services. They were
duly notified once a woman became pregnant in the locality, and they visited the woman's residence at least once a month until she gave birth. Similar
to midwives, barber women offered counsel and practical advice during the
course of the pregnancy. In wealthy Mappila and Sayyid households, the barber women were asked to stay overnight from the ninth month onward until
the baby was born. Many barber women told me that they had to follow these
commands because of their dependence on these households, disregarding
their own family lives. In other cases, where barber women were already notified about the pregnancy, the men or other relatives in the house rushed to
the barber household to summon them as soon as the woman went into labor,
experiencing pains. As part of their work, barber women would often need to
drop everything in the house, including their own nightly sleep, to attend a
woman in labor, sometimes in the middle of the night.

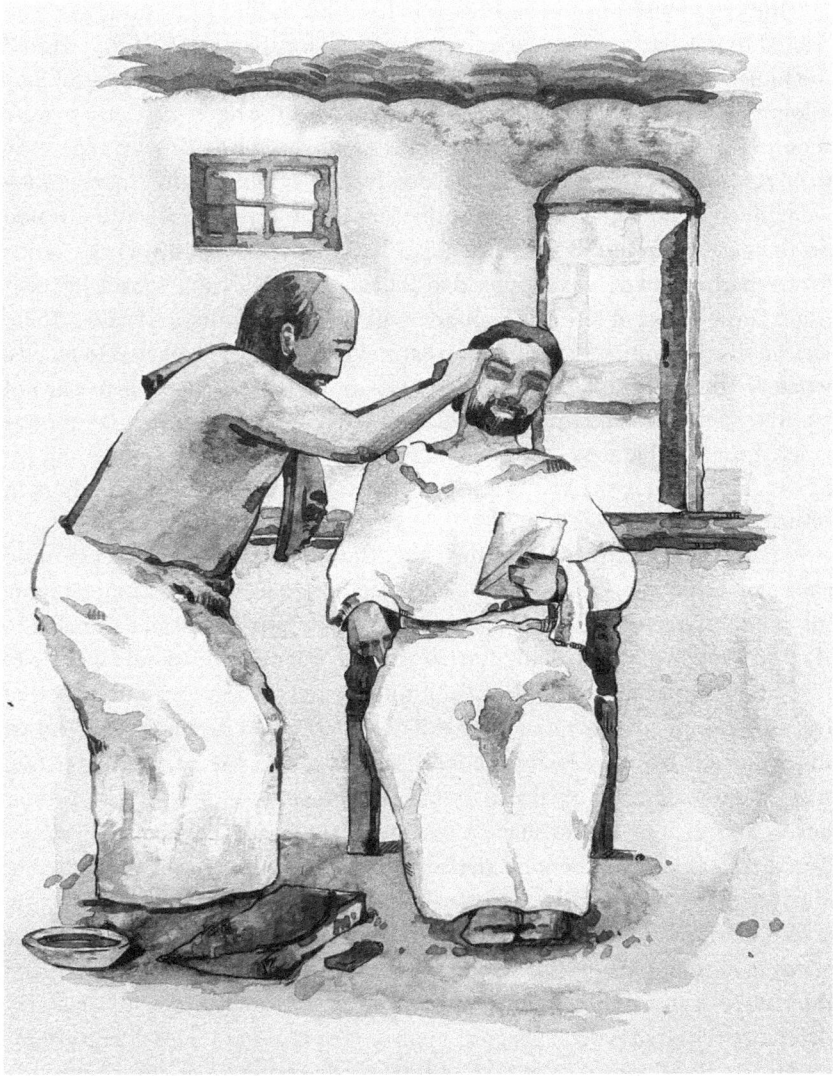

Figure 3. Barber sizing the beard of a patron © Aharika Baskar.

The compensation for barbers was fixed according to custom. As Abu related to me, barbers were not given any wage for their work. If they visited the house of a patron throughout the year, they were entitled to around four kilograms (five *idangazhi*) of rice twice a year after the harvests. Barbers were required to come with a sack and collect it themselves. This was the only fixed reward they received for their work. During other times of the year, they were given a portion of whatever other agricultural produce was cultivated on their patron's land. If something was harvested, a portion was kept aside for the barber and he was supposed to collect it when he came for the job next time. These seasonal rewards included vegetables, coconuts, and yams. There was no fixed quantity for these rewards, and barbers were expected to receive whatever they were offered without any negotiations. The patronage was not based on a financial contract as is the case today where the amount of money is fixed for specific jobs. A barber was not considered a person owning his labor; rather, he or she was an instrument to provide services for others in return for whatever was offered.

Like similar occupations at the time, the socialization of a barber child started at a young age. A barber boy learned his profession by accompanying his father on his rounds, providing services to the households in the mahallu. As Abu explained, this usually started when a boy was able to hold a knife in his hands properly, around the age of nine or ten. A boy commonly started learning at home, working on the head of his father. As the boy accompanied the father on his rounds, he was also introduced to the patrons. Abu said that, in some cases, the patrons would encourage the boy to learn on their heads, and the boy would shave a portion of the head, and his father would do the rest. In such encounters, the boy was given some coins by the patron to encourage and congratulate him for the excellent work he has done. Through such initiation and imitation, barber boys learned not only to provide the services to their patrons but also to internalize the bodily comportment and the nature of social interactions built into these encounters; for instance, the deference required while engaging a patron, the types of topics that are commonly discussed, or how the exchange of goods and services course through the year in line with the harvest, and so on.

In the case of women, girls, too, start accompanying their mothers at a young age during the course of their workday. The experience Ayisha, a sixty-two-year-old woman, shared with me is quite revealing in this regard. Ayisha conducted midwifery alone. "It began as an adventure," she said—when she was just twelve years old, though she had accompanied her mother many

times without participating directly in the process. When she was in the third
class in school, her mother suffered a stroke and was shifted to her maternal
house to get better care. Because there was no one to look after the house
and her younger siblings, Ayisha had to stop going to school. Her mother
was bedridden for around six months. It was during this time that Ayisha
was forced to act as a midwife even though she did not have any prior experience as a midwife. One morning, the husband of a woman in their locality
came anxiously to their house to call upon Ayisha's mother. When the person
learned about her mother's illness, he beseeched her father to tell him what
he should do now. "My father told him that my daughter is just twelve years
old, but you can take her along with you, and I am sure Allah will be with
her," Ayisha told me. Because she approximates her age at around sixty-two
years, she believes this incident might have occurred in the late 1960s. She
recalled how her father handed her the sharp knife with which the umbilical
cord is cut. It was eleven in the morning when they walked to the woman's
house. When they arrived, Ayisha found that it was a mud house thatched
with grass, and it had two rooms, a kitchen, and a front yard. She saw the
woman writhing in pain in the darkest room in the house, lit only by the light
from a kerosene lamp. A middle-aged woman, a neighbor, was keeping vigil.
This woman instructed Ayisha on how her mother would have undertaken
labor, had she been there. It was the pregnant woman's fifth childbirth. While
the first four were all female infants, the fifth was delivered by Ayisha on her
first job as a midwife, and it was a boy. There is a strong preference for sons in
India, and particularly if the firstborn is a girl, parents expect the next child
to be a boy (Kugler and Kumar 2017). Muslims in Malabar usually prolong
fertility until a son is born and Ayisha was happy to be part of such an occasion for the family. The infant, born around the time of the noon prayer, was
laid out on an areca-nut leaf. When I asked her whether an areca-nut leaf had
any ritual implication, she simply said that she doesn't know but added that
this leaf had practical use as it was wide, long, and smooth. As both its sides
bend inward, it provides a safe and cozy support for the newborn. When
everything was done, Ayisha emerged from the dark room to find her father
sitting in the front yard of the house. In fact, her father, unbeknownst to her,
had followed her all the way. As she describes it, her father felt that she would
lose confidence if she saw he was anxious. This type of initiation by fire, as it
were, is not at all uncommon, she tells me. Many barbers, mostly men, spoke
of their wives or mothers being introduced to the profession through such
emergency calls. Like boys who were expected to follow in the footsteps of

their fathers, girls were expected to follow in the footsteps of their mothers and operate as midwives and provide other barbering services.

In the past, a barber usually served members in at least ten houses in the neighborhood. Barbers arranged their work by going to the houses of their potential patrons and submitting themselves as the barber for the family. Every barber wanted to go to the wealthy and landed Mappila or Sayyid houses where they could expect to receive something as a reward. By serving only poor Muslims, barbers could hardly meet the expenses of their households. This also led to some tension in the intended families, as Abu explained. For instance, siblings often bickered with each other over who would serve a wealthy patron's house in the mahallu. According to the seventy-year-old Abu, vying for a wealthy patron could at times end in animosity between siblings and put a strain on relationships within the family. Abu added that, in some cases, patrons exploited such familial rivalries among and within barber households by ditching a barber for another from the same family. We see barbers as somewhat passive in this equation, subject to the whims of their patrons. In Chapter 6, I will return to this issue and analyze how monetary transactions liberated them from such tensions and passivity.

The rhythms of barbering work were modulated according to the demands and convenience of the barbers' patrons. Barbers could not own and divide the time based on their own comfort and personal choice. If they did not reach their patrons at appointed times, they were abused, humiliated, and sometimes physically harmed. Many barbers related to me stories of harrowing incidents that had happened to their relatives in the past. As I have already noted, the asymmetrical power relations and wealth differences sustained these practices. So far, I have looked at how the services provided by Muslim barbers were structured in an unequal system of social relations. At the same time, one should also note that the relationships between barbers and clients were reciprocal, however skewed they may have been in terms of power imbalance. The patrons needed barbers as much as barbers needed patrons; the patrons wanted to shape and maintain themselves as Muslims, while barbers needed to procure a means of livelihood (and sometimes dwellings) by providing their services. The patrons could couch their request in a demanding manner owing to the political and economic arrangements in the region. Moreover, there was a concurrent discourse that circulated within the community that it was the barbers' social obligation to fashion Muslims according to Islamic conceptions of bodily comportment, hygiene, and moral order. Patronage was not simply an economic relation, but an ethical one, of relating to the other, which called for specific responsibilities of action and moral behavior.

One may tend to think that hierarchical intimacy goes against the grain when considering the rigid boundaries between the dominant and the dominated. I must note that hierarchical intimacy does not mean a level playing field; intimacy is always already shot through hierarchy, which means that there is always a power imbalance. I asked a few barbers: Why did barbers suffer so much? Didn't anyone go against the patrons? The only answer I got was, "It was also in the interest of the barbers to endure the suffering; it was not wise to antagonize the patron." Patronage, it seems, always is a game of carrot and stick. Both methods are used by the patron as an when they are necessary. We can read barbers' agency in two ways here. First, it is possible to think that barbers willingly undertook a role that was imagined for them and imposed upon them. If they acted in the best interest of the patron, they could ensure the favor of the patron. In their willing acceptance, they could ensure the constant flow of care from the patrons in the form of rewards and recognition. While it is possible to consider the moral rules as being imposed from outside and therefore constraining, it can also be seen as being discovered from inside and thus experienced as fulfilling by barbers. Most barbers chose this option, as this was the most rational option within the available choices. Second, there is also the possibility of turning against the patron and asserting an oppositional agency. But such posturing was risky for a barber, as his livelihood and existence could be in danger from the wrath of his patrons. Yet, a few barbers, I was told, took such steps to assert their distinctive sense of freedom and agency. A story from Muhammad's childhood illustrates the vicissitudes of such a choice. Sitting at his home in Valanchery, a small town in south Malabar, one evening in the summer of 2023, Muhammad recounted the incident. It was 1965 or 1966. Muhammad was seventeen years old then. His brother-in-law was running a barbershop near their house, which his late father had opened a few years earlier. Following in his father's footsteps, Muhammad both worked at the shop and visited the houses of patrons in the neighborhood.

Muhammad had a chronic leg ulcer in those days and blood would ooze out of it while he was walking. At that time, barbers were not allowed to wear sandals. They were mandated to walk barefooted. If a barber was seen wearing a sandal, he would be confronted and abused. Muhammad developed an awkward gait because of his ulcer. Seeing his difficulty, someone in the neighborhood suggested that he should get a leather sandal, which would reduce the pain so that Muhammad would be able to walk properly. Muhammad went to the next weekly fair in Valanchery town, which happened on Tuesdays and entrusted a cobbler to make a leather sandal. When Muhammad collected it the next week, he found that the cobbler had done an ingenious job; the top piece was also made of steel. The next day, Muhammad had to visit Māyin Haji, the landlord in the mahallu, *muthavalli* (manager) of the mosque and *kāranavar* (prominent person) in the locality. His house was located on the valley of a small hillock. Walking down on the winding graveled path, Muhammad could hear the "ting" sound of the steel on his sandal. He felt at ease wearing the sandal and his legs no longer hurt. When he entered the gatehouse, Muhammad saw that Haji was sitting on the enclosure wall of the veranda. As soon as Muhammad reached nearby, Haji's face contorted, blood rushed to his face, and he hollered, "You, son of a bitch! Who do you think you are! Your father has not come in front of me wearing sandals. Then, you are!" As Haji continued his abuse, Muhammad started shivering out of fear. Hearing all the noise, Haji's wife emerged from the indoors and inspected the scene.

For a moment, Muhammad did not know what to say. He mustered his courage and stammered, "Oh Hājiyār, my legs have been hurting and bleeding. Someone suggested that leather sandals would reduce the pain. But the wicked cobbler put in a steel top piece. It was not my intention. I did not want to disrespect you. Please understand." Haji was not ready to accept any pleading from his barber and continued his tirade. When Muhammad realized that Haji was not interested in understanding his condition, he said, "Oh Hājiyār, if things are like this, I am no longer coming to do barbering work for you." Haji retorted, "You rascal, you don't need to come; there are several barbers here who will come to serve me. They are not like you, disrespectful bastard." Then Muhammad said, "I am no longer coming here; I should now get whatever is due to me." Haji did not relent and continued his abuse. Hearing all the war of words, Haji's wife intervened, "If you don't need his service, pay him off and let him go." Haji then told his wife to gauge whatever was due to Muhammad and disburse him. Then he turned to Muhammad, "I will not give you anything to carry the paddy (rice) from here." Muhammad immediately unwound his dhoti and spread it on the veranda and told Haji's wife to pour the paddy onto it. He tied the four ends of the dhoti and carried the paddy home.

As soon as Muhammad reached home, he recounted the whole incident to his sister and then to others. It was agreed that it would not be safe for

Muhammad to stay at home and continue working. If he stayed, the whole household would be subjected to severe punishment from Haji. Influential landlords could resort to various measures from physical manhandling to social boycott from the mahallu. Muhammad narrated to me such incidents from other neighborhoods. Accordingly, it was decided that Muhammad would go and stay with one of his distant relatives thirty kilometers away and would work in his shop. Muhammad stayed in the relative's place for four years, and the issue subsided over time. But, for him, and for other barbers in this position, jumping to such drastic actions was costly for their personal and family lives. They could not live in a locality where they had antagonized an influential patron. As much as patronage is a constant flow of goods and goodwill, it is also a regime whereby the client should always act in good faith and rectitude.

What is generated through these reciprocal needs and interactions was also a kind of intimacy. As social theorist Anthony Giddens (1992, 3) understands it, intimacy can be construed as a "transactional negotiation of personal ties," constructed through long-standing physical and social engagements between two individuals. These transactions not only include sentiments, sensibilities, and trust but also manual labor and material provisions. A barber gains the trust of his or her patron not only by providing services and treating the patrons' bodies in a particular manner but also by talking and listening to their stories and partaking in their secrets. A patron, in turn, may reciprocate this trust by showing his generosity in the material provisions he offers to the barber. However, the physical and emotional engagements, enacted through proximity and touch are processed and mediated through the involvement in bodily manipulation and waste. Sometimes the patron might even have certain vulnerabilities—bodily or otherwise—that only the barber is privy to by virtue of attending to the patron's body on a regular basis. It is this invariable link between intimacy and the undesirable waste products handled by the barber that also shapes this "hierarchical intimacy" between the patron and the client.

Patronage takes a material form through agrarian relationships. The patron-client relationship I have outlined through the lifeworld of Muslim barbers is a product of common property and agrarian relations in Malabar. As I noted in Chapter 2, many castes among Hindus, such as Nairs and Ezhavas, had their own barbers. Apart from providing barbering services, Hindu barbers also acted as funeral priests to remove or absorb the pollution associated with death. Both Muslim and Hindu barbers were integrated into a common system of agrarian and property relations in Malabar. Studying the agrarian relations in colonial Malabar, Dilip Menon (1994a) identifies asymmetrical and hierarchical social relations in Malabar. Namboodiri Brahmins and some of the upper-caste Nairs were *janmis* (hereditary landlords) of almost the entire lands. As janmis, they could not sell the lands outright, but they were entitled to a portion of the produce cultivated on the land. Moreover, they commanded broader allegiance, including various economic and ritual services from the subordinate castes, such as providing customary agricultural or other sorts of labor, offerings, or services during festivals. The janmis never cultivated the land on their own; rather, they gave to the matrilineal households of Nairs the responsibility of managing and cultivating the land (Radhakrishnan 1989). These Nairs enjoyed extensive and virtual powers of ownership and control with a monopoly over wetlands in a region deficient in the production of food grains. Rural settlements tended to be centered on such matrilineal households encompassing the lands and labor they commanded. Around each such household, there were families of service castes—oil pressers, washermen, blacksmiths, potters—who held hereditary rights and privileges on the produce as well as on the family and local shrine. Very often, the subordinate castes cultivated lands held in lease from shrines or households, which were just sufficient for subsistence (Harikrishnan 2023). As the majority of Mappilas were poor agricultural labor and intermediate tenants, they too were subject to the jurisdiction of the matrilineal households. These Mappilas also had rights and privileges, including in the local shrine. Although most of the landlords were Hindu high castes that benefited from this patronage system, the Muslim landlords, though few in number, reproduced these structures with similar relations with artisanal and service castes. Moreover, within a village, Mappila Muslims too shared a right to the services of artisans and other lower-caste Hindus, such as potters, blacksmiths, and washermen. So, there were multiple strands of patron webs that even subservient Mappilas deployed to their benefit within the village. The occupations of these service groups reflected community obligations within a feudal mode of production rather than their position within a religious framework of responsibilities toward their Nair patrons alone.

The caste system created both opportunities and challenges among Muslims. Many lower castes among Hindus converted to Islam to get away from oppressive caste inequality, which freed them to pursue other professions if they so wanted. From the nineteenth century, the British increased their interventions in the patronage system, undermining the existing political arrangements in Malabar. This meant that the patronage system predicated largely on the Hindu caste structure in Malabar became a point of conflict between Muslim tenants, agricultural labor, and their landlords in the nineteenth century. According to some studies, this was the time when the British colonial authorities began to demolish the customary structures by considering janmis as legal owners of the property and therefore eligible to decide their terms of arrangement with the clients (Menon 1994b; Radhakrishnan 1989).

Caste shaped and sustained the inequality inherent in the political economy among Hindus in Malabar. It created territorial segmentation, which promoted both localized interdependent relationships between castes as well as a hierarchical order of castes. It also prohibited those at the bottom of the hierarchy from engaging in greater activities outside the strict limits imposed on their castes (E. J. Miller 1954, 410). Most of the manual labor in the fields was undertaken by the untouchable castes, who were attached to the plots of land of their patrons and transacted along with these lands, if the ownership of the property was transferred. They were, in effect, enslaved, considered part of the property.

With the abolishment of slavery in 1843, untouchability in 1955, and with democratization movements and land reforms undertaken by the communist governments in Kerala, such established structures of caste had changed, with far-reaching implications for lower castes, thus giving them more occupational possibilities, mobility, and land. Nevertheless, in a recent study conducted in south Malabar, Sharika Thiranagama (2019) found that many of the welfare programs and citizenship promises have not benefited former untouchable castes. In fact, the social and material inequalities between the former untouchables and caste Hindus persist as enduring structures of discrimination.

Debating the Jajmani System

Across the subcontinent, a number of scholars have sought to detail the nature of the relationships between service providers and their patrons, under the rubric of the jajmani system (Clark-Decès 2018; Fuller 1989; Kumar 2016). The term is said to originally refer to the relationship between a priest and his patron but has now come to be generally used to refer to any patron-client relationship (Kumar 2016). One of the most useful working definitions points to both ritual and practical aspects of these relations. For instance, Beidelman (1959, 6) describes it as a "feudalistic system of prescribed, hereditary

obligations of payment and of occupational and ceremonial duties between
two or more specific families of different castes in the same locality." For
Miller (1986, 537) who studied the intercaste relations between potters and
their patrons in central India, a jajmani relationship was one he conceived as
"synonymous with the internal village economic system centered on patron-
client relations." Some scholars emphasized the more contractual basis of the
relations, as a contract between wealthy landlords and other members of the
village providing service to them (Gould 1967; Shah 2002). Other scholars
considered it as a holistic arrangement by which the entire membership of
a village that otherwise is divided by restricted caste organization is brought
together (Dumont [1980] 1998; Wiser 1936). Based on my own examination
of the changing relations in Kerala, I make two observations. First, the key
to any understanding of the jajmani relationship as often conceived by these
authors tends to focus on the village setting and religious background. Yet,
in the case of Muslims, it is not the village but the mahallu, which, as I have
argued, is the focus of patron-client relationships between barbers and other
Muslim groups. Second, the jajmani relationship is usually anchored in the
relationship between landlords and service providers. However, many scholars have also noted that the identification of the jajmani with the landlord
class is an oversimplification of the networks of relationships that exist within
a village (Gould 1967, 40). The services provided often extend far beyond a
particular propertied class to the entire village or to all village members in
one form or another. The barber community rendered their services to all the
Muslims within a mahallu, irrespective of their wealth and economic standing. To be sure, some barbers would prefer a wealthier patron who could provide a more reliable economic source, but this was not the sole consideration
or even a primary one.

Among Hindus, hierarchical ideas of caste underscored the rationale for
the jajmani system, while the asymmetrical economic relationship sustained
these arrangements. In the case of Muslims, the barber family was attached
to the system of mahallu; it was first and foremost couched as a religious
arrangement rather than purely as an economic relationship. In practice,
however, the workings of the system depended on the asymmetrical economic relationships in the given mahallu between barbers and their patrons.
While the barber was collectively attached to the mahallu, the arrangements
of payments in kind were organized between barbers and individual families in a given mahallu. A barber was thus an indispensable part of Muslim
social life in Malabar and barber families were often resettled in new Muslim

settlements to provide their services to the whole community. While the services of barbers were conceived, primarily, as a moral obligation toward the Muslim community, among Hindus, the jajmani system revolved largely around the caste obligations between a client and a patron in a locality.

Factors of Hierarchy

The asymmetries of wealth and power operated at multiple levels during the meetings between barbers and their patrons. The patron controlled the running of the household, and the barber was a welcome intrusion into the patron's domain. This can be observed if we attend to the transactions and work arrangements and symbolic interactions between barbers and Mappilas and Sayyids. When a barber visited the house of a patron, he was expected to wear a somewhat well-worn shirt and mundu—befitting his occupation. As a forty-year-old barber told me, if they were dressed spotlessly, the patron might chide them for behaving above their station. Likewise, when the barber performed a service for his patron, he was required to crouch on the ground while the patron sat on a wooden plank or on the exposed root of a mango or jackfruit tree. Such symbolic interactions were a clear indication of the hierarchies involved, so authority was not challenged or questioned. Similarly, when the barbers were given a reward, they were not supposed to inspect the amount or the quality of what was offered to them. For instance, Abu told me that during the ritual ceremonies, such as tonsure or circumcision, the money would be given to them by the patron in a clenched fist. The closed fist of the patron would be placed above, and the barber had to place his right hand just below in a submissive gesture of the receiver. As soon as the patron placed the money in his hand, the barber had to clench his fist and put the money into his pocket without inspecting it. Such forms of embodied exchanges suggested that barbers were supposed to receive the offerings from their patrons as a type of gift, not to be scrutinized or questioned. This gift-like exchange suggests a hierarchical relationship in which the subordinated party receives it with grace.

Apart from wealth and power, a key factor in shaping hierarchical relationships between barbers and other Muslims was Islam. People often engaged in projects of defining and separating activities in the domains of wealth and power using religious sensibilities. For example, they were motivated to undertake such projects of self-fashioning and self-improvement because

Islam provided a strong moral marking to the distribution of wealth and exercise of power. The services provided by barbers were attributed Islamic significance among Muslims. To this end, the social, economic, and religious arrangements anchored within the habitus, in Bourdieu's (1984) terms, was the basis for the social organization of the mahallu. Many barbers continued with their profession because they gained their inherited experience and know-how, but it also limited their aspirations and constrained avenues for social mobility. The institution of mahallu acted as a powerful structuring mechanism that shaped their occupational identity and relations with other communities. Many older barbers also noted that their forefathers looked at their services as a social and religious obligation toward other Muslims. As Abu told me, his father's generation believed that "it is we who fashioned everyone as a Muslim." Such moral assertions were further supported to an extent by barbers' origin myths that highlighted their proximity to Muslims in Malabar and the vital role of their occupation. The myth described their profession as one that realizes a social obligation rooted in culturally meaningful religious conceptions.

While the barbering profession was portrayed in such laudatory terms using Islam, the official morality of Islam itself became a key dilemma in another service demanded from the barbers. Consider that in the past barbers were also asked to shave the armpit and were sometimes forced to shave the pubic hair of their patrons. While discussing this matter, an elder in the barber community reflected, "We should not understand these actions as voluntary, our forefathers were helpless." Whatever the justification offered for such acts, it seems that these demands did elicit much discomfort and resentment on the part of barbers. Because the engagement with armpit and crotch necessitated involvement with bodily sweat and smell and it was considered an intimate part of one's body, such acts were detested by the barbers. Moreover, the sight and touch of a crotch was considered *harām*, a forbidden activity in Islam, which certainly invites Allah's punishment. So, if barbers were forced to shave the crotch, they were also involving themselves in an un-Islamic activity. While engaging with the crotch was regarded as harām, shaving the armpit was more ambiguous as it was a common service provided by all barbers irrespective of their religious backgrounds. It should be noted that the idea of privacy associated with the body was changing in Malabar in the 1970s. Karinkurayil (2022, 129–131) has observed that most men in Malabar did not wear a shirt until the 1980s; they only wore a half mundu, which covered the parts of their body between naval and knee. As shirts became common, people started conceiving upper parts of their body also as private, and engagement with the armpit became a far more contested issue. It is no surprise that this part of barbers' work was one that over time came to be conceived as especially humiliating. Indeed, in the wake of their unionization activities and empowerment in the 1970s, it was the practice of shaving armpits that barbers first eliminated from their services at barbershops. I examine these concerns in more detail in Chapter 6.

Islam and Hinduism

In this section, I focus on a ritual ceremony among Muslims that offers an excellent opportunity to probe how Islam and broader cultural elements of the region, including those of Hinduism are embedded, coproduced, or inseparably connected in Muslim social life. The tonsure ceremony of a baby is usually conducted by Muslims in Malabar on the seventh day after birth. The ceremony is accompanied by a few ritual materials such as rice, shelled coconut, and betel leaves, which should be placed near the ceremony. These materials are set down in an aluminum or a copper plate, depending on one's wealth. A white folded dhoti, varying in quality according to the patron's wealth; a bath towel; and some money are also put in one corner of the plate. The components of the ritual plate ultimately belong to the barber. As many barbers noted, in the past, barbers collected these things in a sack they would have brought with them. Today, the barber picks up only the money from the plate.

The ritual components of this ceremony hark back to a past when barbers were dependent on rewards in kind from their patrons. However, Ummar, the current president of the Kerala State Barbers' Association (KSBA) had another take on these ritual elements. He noted that the materials associated with the ritual of tonsure indicate that it is a caste-based practice among Muslims. He emphasized that "the placing of betel, rice, coconut, and cloth in a large plate near the ceremony of tonsure does not have any foundation in Islam. These paraphernalia are an integral part of the Hindu ritual of tonsure ceremony as well." In Ummar's estimation, "Muslims have continued to practice the Hindu ritual even after their acceptance of Islam, and one of the main reasons for this continuation has been the presence of vicious religious scholars." According to Ummar, "the religious scholars have done nothing to wean Muslims from their earlier cultural practices. Well-versed in Islamic sciences, religious scholars know the correct beliefs and practices of Islam. They are supposed to educate Muslim masses to do away with non-Islamic elements in their everyday, but they have failed." The reasoning provided by Ummar echoes with an argument much rehearsed in South Asian scholarship on Islam about the collusion between religious scholars and vested interests in the community and the ignorance of the masses. The reformists accuse traditionalist religious scholars of supporting and perpetuating "non-Islamic" practices in Muslim lives. For example, in their study of reformist movements in Kerala, Caroline and Filippo Osella (2008, 323) observe that reformists condemn rituals such as shrine festivals as "prime example[s] of shirk or attributing partners to God (especially, 'saint worship' as they would put it) and as something undertaken by the unreformed, the lower class or by the rural ignorant."

I suggest that we might interpret this practice in another sense beyond these debates, probing the values underlying it. Among the Hindus, too, I was told,[9] these materials are widely used in rituals, particularly on auspicious occasions such as naming ceremonies, housewarmings, or marriages. While similarities in these practices among Hindus and Muslims can be observed, it is better explained by nonreligious terms and by specific values within which they are embedded. I suggest that these materials are residues and symbols of a feudal practice, which is a common heritage to both communities in Malabar. As Ummar noted, one cannot find any religious explanations for placing these materials during the ceremony. Whenever I talked to Muslims who engaged in these practices, they noted that this is a custom that has been followed for generations among Muslims in Malabar. Although they were not ready to accept that it was specifically a Hindu caste practice, they also could not provide any justifications for continuing these practices. I will return later in this chapter to the question of Muslims' engagements with broader cultural practices in the region.

If the meanings and significance of some ritual accompaniments remained an obscure puzzle for some, the tonsure is undoubtedly an Islamic practice. It is recommended in various Islamic jurisprudential texts such as *Fath-ul-Mueen* and texts taught in various madrassa grades (see fifth-, sixth-, and seventh-grade texts produced by *Al Fiqhul Islami*)[10] that tonsure for a newborn should be conducted on the seventh day or on the fourteenth or on the twenty-first, and so on. Following the procedures outlined in Islamic jurisprudential texts, the barber shaves the head of the newborn, starting from the top of the head and shaves to the right side. As I was told by an elder barber,

"We should prefer the right side to the left according to Islamic principles." The preference for the right hand, leg, and side is in accordance with the tradition of the prophet Muhammad and much emphasized in many everyday practices, including eating, drinking, and gifting. The jurisprudential imperatives were also emphasized in various other instances, including in the reward given to the female barber on the day of tonsure ceremony. As part of the tonsure ceremony, slaughtering an animal—a bull, buffalo, cow, or sheep—has also been a matter of prestige in the past. Only a few wealthy Mappilas and Sayyids could afford to slaughter an animal for the ceremony. In accordance with Islamic jurisprudential rules, illustrated in a seventh standard *fiqh* text in the Sunni madrassa (*Al Fiqhul Islami*, 62), a barber woman who conducted midwifery should be offered the entire right leg of the animal as her reward. The reward provided to the midwife, much to the dismay of poor Mappilas, also emphasized the following of Islamic injunctions. People from the neighborhood came and waited to collect some meat, which was distributed during the occasion.[11] They were usually given two pieces of meat and a piece of bone. Many barbers told me that poor Mappilas were offended by the disparity in the offerings provided to them and barbers. Yet, they maintained that such offering was done in accordance with Islamic injunctions, which privileged their own community over that of other Muslims.

My point is that, while the spheres of wealth and power were clearly identifiable in the nature of patronage networks outlined throughout this chapter, Islam often shaped these relationships both by locating its own practices within them as well as by providing the required moral registers for these actions. At the same time, there were other elements in these practices whose origins and reasonings could not be marked as Islamic, with any certainty. As often is the case with established customs, some practices draw from (and are influenced by) the broader cultural environment of the region. Yet, we cannot simply categorize these practices as belonging to the cultural universe of one particular group. Such a reduction would be doing an injustice to the force of Islam that structures the meanings of these practices for Muslims. The idea of acculturation, so central to understanding Muslim social structures in South Asian scholarship narrows these practices down to mere derivative forms, without attending to the myriad ways in which Muslims shape and bring meanings and values to bear on these practices. The unique ways in which these practices operate among Muslims also say something about Islam in this region. Perhaps this is how Islam could operate best, serving as a capacious religious vehicle that avoids clearly demarcating and banishing other cultural practices, while at the same time infusing these with its own sensibilities and meanings.

Conclusion

In inland Malabar, we see a tripartite hierarchical division among Muslims. At the top of the hierarchy are Sayyids, followed by the vast majority of Mappilas. At the lower end are barbers. The station assigned to the Sayyids is justified owing to their family association with the prophet Muhammad and their potentiality to realize the religious principle of piety. Both Mappilas and barbers, in general, accept this gradation. Mappilas are constituted by landed gentry, who claim to be converted from various Hindu upper castes, and the majority are converts from various Hindu lower castes, including former untouchables. Notwithstanding the material inequalities and status distinctions within Mappilas that are based on family lineages and wealth, Mappilas are considered a single group in contradistinction to barbers.

Muslim barbers have been viewed as a distinct social group among Muslims because of their hereditary occupation and family lineage. This social differentiation was sustained through political-economic arrangements of patronage that existed between barbers and other Muslim groups. It was emphasized through bodily encounters between barbers and their patrons as well as the subordination that is built into the interactions between them. By closely working on the bodies of patrons, barbers generated a hierarchically mediated intimacy with their patrons that borders on the religious conception of the pir and murid. Barbers depended for their livelihood on rewards in kind provided by their patrons for the services they offered. The subordination of barbers was not executed merely through these arrangements; along with these, there was a discourse of social obligation thrust upon barbers, but which barbers deployed to their own ends to highlight their vital place in the Muslim social order. This was cast in terms of religious duty incumbent upon them for maintaining the correct comportment of a Muslim. Barbers themselves conceived their services as a moral obligation toward the Muslim community.

Many scholars have emphasized political and economic power as the key factors sustaining social hierarchy (Bailey 1983; Deshpande 2011; Dirks 1987; Jodhka 2015). While the hierarchies produced may not correspond to the ritual hierarchy as defined by Dumont, the hierarchical structure operates and is based on the asymmetrical power relations between the groups. Those at the top of the hierarchy have available both a carrot and a stick. Insofar as they do not resort to the latter, they must employ the former. It is essentially in their interest to have the system construed along moral lines, even as this requires a certain measure of responsibility on the part of those who benefit most from it. Consensus and power are not antithetical but, in fact, are closely interconnected in Muslim hierarchy. One need not portray the consensual aspects of hierarchy from the point of view of barbers only in terms of noblesse oblige, of community responsibility. Rather, the consensual aspects seem to derive from and remain intimately connected with dominance by those in the higher stations of hierarchy. This is the dynamic nature of hierarchical intimacy. In part, the qualified acceptance of inferiority was coupled with barbers often casting it in a positive light—as part of their duty and obligation to the wider Muslim community. In part, it should also be seen in the context of long-standing experience, as a community whose economic standing and political power was limited. As soon as opportunities for economic and political advance appeared, such "resignation" to a lowly social position was tested and challenged, as we will see in Chapter 6. But first we will turn to see how patronage worked on the ground, employing humiliation and subordination as its key operating mechanisms.

CHAPTER 4

Humiliation and Subordination

The subordination of a social group in a locality cannot be understood simply as a product of economic differences or occupational distinctions. The economic inequalities and occupational distinctions are visible references of class and caste differences. Underlying these visible markers is a range of discourses that accompany and justify social subordination and humiliation. I find Michel Foucault's idea of discourse quite useful to think about subordination and humiliation, as he helps us to radically historicize these ideas. For Foucault, "Things meant something and were 'true' . . . only *within a specific historical context*" (Hall 2001, 74). There was no absolute truth about anything social. He thought that the same phenomena may not be found across different historical periods, without any changes to their meanings, constituent elements and their social organization. As a set of statements about a particular object or event at a specific time and space, discourses construct what is true for each society. They are operational in various domains of social life, both religious and secular, through mundane, everyday actions. These discourses often come to rupture the operational logic of these social spheres and may potentially become sites of social tensions. This chapter showcases a range of stories and practices among Muslims in Malabar that accompanied the political economy of hierarchy delineated in the previous chapter. They highlight the complex nature of subordination of barbers, which cannot be seen simply as a result of economic dependence on other Muslim social groups. Rather, these stories and practices provide ways of thinking, justification, reasoning, and ideological underpinning to the hierarchy. I show that economic inequalities are often accompanied by cultural notions and ideas propagated through stories and practices that seek to establish the hierarchical social order as a natural phenomenon.

In his study on Muslim barbers in Malabar, Safwan Amir (2019, 4) identifies contempt as the general behavior of Muslims toward barbers and how it is negotiated and challenged by barbers using cultural considerations and various ethical registers in Islam. For instance, let us look at how barbers challenge conceiving their profession as low with reference to their engagements with blood. They challenge this equivalence between blood and social status by referring to the doctors. Doctors too engage with blood, more so than barbers do, but "aversion to particular professions, career preferences and occupational trends are based on differential comparisons—one kind of labor in contrast to another." Barbers use such available tropes and comparisons to challenge contempt associated with their work. I extend this conversation to identity antassu as a key value of barbers' construction of identity in Chapter 6. Now I want to focus and reflect more on how barbers experienced the contempt directed at them. Unpacking the stories, experiences, and practices of subordination, I identify humiliation as a key motive and organizing principle underpinning social relations that Mappilas and Sayyids nurture with barbers. As Joel Lee (2021a, 311) has put it, "Social structure differentially shapes the cultivation of emotion, encouraging particular classes to develop particular emotional repertoires," thus assisting in the reproduction of hierarchy. In delineating discourses of humiliation, I describe how they operate in mundane activities such as at play, in schools, in religious institutions, and within commensal relationships. Such discourses cast the worth of individuals and communities as degraded and unsuitable for any longstanding social relationships. We often see such discourses about groups in the lower rungs of social hierarchies, which are sometimes accepted, tolerated, or contested by the dominated in various ways. In the context of India, many scholars have studied the discourses of humiliation attached to the former untouchables among Hindus (Ambedkar [1948] 2008; Rawat 2011). They have been considered ritually polluting and degraded. The disgust-arousing significance attached to a lower-caste body is justified through a cosmological framework of pollution, which works as a source of marginalization and oppression (Chakrabarty 2018, 4). Thus, the untouchables remain ritually marginalized, economically dispossessed, and politically powerless. Moreover, among Hindus, "It is the notion of untouchability that foregrounds the form and content of humiliation" (Guru 2009, 1). The worth of the individual was constructed on the basis of possibility of touch and non-touch. While humiliation, as analyzed by Gopal Guru, provides an instructive frame within which to compare and contrast the practices among Hindus and Muslims, I illustrate that humiliation in the case of barbers is based on the notions of patronage and morality.

Lawrence Babb (1983a, 167), analyzing the role of karma in popular Hinduism, notes that the doctrine of karma is essentially used to explain misfortune. As he writes, "It is a theory of causation that supplies reasons for human fortune, good or bad, and that at least in theory it can provide convincing explanations for human misfortune." It provides reasons and explanations to each caste for the caste members' current fate. Karma is a key idea of hierarchy among Hindus, which, according to dominant interpretation found in the writings of Ambedkar (2011) and others (Chapple 1986; Obeyesekere 2005), is designed in part to enhance a religiously sanctioned false consciousness—that is, to manipulate the members of the untouchable group into acknowledging their contemptible, repulsive, and lowly standing as part of a natural social arrangement. This compelling acquiescence necessarily leads to the diminishing of a moral initiative that is important for making a stand against humiliation. We have evidence to suggest that Dalits have historically challenged and contested such upper-caste portrayals and stereotyping (Omvedt [1995] 2006). Yet scriptural authority was always used to depict untouchables as passively accepting their designation. This was seen in the doctrine of karma that largely applied to individual conduct based on the Laws of Manu. Laws of Manu also propagated the varna system that cast the untouchables as a group condemned to defiling practices. The karmic load, as it were, limits the scope for the lower-caste untouchables to stake a claim against humiliation. The theory of karma constructs a person in such a way that she or he finds it unnecessary to take the moral initiative required for taking a stand. With the arrival of the state and citizenship rights, many scholars maintained (Ambedkar 1987; Gorringe 2005; Guru 2009), the untouchables sought to acquire the moral stamina to stand up against humiliation. The ideological spell that necessarily arrests the growth of assertion against humiliation begins to fade away, particularly in modern social conditions, fueled by urbanization, education, and avenues for diverse employment.

In the case of Muslims, however, cosmological references and a theory of karma for categorizing a social group as untouchable does not exist. Some have argued that this was part of the attraction for converts, who saw Islam and its promise of egalitarianism, as an escape from the ritual and social oppression of Hinduism (Aslam 2013; Robinson and Clarke 2007). Rather than a single idea, like untouchability among Hindus, there is a range of ideas and practices among Muslims to operationalize humiliation. In most of those ideas and practices, we find Islamic juristic notions playing a key role; in others, broader cultural notions of humiliation play out as the ideological mechanism. While karma and piety are noncomparable, they resonate very strongly with each other as sorting processes with the moral lesson "you get what you deserve." They do much of the same work (sorting people into hierarchies) with the same underlying moral expectation that social order is divinely sanctioned. Yet, piety does not fix permanently the kind of subject positionality you can achieve in this world. In that sense, it is an achieved status with radical potential for anti-caste mobilization within the frame of Islam.

The moral boundaries for a barber were constructed by other Muslims, and violating those boundaries became the context for barbers' humiliation. The boundaries, however, remained in the imagination of the dominant groups who circulated notions of the boundaries through habits, stories, and reasonings. Barbers were often instructed in these matters whenever they set about acting on their own. In this sense, it is not difficult to see how humiliation can be activated within a dialogue of claims and counterclaims. For Muslim barbers, Islam provides a key ideological ground for countering the humiliation at various levels. In this chapter, I seek to show how a discourse of humiliation plays out among Muslims. I categorize the realm of these stories and practices into "religious" and "secular" domains for analytical purposes. While the term *secular* is generally used to mean separation of religious spheres from political power, these two domains coexist and overlap in the Indian lifeworld. As I mentioned in Chapter 1, I use the terms *religious* and *secular* in this book as heuristic instruments and foils, to distinguish between spaces that are conceived as embodying different systems of values. These terms are not intended to signify, in any sense, separate spheres of activity. They often overlap, making it difficult to draw a strict boundary in everyday practices.

In a context where Muslims claim the absence of caste, barbers have to posit their experience as the proof of hierarchy because the presupposition of the absence of caste also denies the existence of social hierarchy. Maybe that is why there is such a fierce grit among Muslims to deny caste. In one single shot, both caste and hierarchy could be dismissed, and the social gradations could be naturalized as simply an effect of division of labor or as a result of ignorance of a foregone generation of Muslims. Barbers, by positing their experience, establish the hierarchy as the social form among Muslims. I am inspired by the arguments put forth by Sundar Sarukkai (2012, 34–35) who argues that lived experience is a domain that cannot be denied or wished

away. It is, of necessity, that groups of people (in his case, Dalits) are forced
to lead their lives in a certain way. They cannot leave that experience if they
wished so. If the subject has no choice over the experiences, these experiences
become key to formulating some notions of authenticity. In this way, lived
experience becomes an ethical and epistemological category to the subject. It
becomes ethical in the sense that the subject constructs a notion of the good
out of the necessary experience, even if this good has to be achieved by challenging the root cause of the experience. It becomes epistemological in the
sense that the subject learns of himself, his surroundings, and his relations
with others through the lived experience. In the same manner, barbers in
Malabar narrate their lived experiences, which are characterized by humiliation, to make a moral claim on other Muslims to challenge them to think
about the ethics of their subordination. Other Muslims usually dismiss the
domain of the lived experience as that of the past, as having no direct bearing on the present or, at most, as fast disappearing, which does not need any
invocation and reflection. This moral claim on the community is what distinguishes Muslim subordination from that of the lower-caste Hindus. By fore-
grounding the lived experience, the lower-caste Hindus call upon the state
to intervene to remedy humiliation and subordination. At the same time, as
Gopal Guru has said, the lower castes also urge the upper castes to reform
their ways. Since caste is a "legitimate" institution among Hindus, upper
castes are not challenged by the moral claims of the lower castes. However,
the moral claim made by the barbers is directed at the Muslim community; it
is not a claim on the state. Barbers want recuperation of their predicament by
reforming the community through the egalitarian impulses of Islam.

Discourses of humiliation tend to normalize and provide moral justifications for existing hierarchies. Studying the hierarchical thinking in Islamic
thought, Louis Marlow (1997, 57) has suggested that hierarchical discourses
seek to explain differences in social functions as reflections of people's intellectual capacities and moral qualities. The humiliating discourses are often
used with the assumption that every human being is endowed with an innate
disposition to perform certain functions, and this will be an occupation indicated by the category to which a person is born. They suggest that one should
only undertake the tasks to which one is naturally disposed and avoid those for
which one is not suited. The case of Muslims in Malabar provides an excellent
case study to analyze how discourses of humiliation operate within Muslim
societies. While some of these practices have been less pronounced over time
due to professionalization of barbering and socioeconomic improvements,

my informants had plenty of memories both from their own childhoods and about their parents. Even if these practices may be less relevant today, they continue to reverberate in contemporary discourses of humiliation attached to barbers these days.

Religious Contexts

The religious ideas, sites, and practices often construct and demarcate social identities in their quest to defining and formulating a moral subject. We can observe how this works in various sites such as madrassas, *dars*, and mosques. A child usually enters a madrassa when she is five years old and learns the correct rituals and practices necessary to fashion her life according to Islamic norms. One also learns about the socially necessary roles provided by various groups, such as barbers, for the upkeep of a moral subject and begins to understand them as distinct. While these social roles have been historically unique and mandatory, ideas about them also created an othering among Muslims. This othering was corroborated by a host of practices that took inspiration from Islamic cultural considerations.

The denigration of certain occupations like that of barbers was socialized from the madrassas. A barber child was forced to understand himself or herself as socially inferior to others. This othering, many barbers explained to me, challenged their self-respect and often resulted in lower self-esteem as they grew up. This low self-esteem was viewed as the product of their every-day socialization in the community. This can be very well illustrated by an incident Bāvākka recollected from his childhood. We were sitting in adjacent barber chairs one afternoon in early 2019 at his shop in a small neighborhood in south Malabar. He has been an active participant in the union activities of barbers and has owned and operated the barbershop for more than twenty years. He operated the shop with two workers, and he served only his old and regular customers. He was financially well-off, and his two children were working in the Middle East. The incident he related occurred in the 1960s when his father was still involved in the patronage system in their locality. A Thangal (lineal descendant of the prophet) had come to their locality to teach the kids *duff-muttu* (an art form using a percussion instrument called *duff*, made of wood and ox skin), which was to be performed during the procession on the day of the birth of the prophet Muhammed. Bāvākka had also joined the classes. The arrangement was that the meal for the teacher on a daily basis was to be provided by the households of each child. When Bāvākka's turn came to feed the teacher, someone in the locality informed Thangal (the teacher) that the child belonged to an ossān family. Thangal subsequently told Bāvākka that he need not bring food.

Bāvākka's family refused to be silent and raised the matter with the mosque committee and the issue became widely known in the locality. Thangal defended himself saying that receiving food from barbers is *mak-rooh* (undesirable), a term derived from an Islamic juristic category called *karāhath* in Arabic, which refers to actions that one must avoid for the sake of prudence but if conducted do not invite godly punishment. The issue created a stalemate as no one on the mosque committee dared to defy the arguments posed by a descendant of the prophet, who is thought to be embodying the spirit of Islam. Bāvākka's father refused to tolerate such a humiliation and withdrew his son from classes and learning *duff-muttu*. Since Thangals are held in high esteem among Muslims in Malabar, their decision would be taken as the last word on a matter. Added to this is the assumption that such a restriction on the transaction of the food is Islamic, as evidenced by the Thangals' use of an Islamic juristic category to defend his action. Bāvākka's family expected otherwise; they thought that distinctions of status would be immaterial in the case of actions that fall within the purview of Islam. They hoped that religious figures like Thangals would reshape hierarchical legacies in order to proclaim the egalitarianism of Islam. Not only did such assertions not happen, but figures of authority themselves contributed Islamic reasonings to perpetuate unequal social relations.

Such experiences cannot be brushed aside as individualistic, or as a matter of aberration and uniqueness. Hierarchical thinking and humiliation permeate religious institutions in general, as a rubric of establishing and organizing social relations. The institutions of higher religious learning also either tried to discourage barbers from seeking to be scholars or undermined their intellectual and spiritual capabilities to become scholars. Jabbār, a barber religious scholar, recollected that when he joined a dars after finishing high school, there were covert insinuations from Mappilas in his locality that he was not made for being a religious scholar. Some alluded to him that it was better for him to learn the well-paying barber job than to study to become a religious scholar, which would not earn him an attractive salary. Others were more explicit in saying that he had to follow his family's traditional profession. Such insinuations happened during interpersonal discussions and therefore were not matters of public scrutiny. Many barber religious scholars and those with secular employment have recounted such narratives to me. One of them even said that because caste is not recognized among Muslims, these individuals making covert and subtle statements against barbers cannot even be booked under the law. In India, untouchability was abolished in 1955 through Article 17 in the Indian Constitution and, in some states, a person can be booked under the law and imprisoned for perpetrating untouchability (Gorringe 2005). Because caste is not recognized as an institution of social hierarchy among Muslims by law in India, barbers cannot resort to constitutional or legal measures to alleviate their plight.

Jabbār further recollected that there is a saying among Muslims in Malabar—*ōthi ōthi otthānāvuka*, meaning "learn and learn and eventually you become an ossān." The saying meant that regardless of the deep religious education aspired to and sought by a barber, he will eventually fail in this endeavor due to his intellectual incapacity or moral degradation. He can only turn out, eventually, to be a barber. One might contrast this with secular education, to the extent that it holds the promise of social mobility among Muslims in Malabar. Yet, as I will discuss in Chapter 7, that also needs to be qualified, as secular education might be a necessary but insufficient path to social mobility and liberation from the shackles of ascribed status. When the saying is used in the context of religious education, there is an idea that barbers are not suited for religious scholarship. As an occupational group, they should be delimited to learning their own traditional profession rather than abandoning it for other pursuits, including religious ones. Among Muslims, religious education is held in high esteem and being a religious scholar accrues respect not only within the family but also within the community. Sending at least one child to pursue religious education is proclaimed to be a good investment for the hereafter as far as the parents are concerned. Muslims in Malabar believe that if they send their children to pursue religious education, the children may be pious and fulfill duties and obligations incumbent upon a child after a parent's death, such as praying at the grave and commemorating the parent through their routine prayers. It is also believed that children pursuing secular education and employment are less likely to engage in such activities with the same intensity and frequency. Though such considerations generally exist among Muslims, as far as a barber child was concerned, he was meant only to follow the community occupation. As such, these practices can be understood as contributing to the discourse of humiliation I have sought to outline throughout this chapter. It is designed to keep the barber community employed in their traditional profession, limiting their prospects of social mobility. This was usually used to allude to the fact that a barber would not have the required intellectual and spiritual abilities to progress in religious education and would eventually fall back on his traditional profession for a living. The discourses of humiliation construct a barber as an individual inherently incapable of achieving piety; for this reason, the exclusion or the relative discrimination of a barber in these spaces is considered unproblematic. For some barbers, such views that cast them as lowly are further indication of how certain Muslim groups seek to dominate and exclude them.

Distinguishing Gifts

Muslim religious institutions and sites are conceived as egalitarian spaces because of their entrenchment in a divine realm that purports to be egalitarian. While Allah's conception of these spaces is an important register, local status and power get implicated in them. Most of the lands for constructing these institutions are gifted by individuals belonging to landed families in a locality. Because it was a gift, the members of these families have special rights in the mosque, such as positions on the management and special places to do their prayers. At the same time, these gifts are deemed to be given in the name of Allah. Like any gift, it cannot be retraced or called back as private property. Once devoted to Allah, the ownership of property is transferred from the individual, and the previous owner can no longer make any demand of ownership on that property. The market economy can no longer make speculations on that property. As spaces of divine gift, these should ideally be egalitarian without much regard to social distinctions. Of course, such ideals are rarely realized in practice, but they are nonetheless important as normative principles because they provide moral registers of action. As spaces devoted to Allah and therefore indistinguishable from the realm of the divine, there is a normative assumption that piety—the only distinction valued by Allah among his subjects—should be the touchstone for distinction in these places. However, even such spaces become sites and environments of routinized humiliation for the barber community.

Attending to the architectural specificities, spatial demarcation, and general management of the mosque can reveal the hierarchical nature of these spaces. The older mosques in Malabar had a typical structure, which included a small inner hall, a big entrance hall, and narrow stretches on both sides of the inner hall. Many older barbers told me that they were not allowed to do their prayers in the inner hall. The inner hall was reserved for the wealthy Mappilas in the locality and some of them even had reserved spaces in the mosque for doing the Friday prayer. To understand the claims of space within the mosque, we should attend to the construction of the mosque in a locality among Muslims in Malabar. In most localities, a few Mappila families owned most of the lands. The land for a mosque and graveyard was often gifted by one of these family members. Sometimes, the mosque itself was constructed by the family for the benefit of the community. In other cases, the land was gifted by a family and the mosque was built by the community collectively. The family that gifted the land had clear prerogatives in the mosque; their family members were often in charge of the mosque, and in managing everything related to the mosque. They will be involved in managing the mosque, including the payment of salary to the religious scholar who would be leading the prayer. In some mosques, spaces inside the inner hall, such as the first row, was reserved for the family. In some mosques, some Mappila members brought from home prayer mats during the morning prayer on Fridays and kept it in a space in the inner hall. The place where they put the prayer mat would be reserved for them during the Friday prayer. Such distinctions existed inside the mosque.

In the older mosques, barbers were directed to pray in the narrow stretches on both sides of the inner hall. They could not venture into the inner hall. The spatial distinctions during religious functions were not restricted just to the mosque. In every social gathering where religious texts such as mawlids were recited, barbers were not allowed to sit with Mappilas. The idea of space, with ideas of openness, accessibility and acceptance, was not a given in a hierarchical society like India. Harikrishnan (2023) has observed in the case of twentieth century Kerala that space with its modern embellishments were constructed by the Dalits and other lower castes through political struggles and physical confrontations with upper caste Hindus. Similar complexities structured ideas of space among Muslims too. They also activated hierarchical conceptions of spaces, despite the impulses of egalitarian spaces advocated by Islam. In practice, the normative idea in Islam that religious spaces are egalitarian seems unfounded. What we observe in Malabar is that the ownership of resources and livelihood in a locality determined the access into religious spaces. The hierarchical relationship was marked in ritual spaces, though it was conceived to be devoted to Allah and therefore beyond the mundane considerations of life.

Barbers assert that mosques, because they belong to Allah, should exemplify piety—Allah's axis of ranking—as the distinguishing marker of hierarchy. This is also operationalized in various practices and rituals at the mosque. Ward Keeler (2017) has also observed in the context of a range of relationships between monks and laity in Myanmar that religiously sanctioned hierarchies are valued social dimensions in various contexts. In the case of Muslims too, this is true if we consider the relationship between the imam— the leader of the prayer—and the masses who stand behind him worshipping. The hierarchical relationship between the religious scholar and the laity is structured by notions of knowledge and the possibility of embodying piety. But this is not the only hierarchy begotten at the mosque. Muslims in Malabar still retain the memories of particular lands that were gifted by certain families for constructing the mosque, the graveyard, or the madrassa, or for running some religious educational institutions. Until the 1970s, most of the mosques across Malabar were under the control of such families and the male who managed the mosque was called a *muthavalli* (manager). Though the Waqf Board came into operation in 1956, most of these gifted lands were not registered under these legal bodies until the 1970s. It was a board instituted by the central government to ensure the safety and management of the gifted lands in the way of Allah. Even today, one can find a few mosques across Malabar being managed by certain families. When the mosques were registered with the Waqf Board, it was a requirement that each mosque should have a committee incorporating people from the locality who are associated with the mosque. Because of this democratization drive, the dominance of certain families came to an end in the case of mosques. Even when the management of the mosque became a community affair and every household within the mahallu became attached to the mosque through a monthly subscription, the barbers were mostly kept from giving any contribution to the running of the mosque. Barbers were not allowed to be part of the general mechanism of running the religious institutions in the locality. The money they earned by barbering was not deemed suitable to be expended for community purposes in the past, many Mappilas observed. Barbers were actually the recipients of the gifts the community provided to them. They were not supposed to use the gifts to serve the community and return the favor to partake in the management of a religious community in each mahallu. They had to remain as receivers and could never become givers.

Studying the agricultural economy and peasant resistance in southeast Asia, James Scott (1990, 23) has pointed out that the relationships of subordination generate practices and rituals of insult, denigration, and "assaults on the body that seem to occupy a large space in the hidden transcripts of their victims." These forms of oppression deny the subordinates the ordinary luxury of negative reciprocity, a tit for tat, trading an insult for an insult. In all the stories I have narrated above, we can see a moral force and energy infused by barbers into the humiliating practices faced by them, which originates from Islamic ideas of egalitarianism. To counter such humiliation, barbers often draw on, to use a concept developed by Scott, "public transcripts"—discourses and practices deemed by the dominant group as worthy and legitimate. This was revealed to me in various statements and stories narrated by a seventy-two-year-old barber named Pokker Haji. As someone who has conducted the pilgrimage to Mecca, he was called a haji. I have not met many barbers who had been on the pilgrimage and without hard cash, it was not easy for ordinary barbers to think about hajj until the 1970s. Haji lamented that barbers have faced a lot of humiliation from other Muslims and had been kept separate from social transactions. But Islam professes universal brotherhood, and he cited a hadith from Abu Bakr Siddiq, the companion of the prophet, *Innamal Mu'minoona Ikhvathun*, meaning "certainly the believers are united by brotherhood." He said that Muslims are practicing something that is unheard of in the history of Islam. Another barber told me that during the Makkah victory (629–630 AD), the prophet Muhammad exhorted that "today I have completed Islam for you and there is no distinction among believers except in terms of piety." He opined that to realize this vision of true Islam, the religious scholars should publicly propagate the true notions of Islam, which they do not do. Pokker Haji added that whatever public declarations are made, they need to be backed up in practice; for instance, in facilitating marriage alliances between barbers and other Muslim social groups. He averred that the barber community has given great service to the society and the society has not given barbers due respect.

A key aspect of religious spaces among Muslims in Malabar is that all people could populate these spaces unevenly, with zones of inclusion and exclusion based on the identity of a social group. The hierarchy thus created in such spaces challenged the divine logic that should have been the organizing principle here. While piety should have been the accepted ideal of this accommodation, other considerations, such as genealogy and wealth, also formalized distinctions in these spaces. In contrast, the religious spaces, and access to them among Hindus, were categorized in the past on the basis of one's caste, which controlled one's proximity to and distance from the divine. The godly realm was largely restricted to people in the upper castes, who were endowed with the moral and religious authority to attend to the divine. The groups in the lower hierarchy were seen as ritually polluting and therefore were allowed only limited access to the divine realm. Even with the temple entry movements and initiatives from the state, many prominent worshipping places, such as temples, mostly remain inaccessible to the untouchables (Viswanath 2014). Conversely, Islam on the Malabar coast sought to accommodate most Muslims into the devotional and discursive spaces hierarchically.

Secular Contexts

Secular educational institutions are those that are run with the logic of equality, are represented by the state, and carry notions of citizenship as their underlying conception of individual. In these spaces, children are seen as tomorrow's model citizens of the state. Despite these normative assumptions, social hierarchies continue operating in these spheres with institutional support. Studying the successive Indian governments' programs for creating a clean India, Assa Doron (2016, 720) has posited that the "proper citizen" was often portrayed through various projects at the school level, including the widely circulated educational charts from the 1960s onward that foregrounded the child as an embodiment of a modern secular state. The images portrayed in these charts, however, exuded middle-class sensibilities and simultaneously excluded the diverse modes of life that existed in India, especially those "unruly" spaces inhabited by the lower orders of the society. In the same manner, many of my barber interlocutors experienced the educational spaces as discriminatory and exclusionary in nature. Abu's case illustrates how even primary schools colluded in sustaining hierarchies. He was enrolled in the local government primary school when he was six years old. But he could not continue his studies beyond a few months because of circumstances of humiliation, which led him to act against the school authorities. Throughout those months, he recollected, "I was called by all the other students as otthān" (unpolished version of ossān)—clearly marking his community background, which was considered lowly and degrading. He continued, "the feeling of humiliation made me shudder with rage and sometimes made my eyes well up." Abu felt that he did not command any dignity from other children because of his social identity. No one wanted to play with him or to include him in their company. He became the butt of jokes and harassment from other students. One day, he confided in his favorite teacher about his feelings of humiliation. The teacher consoled him, saying that such things would happen, that they were a normal part of life, and that he should not be concerned by such abuse. Abu was seeking intervention from the teacher on his behalf because he felt that it was unnatural for others to insult him at the school. One could also say that Abu was calling upon the equality enshrined in the founding of the school as a public institution. Rather than confronting the students who had called Abu names, Abu noted, the teacher normalized such abuses, seeing them as an inevitable part of Abu's life. He was instructed by the teacher "to be brave and to withstand such personal insults."

The abuse did not stop and, as a last resort, Abu went to the headmaster and poured out his heart. Abu thought that if his own teacher could not do anything, surely the headmaster the head of the school—would harangue the students who were accosting him. To his shock, the headmaster retorted, "What else can you be called other than otthān?" Abu recalled feeling numb for a second, followed by outrage. It was a blow to his already wounded young mind. He came out of the headmaster's office and folded the red sarong he wore to school every day. He kept his slate in its folds. He bent down and picked up two stray stones from the front yard of the school and pelted them at the headmaster. Fortunately, for him, he told me, "Neither stone hit the headmaster." Still, this very act of defiance had severe repercussions that would haunt him all his life. First, the school peon and other kids ran to catch Abu and punish him. Abu quickly fled from the school and ran non-stop for ten kilometers, until he reached his maternal uncle's house. In the evening, Abu's father came there looking for him, and Abu's grandmother told his father that she would bring him home the next day. Abu stopped going to the school thereafter. He then started accompanying his father to the barbershop every day. The humiliation he faced became the cause of the end of his schooling. Ironically, although he had stopped going to the school, Abu recalled, whenever there was an inspection by the assistant educational officer (AEO), a senior state official, the teachers would instruct Abu's father to send him to the school to make up the numbers. It seemed everyone was in on the performance of civility so long as it did not disrupt established order.

The school, as an institution of the state, was perceived by Abu as advancing equality and civility. Since public schools are not controlled by the mahallu or a religious community, Abu was of the opinion that it should not be acting upon ideas that denigrate on the basis of caste or community. The institutional humiliation suffered in schools is powerfully portrayed in the Marathi film *Fandry* (Manjule 2013). The movie depicts the story of an untouchable boy and his family who are charged with handling the pigs in the village, and other polluting tasks. The main character is the boy who attends the local school and routinely gets humiliated by his peers for his social background and is called *fandry* (pig). At one point, the pigs wreak havoc in the village and the family is called to catch the pigs. The boy is forced to join his family in catching the pigs and therefore misses school. In the last scene of the film, he walks in front of the school carrying the pig caught on a bamboo pole. On the walls of the school, we see large painted portraits of figures like Dr. B. R. Ambedkar, Periyar E. V. Ramasamy, and Jyotirao Phule—figures of anti-caste and self-respect movements in India. The movie is a poignant comment on contemporary forms of humiliation faced by Dalits, even in spaces that are "secular." It also showcases the plight of Dalits in contemporary India even after the abolition of untouchability and promises of citizenship and social upliftment.

Schools are professed to be producing tomorrow's citizens through education and by cultivating a civic sense. They avow to promote ideals associated with modern citizenship, unencumbered by the "pre-modern" sensibilities of caste and religion. This is very much the gist of the constitution, too, drafted by Dr. B. R Ambedkar, who sought to do away with enduring structures of inequality based on caste, ethnicity, and religion. Hence, public schools were seen as one of the primary vehicles for promoting this secular vision. The story of Abu offers a powerful illustration of how the ideals were dashed in practice. Despite Abu's anchoring his hopes on those ideals, the reality proved much harsher. Both in the government school and within the wider neighborhood, Abu remained the son of a barber.

Abu went to school in the 1960s and many changes have occurred in Malabar in the subsequent decades. While one may assume that such institutional humiliation may have given way to more egalitarian treatment of barbers, that is still not the case, as the experience of Basheer reveals. Basheer belongs to a barber family and holds a doctorate degree in management and works as a college lecturer. But he has faced discrimination throughout his life. He recalled, "When I graduated from high school with the highest marks in the whole school, my achievement was not publicly acknowledged. Every year, the school conducted a program to celebrate students with the highest score in the examination, but that particular year, the practice was abandoned. The next year, it continued." Basheer observed that while schools, as an institution of the state, should ideally promote equality of all pupils and recognize merit, it failed at observing these ideals by concealing his achievement. As Ajantha Subramanian (2019) has emphasized in her study of merit, which is central to the elite science educational institutions in India (Indian Institutes of Technology, IITs), ideals of merit appear in conditions that support existing structures of inequality.

Most of these personal narratives suggest that a barber's social identity follows him or her throughout his or her life in Malabar, even in the spaces where one might have hoped to shed prejudice in favor of a more progressive outlook that prioritizes equality, merit, and social justice. I want to give a few more examples of why such domination remains so difficult to overcome, especially at the local level. It is the involvement of barbers in ritual ceremonies such as tonsure and the bathing of the newborn and mother, as well as the running of shops in the neighborhood of their own residences that creates and sustains this local knowledge in the community. But even in cases where social identities are not easily recognizable, such as in educational institutions and places of secular employment, people often ask about one's family lineage and father's profession. If the identity of a barber is thus revealed, it is then used to stereotype and malign his or her behavior. Basheer's second story illustrates this very clearly. Basheer was admitted to a master's program in management at Aligarh Muslim University, a reputable public institution in the state of Uttar Pradesh in India. He topped the admission list and secured a scholarship from the university's alumni group in the United States. There was also a competition for a fellowship to those belonging to economically weaker sections in the Muslim community. Basheer applied for that fellowship too. He said, "In the course of filling out the forms, there was a column asking for one's father's occupation, to which I wrote 'barber.'" Once the applications were reviewed, the person in charge of reviewing applications, who was one of Basheer's Muslim professors, summoned Basheer for an explanation. Basheer continued, "The professor refused to believe that I belong to the barber community and suggested that I had lied in the application just to secure the fellowship. I was told that my application was a ploy designed to gain access to the affirmative action policies."

Though Basheer tried his best to convince the Muslim professor that his father was indeed a barber, "my professor refused to believe it, and he tore my application in front of me, and accused me of using subterfuge." Basheer continued the story, saying, "I felt really shocked and could not understand what happened at that time." Now that he tries to make sense of this incident, he tells me, "This Muslim professor could not believe that a Muslim barber's son could be equally talented to secure the first rank in the entrance test. He thrust his own disbelief upon me and dismissed me as a liar!" The point is that regardless of one's faith and economic circumstances, it is the occupational designation and station in life that seems to determine one's life chances. In his behavior, the professor—a figure of authority—revealed an entrenched belief that social identity was fixed and was equivalent to one's intellectual capacities. This further illustrates how hierarchy is constructed and sustained throughout society, even when there are structures (e.g., affirmative action) that are supposed to mitigate it.

Like religious spaces, secular educational spaces also stigmatize barbers as possessing low intelligence and low moral worth and, therefore, consider them unsuitable to deviate from their traditional profession. What is striking about these two spheres is that they operate with distinct ideals as the organizing principles of their operation. While piety was the key to religious ideas of moral personhood, notions of citizenship and equal rights were prerequisites for the conceiving of secular spaces such as educational institutions. It is important to note that it is the construction of barbers' social inferiority—which originated in their earlier involvement in the patronage network in every locality—that trumps any possibility of imagining social relations in these spaces as egalitarian.

Everyday Spaces

I have so far delineated the practices of humiliation that seep into institutional spaces. In the following, I want to consider how everyday space is constructed for barbers as a site of routine humiliation. Everyday life can be thought of in multiple ways. It can be seen as the site of habit and routine, within which struggles for culturally meaningful values such as piety, wealth, and status take place (see also Doron 2013). But it is also often a site of trance, illusion, and danger, as Veena Das (2007; 2010) has argued. This aspect of the everyday—a location of contestation and vulnerability—is clearly visible in the lifeworld of the subordinated. In my own case, I suggest that barbers' everyday is in part constituted by the humiliation to which they are constantly subjected. While institutional domains provide cases for analyzing how different logic, discourses, and values are contested, analyzing everyday helps us unearth the vulnerabilities of imagining a dignified life in the presence of the other. The hierarchy was enforced through physical and punitive action, which often denied possibilities of imagining a dignified life for subordinated groups like the barber community.

Abu, who threw stones at the headmaster, told me a revealing story about his childhood, which showcases the asymmetry of power relations and humiliation built into the hierarchy between barbers' and other Muslims' everyday spaces. While Abu was working at his father's shop as a youngster, he would sneak out of the house after lunch to play cricket with his peers. He used to play with kids in the neighborhood. One day, Abu, who was balling against a kid from a wealthy Mappila family, caught the kid in front of the wicket. The boy did not concede his wicket and called it a no-ball. A scuffle ensued; Abu was called an otthān and a liar, and he was told not to play with them. During the name calling, Abu was pushed around and asked by the Mappila boy to leave the ground. Abu retaliated by slapping the Mappila boy twice with all the force that he could muster. The kid fell to the ground, cried and ran to his house. Abu's playmates warned Abu that he may be shot dead by the boy's father, and he should run for his life. The boy's father was the first president of the local *panchayath* (local administrative body), and he had cordial relations with most of the important political leaders in Kerala at that time. Abu ran from the spot and hid in the bushes of a nearby hillock till late evening. Once it was dark, he sneaked back home where he realized that the matter had already reached his father, and he would have to face the consequences. The hungry boy quickly gulped down a few ladles of gruel and pretended to be sleeping when his father came from the barbershop. He overheard his parents talk about the incident and the danger that it could put the family in. From the next day onward, Abu's father took him to the shop daily, and, when they returned for lunch, Abu was locked in a room where he stayed until after his father's afternoon nap. Abu then accompanied his father back to the shop. Here, a barber child was collectively humiliated, while non-barber children colluded in the humiliation by their silence or by their attempt to physically attack him. The social subordination here implied that there could be unparalleled violence that may be perpetrated against Abu.

Such humiliations carried into Abu's adult life in the 1960s and 1970s, when there were strict injunctions against the commensality of barbers during social ceremonies. During the meals given as part of ritual ceremonies such as tonsure and circumcision, barbers were not allowed to sit with other Muslims for the meal after the ceremony. One of my barber interlocutors noted that his forefathers were served separately in a corner during public functions, and if they dared to sit in the hall, the male host of the household showed a barber his place often through physical action. Abu recounted his own experience in a Mappila house where he was sitting with his friends for a meal. "Some-one among the guests who knew my father and my barber identity pulled me out of the gathering, as if he was pulling a kitten, and told me that my meal was arranged in another corner." Social spaces were structured by hierarchi-cal inequality and any transgression was policed and punished immediately. Unlike in Malabar, in southern Kerala, I was told that the barbers were not even allowed to enter the host's house during marriage functions. An incident to this effect was narrated to me by the late Latheef from Alappuzha. He was a barber and a follower of Jama'athe Islami, a reformist organization in Kerala. He noted that his organization accepted the fact that there are hierarchical practices among Muslims and, yet they could not engender any structural changes to them. He told me that in the past his grandfather had to wait out-side the house at a marriage feast, and he would be carrying a bath towel with him. He was to wait there until the owner of the house came looking for him and took his towel. The owner would fill up the towel with the meal and he would carry it back to the barber. The barber would take the food home and share it with his entire family. We see two kinds of engagements with subor-dination here. In one case, the behavior of the barber is watched over if he were to mingle in social gatherings. In the second case, any such possibility of intermingling is forestalled at the start. In effect, barbers were treated as social outcasts who could not be invited to partake in the commensal relationships.

Maybe till the 1970s, not only were barbers barred from participating in commensal activities, but other Muslims refused to engage in any meaningful way in social ceremonies conducted by barbers. While Muslims attended the ceremonies, such as marriages of barbers, they did not eat anything from bar-ber houses. The food cooked by barbers, as I have remarked earlier, was con-ceived to be makrooh (undesirable). In one sense, an ideal Muslim would try to avoid such actions to keep his piety. The reasoning for categorizing food cooked by barbers as makrooh was said to be their involvement with blood, which is an impure substance in Islam. By linking the avoidance of accepting food to the attainment of piety, religious scholars provided an Islamic theo-logical underpinning for this practice. Many Mappilas I talked to reiterated this sentiment, which was commonly held in the past and, accordingly, bar-bers were treated as inferior to other Muslims.

Because Mappila leaders asserted this exclusion in religious terms, a few barbers told me that some members of the community were resigned to accept their fate. Many thought aloud, "It is true that our ancestors were engaged in blood-related jobs such as midwifery, circumcision, bloodletting, but we need not be profiled for the past actions of our forefathers." One could argue that such statements, rather than contesting the basis of such claims, offer an implicit acceptance of the religious foundation that their occupation is polluting and degradable. However, that would simply reproduce one part of the story and ignore the dynamic nature of everyday interactions and ever-changing social relations and ambitions on the part of barbers. Many barbers openly and vociferously challenged any implication of lowliness that may be attributed to their occupation using various ideas. For instance, Shafeeq, a barber who has undertaken a few years of religious training, fiercely contested this declaration of impurity associated with the occupation. He noted that there are many professions where people come close to or handle blood, such as nurse practitioners and doctors, but they have not been stereotyped and marginalized as the barbers were. Neither were religious scholars who encountered blood regularly stigmatized. One of my key barber interlocutors, Saidalavi illustrated his contention this way: "Take the case of the tonsure ceremony. A barber and a *musliyār* (religious scholar) go together for the ceremony. The musliyār gets a sarong from the house for conducting the 'haqeeqah' (animal sacrifice). He becomes embroiled in blood due to the butchering and the barber conducts the tonsure ceremony. Here the person who comes in touch with the blood does not have any stigma but the barber who does not have any contact with blood is stereotyped." While exclusionary practices seem less commonplace these days, many older barbers said that reluctance to eat at a barber's house was very much part of their childhood experiences. It can then be deduced that such behavior may have been common until the 1970s, at least in Malabar. The point is that hierarchy was expressed across multiple lines that were part of everyday experiences of humiliation. So far, I have shown that everyday spaces and communitarian gatherings operate in ways that perpetuate humiliation and sustain hierarchy by reference to both Islamic jurisprudential categories and mundane forms of social inequalities. In the following section, I turn to the question of women to take a close look at the domestic spaces to illustrate the interpersonal nature of humiliation.

Women

The experiences that a few barber women shared with me provide insights into the intimate encounters and also humiliating practices among Muslim women in Malabar. Ayisha, one of my key female informants, recounted that she has come away from many houses in the past angry with what she deemed as "un-Islamic behavior of Mappilas." In fact, she has been very outspoken in telling some of them that their conduct was immoral. Most of the incidents she described occurred at least twenty years ago. When I asked about her experiences, she did not mince words and her rage was evident through her statement, "What they kick from their legs, we deal with using our hands; we clean their bodies and wash their babies and they need us for all that, but we are not suitable to eat with them, that's what they thought. Do we tie something or paste something on our hands when we go to their houses?" As I asked her to explain what she had uttered, she said, "We are needed by our patrons. They politely request us to come and serve their women and newborn. We go happily and do all their dirty work. We are inside their houses, and we know their secrets, body or otherwise. But they think that we are ill-suited to eating with them." I asked her if she could provide more details about her experiences. She mentioned that even when she was invited by the relatives of the newborn's father to join the meal with the guests, during the tonsure or bathing ceremony on the fortieth day, the issue was contested. She would only be able to join in if the women in the household hosting the event were supportive. In one such gathering for the tonsure ceremony on the seventh day, even when the guests did not exhibit feelings of superiority, it was up to the host to welcome her properly. As this was not done, Ayisha sought to save face by "collecting everything that was given to me including money and other rewards and then told them that it is already late, and I have to go to another house to do the work. I said that I would come while returning after finishing the next job." She bid goodbye to those who were eating and then left. She went back only the next morning, and when they asked her why she couldn't join them, she told them that she ate from the other house and did not feel like having one more meal. The same experience repeated in the same house on the fortieth day (where the mother takes the ritual bath to end her maternity rest) and the invited guests urged her to eat with them, but again the female host was not interested in seating her with them. Then she told the gathering that she had another fortieth-day ceremony to go to nearby and they would be waiting for her. Like last time, she took her leave, saying she would come back as soon as she was done with the ceremony there, but she did not go back. Then, after a few days, when she was invited to shave the head of the baby, the female host asked her why she had not come back on either occasion. To this, as Ayisha recalled, she responded in no uncertain terms:

I am not a bitch tied behind your back; I too am born into Islam.
There are still people like you who have not realized the dawn that
has already unfurled. When I am coming to do the job in your house,
I am not sweaty or dirty or bringing any bad smell or bringing the
dirty clothes from the previous houses where I have worked. Even
when I am doing my work, I keep myself cleaner than you people are.
I did not come back precisely because you saw me and you as two
distinct people. In the other house, I did not face any of this humiliation; they seated me along with them and we ate together.

She concluded the interview with me by saying, "I am not made for that; that
was in the past; that is all over." She was certain that she would not allow others
to humiliate her on the basis of her work, which she considered as dignified,
like any other job permissible as per Islamic jurisprudential norms. There are
many interesting points to this story. First, Ayisha's assertion that she is not a
bitch tied behind the female host's back reworks a Malayalam word *vālātip-
patti*, a tail-wagging pet-dog. The idea is that a pet dog always wags its tails
out of love for its owner. Ayisha was proclaiming that, as a barber, she was
independent now and was no longer tied to the patronage system whereby
she might have been compelled to accede to such humiliation. She also asserts
an ideal of equality in Islam where she should be treated as equal to other
Muslims. The other point she notes is about hygiene, which is conceived as
a personal affair, closely tied to one's body, rather than social identity.[1] The
points raised by Assa Doron (2016, 727) in his study of clean-India campaigns
is relevant here. He observes that in the secular citizenship model, hygiene is
often defined "as that which contributes to the good of the body politic" and
is achievable with the right mindset and practices. We can stretch this observation to argue that Ayisha uses this notion of a "public hygiene" to argue
that such hygiene should inform the domestic sphere as well, in the case of
barbers and other Muslim groups. If she were unclean while coming to the
clients' house, that can be a sound reason to keep her from mingling with the
guests who are clean, she asserts. But she had made sure that she kept herself
cleaner than the people in whose house she had arrived. She also observed that
this discrimination was not a general practice among Muslims. Many Muslims
no longer harbor such prejudice, or they at least do not express it in these
ways. Some are willing to recognize the social worth of barbers as Muslims
and behave accordingly. Ayisha suggests that there is an ideal of egalitarianism
in Islam by which all Muslims, irrespective of their social origins, should be

considered equal. While this ideal is anchored in what we may call normative Islam, in practice, it is not often realized. At the same time, we should not understand normative Islam itself as a homogeneous discourse. I describe in Chapter 7 how barbers use competing strains found in normative Islam to challenge and contest hierarchical practices that subjugate them.

Conclusion

The question remains as to what is achieved through the humiliation operationalized against barbers in Malabar. One common answer to this question is that humiliation is intended to reproduce hierarchy. This makes sense if we consider the "traditional" spheres of social action the barbers were involved in. Barbers, by being denigrated in every social sphere they operated in, were constantly reminded of their moral obligation toward the community. They were called upon to conform to this moral obligation imposed on them by virtue of an occupation deemed dirty and ritually polluting and based on Islamic tenets and principles. They were discouraged from following any other occupation and the stigma stuck as a controlling discourse that reproduced this hierarchy. If barbers sought to escape the occupational strictures imposed on them, they had to overcome such stereotypes, which plagued them from every corner. I have shown this in the examples of Bāvakka and Jabbār, who suffered humiliation in the institutions of religious realm that apparently uphold an egalitarian Islam, as in the madrassas and the mosques. So, too, with the more modern educational institutions that purported to encourage civic action, rationality, equality, and merit-based aspirations, as illustrated through the experiences of Abu and Basheer.

In the past, barbers were barred, by the circumstances of dependence on their patrons, from pursuing religious and secular educational opportunities and from participating as equals in social gatherings. Recently, some barbers have attempted to become religious scholars, professionals, and graduates and have sought to reconfigure their relationships by reference to more progressive values espoused by the nation-state. However, the notions of hierarchy have endured, creeping into all these spheres as well, contradicting the logic of these spaces and institutions.

The stories, gestures, and practices of humiliation directed toward barbers are comparable to those directed at the former untouchable castes among Hindus. Why do the experiences of humiliation sound very similar among Hindus and Muslims? I believe that social groups on the lower rungs of hierarchy in India have been embraced into the same structure of patronage irrespective of their caste and religious location. While the duties and obligations expected by the clients may differ in terms of their particular services and the ideological structure underlying them, the structure of deference was the same. The abolition of untouchability by law and the upsurge of political assertions have given a language of rights and equality to the former untouchables with which to challenge the existing hierarchies among Hindus (Narayan 2012). But one should not assume that stereotyping, punitive action, and physical violence have diminished. They continue to appear in everyday interactions and institutional settings (Gorringe 2017). In the case of Muslims, such hierarchy is rarely recognized by the state as a social issue, so the treatment meted out to barbers is not as visibly recognized and barbers have less of a support network that might enable them to appeal to state authorities on the basis of discrimination. This has been one of the demands of various organizations, such as Pasmanda Muslim Mahaz, working among Muslims, particularly in North India (Ansari 2009). To be sure, the vocabulary of rights and dignity is increasingly deployed by the barber communities, and filters to everyday interactions, as the women in this chapter have shown. Yet, this "resistance" is partial at best. It lacks the foundations of support afforded to lower castes in India, whose ambitions—social, political, and economic—have been recognized and at times realized in law and electoral politics (Doron and Jeffrey 2012). Muslim barbers attempt to bring the language of equality available both in Islam and in secular democracy to reflect and challenge the contemporary hierarchical practices among Muslims and call upon the community to live up to their own ideals. Chapter 6 unpacks how barbers used tools and ideas of secular democracy to challenge the enduring social hierarchies and to restructure their social relations with other communities in Kerala. Barbers, and Muslims in general, however, do not conceive the hierarchical relationships among them in terms of caste, as I illustrate in the next chapter.

CHAPTER 5

"There Is No Caste in Islam"

"There is no caste in Islam," Ummar asserts in response to my query as to how caste among Hindus in India has influenced Muslims. Ummar is a Muslim barber, and he runs a barbershop in a coastal town in south Malabar. I was introduced to him through the snowball sampling method I used among barbers in Malabar during fieldwork in 2019. I frequented his shop over several weeks, recording his views on the history and social condition of barbers and the impact of unionization movements. Once, he suggested that I should interview his mother because she acted as a midwife in the locality many years ago and could tell me lot of stories about the conditions of work in those times. Ummar told me about the troubles and tribulations faced by barbers at the hands of other Muslims in Malabar. He enumerated many practices, including endogamy, and occupational distinctions among Muslims to attest to the hierarchy existing among Muslims. At the same time, he was dismissive of my attempts to equate Hindu caste with Muslim hierarchy.

While talking to all Muslim social groups in Malabar, be it barbers, fishers, Sayyids, and Mappilas, I inquired as to how we should understand hierarchical practices among Muslims, if not with reference to caste among Hindus. I got a range of responses, but they can be broadly categorized into three. First, barbers and fishers acknowledged and enumerated several hierarchical practices. Their stories and experiences were filled with pain and pathos. Most of the time, their own grandparents and parents were the lead actors in their stories, and they lamented the unequal and humiliating treatment meted out to them by other Muslims. At the same time, they were reluctant to assign the Muslim hierarchy as caste. They signified these practices as un-Islamic and a result of Muslims not correctly learning the faith and tenets of Islam, which represented egalitarianism.

The second and third responses were posited by Mappilas and Sayyids. The second response, much rehearsed by religious scholars, dismissed any possibility of caste among Muslims. They dismissed hierarchy among Muslims as a thing of the past, a product of asymmetrical political-economic relations. Because it was a matter that no longer existed, hierarchy among Muslims did not warrant any discussion. As far as religious scholars are concerned, acknowledging the existence of caste creates an intellectual and a political problem. If accepted, it complicates the contention of egalitarianism in Islam. Muslims proclaim that Islam is an egalitarian religion, and they draw upon Quranic verses and incidents from the life of the prophet Muhammad and his companions to corroborate such views. I look at the egalitarian tendencies of Islam in the final chapter of this book. If caste is accepted, it needed to be explained using some normative edicts from Islam. It also creates a political problem of fashioning a Muslim community identity in the Indian context, where the overarching political position made available to Muslims is that of the minority (Ansari 2023). Rather than projecting minority as the framing narrative of political identity, something else needs to be constructed, which goes against the homogenous conception of Muslim community identity. An outright dismissal of caste as a non-issue among Muslims ensures non-committal and safety from intellectual dilemma.

The third response, much reiterated in academic and intellectual circles among Muslims, questions the deployment of the term "caste" to signify hierarchy among Muslims. A Sayyid, who manages a Muslim heritage library in Malabar, told me, "It is you, the social scientists who construct caste among Muslims." As a Sayyid, he was agonized by the equation of his community with Brahmins among Hindus. Sayyids are often referred to as the priestly class among Muslims owing to their assertion of being spiritual guardians and leaders of the community (Gautier and Levesque 2020; Niazi 2020). He further asked, "Do you see untouchability and unseeability among Muslims? That is what structures Hindu caste system in Kerala." I concurred with him about these points, but continued probing, "But Muslims do not marry each other!" He retorted, "that is not because of caste; it is because of kufuv. It is your ignorance of Islam that pushes you to call everything caste." While questioning the deployment of "caste" as an analytical category, these Muslims recognized hierarchical practices among Muslims.

The range of responses provided by Muslims in Malabar with reference to the existence of hierarchy foreground the issue of how to analyze caste alongside Muslim hierarchy. When pronouncing that there is no caste in Islam,

Muslims in Malabar advocate that caste is a non-Islamic institution. The idea is that caste is a Hindu institution that does not have any relevance for Muslims. This is a declaration widely held among Muslims in Malabar irrespective of their social belonging. While talking to barbers, Mappilas, and Sayyids, I inquired about the concept that should be used to denote Muslim hierarchy. While no one could suggest an alternative concept, everyone firmly believed in the inapplicability of caste.

The basis of argumentation for the inapplicability and irrelevance of caste in Muslim lives lies in a peculiar conception of Hindu caste, which is popularized and made into a commonsense idea through Dumont's work. In South Asian anthropology, Louis Dumont ([1980] 1998) has been a key theorist who looked at caste in ordering the Indian lifeworld. For his analysis of the caste system, he follows the fourfold division of varnas upheld by the Hindu scriptures, such as *Manusmriti*. The scriptures primarily divide the Hindus into four groups—namely, Brahmins (priests), Kshatriyas (rulers and soldiers), Vaisyas (merchants), and Sudras (service castes). Outside this fourfold system lies a huge number of social groups (*jātis*)[1] engaging in polluting and menial work for the above four castes.

The idea of caste now cannot be thought without invariably linking it to the Dumontian concept of hierarchy based on the purity principle. In Malabar and other parts of Kerala, the caste divisions were so severe that "in no part of India are the unnatural divisions so strongly marked, so anxiously regarded, or the degrading or ennobling associations" so severely established (Ward and Conner 1863, 116). In Malabar, 90 percent of Hindu social groups were untouchable to the Brahmins. Almost 30 percent the Hindu population had to follow particular lengths of distance between various subcastes and also between themselves and the higher castes (Balakrishnan 2004, 186). Enumerating features like untouchability and unseeability among Hindus, all the Muslim groups in Malabar reiterated that one could not find similar practices among Muslims. The point is that Muslims like to signal their religion as virtuous and egalitarian, especially since they operate alongside Hindus. Reconceptualizing caste as a regime of hierarchical inequality based on birth, which is a common inheritance of populations on the Indian subcontinent, this chapter delineates the ways in which Muslims understand, practice, and justify caste, through the institution of endogamy—which is also said to be a key institution of caste among Hindusm. I argue that, notwithstanding the apparent similarities in certain practices among Muslims and Hindus, they are best accounted for by using values and belief systems from their respective religious traditions and cultural contexts. Caste—as a regime of hierarchical inequality based on birth—has distinctive features and modes of operation among Muslims.

Caste and Islam

Caste is the most studied phenomenon of Indian society, and it has generally been used to denote the social structure prevalent among Hindus on the subcontinent. There is no consensus as to what caste is, how it originated, and how it operates. In this section, I will juxtapose studies on the social structures of Hindus and Muslims in India to highlight the similarities, interrelations, and disjunctions between them. One axis of commonality seems to be the centrality of the concept of birth. The whole range of social interactions and relations between the groups is determined by one's birth into the social group. Therefore, the status distinctions, division of labor, marriage relations, commensal restrictions, and even the worth of the individual is predetermined and impervious to change.

Muslims use various categories, such as *baradari, qaum, samaj*, or the English word community to signify hierarchical differences among them (Levesque 2020, 3). Yet, Muslims are usually divided, based on historical literature, into two categories, namely Ashrafs (nobles and foreigners) and Ajlafs (commoners or Indian Muslims). Ahmad (1967) suggests that such a division does not reflect empirical realities, and the analytical unit should be caste-analogous groups among Muslims. However, the Ashraf-Ajlaf distinction has often been used by scholars to portray similarities in the caste structure of Muslims and Hindus; for example, Ashrafs are further divided into four groups. The first two groups in the hierarchy, Sayyids and Sheikhs, in theory of Arab origin and learned, correspond more or less to the literate Brahmins. The other two groups, Mughals and Pathans, ethnic in origin, correspond rather to the Hindu Kshatriyas. "Among the non-Ashrafs, three levels of status can be distinguished." They are converts of Hindu superior castes, "a large number of professional groups corresponding to the artisan castes of the Hindus" and "converted untouchables who have preserved their functions" (Dumont [1980] 1998, 208). In this neat structuring of Muslim hierarchy, social groups remain more or less constant with their former tribal, ethnic, and caste attributes. If Hindu caste conception is provided by scriptures, Muslim hierarchy is merely a replica of sorts, existing without any independent ideological backing.

There have been two strands of studies on Muslim social hierarchy in India. The one strand, following the Dumontian line of reasoning, has attributed to the institution of caste significant authority and influence on how social hierarchy is constructed among Muslims (Ali 2002; Bhatty 1996; Hasnain 2006; Jairath 2011; Madan 2001; Rai 2018; Rathore 2023). What Ahmad observed in 1978 as a significant orientation of such studies is still true today. He noted that many scholars "base their definition of caste on the Hindu phenomenon and then go on to examine the extent to which the social stratification of the communities studied by them corresponds to the Hindu model" (3). These scholars determine the framework from the outset and then look for elements in Muslim social lives that conform to that framework. The discourse of caste has gotten a new lease on life in recent times owing to political assertions and demands being made on the state to recognize it as a significant category shaping marginalization and discrimination among Muslims (Ansari 2009; Ahmad 2023; Ahmed 2023; Azam 2023; Levesque and Niazi 2023; Shah 2023). Within the ambit of state reservations for education and employment, Muslim social groups have been divided into two: Other Backward Classes (OBC) and general category. The very category of OBC has been further divided in some states, like Bihar, to recognize the most vulnerable groups among OBCs. However, there has been persistent demand, particularly from the 1990s, to recognize caste as the principal axis of social divisions, discriminations, and marginalizations among Muslims, just like Hindus. Most vocal among them has been the Pasmanda movement based in Bihar, that emerged in the 1990s. Movements like All India United Muslim Morcha (1993) and All India Pasmanda Muslim Mahaz (1998), Ansari (2009) claims, interrogate the monolithic notions of Muslim community and the benefits the higher social groups hoard based on being a religious minority in India. There have also been demands from such movements that the category of "Scheduled Caste," which enlists the Dalits for reservation purposes by the state in India should be extended and expanded to include the lowest classes among Muslims. Despite such radical claims, these movements have been unsuccessful politically because, as Ansari (2009, 9) posits, they have failed to develop and advance a "comprehensive social/cultural/economic agenda" for the lower classes among Muslims. To overcome this failure, he exhorts that these movements need to engage with the question of the social, which he frames within the strictures of the caste in terms of the ideological and the practical. While the Quran does not seem to uphold caste, it operates, for all practical purposes, "as a category in the Islamic juristic/legal corpus and interpretive tradition as it has evolved in India." So, the trajectory of these movements is easily set out; they "must offer a critique of Islamic interpretive tradition as it has evolved in India and, if possible, construct an alternative Islamic hermeneutics from the perspective of the marginalized." On a practical level, intercaste marriages should be encouraged among Muslims, occupation-based cooperatives should be formed, and attempts should be made to bridge the gap between the unorganized and the organized sectors so that the lower classes predominantly concentrated in the unorganized sector get better opportunities for socioeconomic improvements. Although I am not familiar with the intricacies of the north Indian Muslim lower-class politics,[2] I can confidently say that most of these tendencies are already visible in the case of lower-class Muslim politics in Malabar. Yet, unlike what Ansari would want, these tendencies are not revolving around the issue of caste, but they are within the threshold of Islam.

Following a caste-centric framework to understand status claims of various social groups among Muslims is questionable on a number of counts. First, the caste system has largely been understood as rooted in a religious principle intrinsic to Hinduism. Scholars of Islam have generally taken this assumption as a basis of their analysis without questioning its ideological assumptions. Ahmad (1978, 11) suggests that even "if the formal Islamic ideology rejects caste, the actual beliefs held by the Muslims not only recognize caste distinctions but also seek to rationalize them in religious terms." The difficulty, then, is related to resolving the contradictions between the professed egalitarian notions of Islam and hierarchical notions of the caste system. Such a contradiction is resolved by resorting to notions of syncretism in India. Dumont ([1980] 1998, 206) suggests that Muslims adopted caste as a tacit and reciprocal compromise. Hindus had to live for long periods under political masters who did not recognize Brahminic values. On their side, "Muslims had made and went on making concessions to co-existence," including the acknowledgment and use of caste for ordering their own social relations. It is argued that Islam adapted to hierarchical principles in a multicultural environment in India as a sort of survival mechanism in an alien environment. Muslims subscribed to many Hindu practices and belief systems as they lived alongside each other to make sense of their everyday life (Ahmad 1981; Roy 1983). This line of reasoning does not align well with the history of Islam on the Indian subcontinent. To reiterate an argument advanced by Richard Eaton (2000), Islam did not make much headway in regions where Muslim regimes were concentrated. It was in the outlying regions, such as Bengal, Assam, and Kashmir in North India that Islam made much headway.

As I noted in Chapter 1, the story of Muslims on the Malabar coast also does not fit into the Dumontian picture of political expediency. Moreover, as Tony Stewart (2001, 262) has observed, implicit in the argument of syncretism is an assumption of Hinduism as a stronger historical force compared to other belief systems. In this case, Islam is understood as unable to provide a worldview to the believers and wean them away from their preceding ways of life. But this assertion has not been established by any kind of empirical analysis.

The same problem also persists in studies of social hierarchy in other non-Hindu communities. For example, David Mosse (2012) has recently used these arguments for understanding how a Jesuit mission negotiated in a caste-ridden society in a Tamil region. He notes that while Hindu religious notions of caste were dismissed, Christianity integrated itself into the local social order informed by caste maintaining the hitherto existing social privileges enjoyed by certain groups in ritual and perpetuating endogamous marriage relations. He shows that the ritual contexts in a Christian saint shrine in the town became the locus in which the rights and privileges owned by groups in the indigenous social order were reproduced and transformed. The integration of Christianity into the local caste structure was also noted by C. J. Fuller (1976, 68) in the context of Christians in Kerala.[3] He has noted that "Christians and Hindus share a common orthopraxy—i.e., behave in accordance with the same set of rules concerning caste and pollution." If all religious communities are said to have social structures like caste, we need to rethink caste, rather than seeing it as a derivative of Hinduism.

The second strand looks at Islam as a key category, sometimes also along with Hindu caste, for understanding social hierarchy among Muslims (Bellamy 2021; Lee 2018b, 2021b; Fanselow 1996; Vatuk 1996). Sylvia Vatuk, for example, analyzes how members of a Muslim group in Deccan and Madras— namely, Nawayats—organize their social relations with other Muslims. She finds that in their self-conception, being descendants of Arabs who migrated to India was of paramount importance. This idea, when juxtaposed with the local converts to Islam in India, gave them a sense of difference and superiority. Such notions of distinction were preserved and propagated through endogamous marriage relations. She notes that the idea of kufuv was used to delimit marriage relations within the group. While denying that there is inequality in Islam, they held on to the notion that they were different from other Muslim communities owing to their relations with Arabia and closeness to the prophet Muhammed. The Qureshis (butchers) in Delhi studied by Zarin Ahmad (2018) also portray themselves as closely linked to Arabia and proclaim that the very term *Qureshi* as their group epithet is reminiscent of their connections with the Quresh tribe in Mecca, to which the prophet Muhammed belonged. The works by Bellamy (2021) and Lee (2018b, 2021b) tackle the question of caste as well as of Islam to understand the complexities of Muslim social hierarchy. Studying the scavenging community of Lal Begis in Lucknow, Lee (2021b) posits that this community was categorized as neither Hindu nor Muslim until the late nineteenth century when the colonial officials and administrative mechanisms, along with Arya Samajists, attempted to pigeonhole this community either as Muslim or as Hindu. Until then, the scavenging community was known as the followers of Lal Beg, who has been understood to be a local prophet. The idea that Muslim social groups and the resultant categorization within the schema of the Ashraf-Ajlaf-Arzal distinction also get constructed and formulated within the strictures of colonial and national projects of community-making is an important point to remember. While Lal Begis could not get reservations because of their caste location, Bellamy (2021) shows how Chippas work with both the ideas of Islam to construct dignity and the identity of Chippa to seek the benefits of OBC reservation. While scholarly attempts to understand how a particular social group or local hierarchies get implicated within the frame of statist discourses is an important endeavor, so is it necessary to explore whether Muslim social groups have alternative discourses to engage with hierarchy.

I take the issue of both caste and Islam seriously and think about using these concepts to unearth the elements that make up these ideas in the Muslim lifeworld. With reference to caste, my interest is in examining how Muslim social groups in Malabar are making sense of the phenomenon. I do not accept this category as a given but see it as a terrain of contestation within the community to make certain claims and challenge others, thereby highlighting the issues associated with this concept. Similarly, I take the idea of Islam not as a domain of theology but as a field of ethnographic making whereby my interlocutors construct, reconfigure, and negotiate what Islam meant or should mean within the context of social hierarchy. As a result, I see both the categories of Islam and caste as emergent, not yet fully formed, amenable to change and contestation, and as an idiom for Muslims to understand their own social world, its power structures, and its norms of functioning.

Caste can be understood as a regime of hierarchical inequality based on birth, operating across various communities on the Indian subcontinent. While such an idea of caste based on ascriptive status is a necessary starting point, it is inefficient because caste operates in distinctive ways across political, economic, social, and cultural spheres. In understanding how caste operates across communities, one should pay close attention to how it gets inflected through the values upheld by respective societies and how these values operate in everyday life. What comes out through my ethnography is that Islam is a key principle of organizing caste relations among Muslims, along with the negotiation of local political and economic relations. I discussed the political and economic aspects of Muslim hierarchy in Chapter 3. The importance of Islam to the understanding of social relations among Muslims is elucidated in many studies, particularly when scholars analyze the changing names of social groups among Muslims (Ahmad 1978; Ghosh 1997; Lee 2018b; Mehta 1997). Joel Lee describes how Dalit Muslims, who are engaged as sweepers and scavengers in Uttar Pradesh and Bihar in India, use the term "halalkhor" to re-signify their identity using Islam. The term halalkhor is a combination of *halal* and *khor*. The former is an Islamic juristic category referring to what is allowed by law, and the latter term means a person who eats. So, their group title means someone who eats what is lawful in Islam. Dalit Muslims creatively use this term not only to proclaim the dignity of their labor and income but also to challenge the high-status Muslims by asking, for example, whether they are not halalkhor. To say that someone is not halalkhor flies in the face of their Islamic moral system in what is right or wrong and what is allowed or not. Following these debates, my interest here is to analyze how Muslims in Malabar use categories of Islam to justify and support hierarchy. While hierarchical arrangements such as endogamy display similarities to those of Hinduism in terms of praxis, the underlying rationale draws on a very different reverence framework, anchored in textual traditions and socioeconomic practices.

Endogamy Among Muslims in Malabar

I suggest in this section that Muslims employ certain categories and subvert, manipulate, and reconfigure certain practices to their own advantage in order to sustain and perpetuate caste relations. For that purpose, they also draw upon ideas and beliefs from various traditions of Islam. I do not mean that the textual traditions determine these practices holistically. Rather, even if the textual tradition represents ideals and doesn't always correspond with what people do, it needs to receive some attention as the source of ideals and beliefs. I showcase this by exploring endogamy among Muslims in Malabar.

Endogamy is a key principle of the reproduction of social relations. It is the site where a generation passes over its heritage, wealth, and status to the next generation (Bourdieu 2002). By restricting marriages to within a stipulated circle, each generation reproduces and perpetuates the existing marriage relations based on hierarchy. Among Hindus across India, the marital alliances were often restricted to within the subcastes. That is, say, among Brahmins, there will be a number of subcastes in a given village and members of the subcastes prefer to marry among themselves. Fuller and Narasimhan (2008) have noted that subcaste endogamy has started breaking down in India due to increasing educational, employment, and migration opportunities. But the caste endogamy is guarded among Hindus across India and any transgressions are often met with violent consequences, including honor killing.

Among Muslims in inland Malabar, it is the males who inherit the lineage of their fathers.[4] A woman, however, becomes part of her in-law's house after marriage. Though she retains her father's family name and the status as an individual, her children are considered part of the male's household. Indeed, her lineage is also taken into consideration when a marriage alliance is sought for the children. The status of a family is determined by the lineage, how far in the past they can trace their origins, the ownership of wealth and other resources in the locality, and the control of religious and civil institutions in the locality. The importance associated with the lineage comes out in the experiences of barbers in Malabar.

"Mappilas will not engage in marriage alliance with us," Hassankutty, a seventy-two-year-old barber replied when I asked him whether he sought marriage alliances from Mappilas for his children. We were sitting at his house in June 2019 on a humid evening. His wife served us black tea and banana chips to enliven our discussion. By that time, I had met with him at least four times and conducted many short interviews. I had come today specifically to ask about his family and the marital relationships of Muslim barbers in Malabar. I learned that he has five children, three boys and two girls, and all of them have contracted marital relations with other barber families in nearby localities. In fact, two of his boys refused to learn barbering in their childhood with the intention of pursuing non-barbering professions for their livelihood. One son, Rasheed became an electrician, and, when his family sought marriage alliances through a marriage broker from outside the barber community, they could not succeed. Many Mappilas refused to entertain such a proposal. Hassankutty noted, "the broker told me after a few attempts that it doesn't seem to be working out." Such attempts, particularly for those who pursue secular employment through informal labor, may not be successful. The fact that Rasheed did not follow his community occupation and pursued a secular profession was simply not enough for him to gain the marriage alliance he sought.

Social Control

Scholars studying Muslims in South Asia have observed that endogamy is a defining feature of hierarchical relations among Muslims (Ahmad 1976; Fanselow 1996; Jairath 2011; Levesque 2020; Safdar et al. 2021; Vatuk 1996). Like their Hindu counterparts, each social group among Muslims enforces strategies to restrict marriage alliances to within their endogamous circles. Among Muslims in many parts of India, there are baradari or biraderi[5] councils formed by each social group to manage its affairs, including marriage alliances. In many cases, permission is required from the council to undertake a marriage within the group. Such rules forestall the possibilities of marriages outside endogamous circles. In cases where such councils do not exist, Muslims deploy various means to restrict marriage alliances to within their own social group. Malabar provides a quintessential example of this tendency. It is not restricted to Muslims in Malabar only; in many Muslim societies beyond India, we can see similar ideas operating to keep marriage alliances within a group (Al-Azri 2010; Samin 2012; Ziadeh 1957).

For each social group, endogamy operated in multifarious ways. As for barbers involved in the patronage network in the past, their family affairs such as marriages were looked after by the Mappilas in the locality. If a barber boy or girl reached marriageable age, the father would inform his patrons about his wish to arrange an alliance for his child. It was with the approval of the patrons that the father searched for a potential partner and if a suitable partner, that is, from a barber family, was identified, it was the responsibility of the Mappila patrons to take the matter into their own hands. All the arrangements would be made by the Mappila patrons in a locality collectively and the barber father did not have much say in the conduct of the marriage apart from vouchsafing the boy or the girl in marriage. The Mappilas never allowed barbers to marry out of their own community. If the Mappila patrons decided something, the barbers could not act against that for fear of losing their livelihood. The lack of ownership of resources and means of livelihood forced the barbers to accept the authority of the elites in the locality. The controlling of marriages through such practices was the key factor in reproducing the hierarchy.

A few educated barbers told me that, along with this social control, there was also another mechanism at work among barbers themselves. Until the 1970s, at least, most of the Mappilas in Malabar were poor and struggling to make ends meet. But the barbers had means of livelihood through the rewards in kind they received from their patrons—the wealthier Mappilas and Thangals. According to Basheer, a forty-five-year-old management professional belonging to a barber family, barbers were also reluctant to breach marital conventions because many in the barber community saw marriage with Mappilas as economically disadvantageous, even if it were possible. In any case, barbers would not have received marriage alliances from the wealthy Mappilas on whose mercy their livelihood depended. This idea of social distinction in terms of access to resources was augmented by barbers' feelings of superiority of being descendants of an original Muslim who came along with Mālikibn-Dīnār to propagate Islam in Kerala. In the case of Mappilas, the marriage alliance was determined more by socioeconomic considerations. A poor Mappila married a poor counterpart from the Mappilas; he was not ready to contract a marriage alliance even with a relatively well-off barber. In the case of Thangals, they never gave their daughters to anyone other than Thangals. However, they sometimes accepted girls from wealthy and influential Mappila families in a locality. With the economic improvement barbers have made in recent decades, some Mappila families have come to accept barber women for their sons, but they hesitate to give their daughters in marriage to barber men. In the past, the authority structure of the mahallu controlled most affairs of the barber community, including with whom they should engage in marital alliances. Yet, barbers had a steady source of income, unlike many poor Mappilas who might have been willing to establish a marital alliance. Such possibilities of social transgression did not materialize in a context where wealth and lineage claims were held to be high virtues.

Endogamy operated within the existing socioeconomic differentiations and group identities. It should also be understood as a practice sanctioned by the religious traditions of Islam. If we dismiss the religious mediations that accompany endogamous relations among Muslims, we may fail to understand them fully and equate the practice with endogamous marriages among Hindu castes. Among Hindus, endogamous marriages will be anchored to the notion of purity as understood within the concept of varna and such rationalizations are not the basis for endogamous marriage relations among

Muslims. In the next section, I will look at various religious ideas informing the endogamous marriage alliances and occupational specializations among Muslims. Drawing upon my conversations with barbers and ordinary Mappilas and religious scholars, I will unpack the range of ideas and justifications furnished by them to propagate endogamous marriages in Malabar.

Textual Traditions

I learned the factors that are taken into consideration while evaluating potential marriage alliances in Malabar from a religious scholar named Saleem. He acquired his religious training from a prestigious Sunni college in Malabar.[6] I visited Saleem many times during 2019. Once, I asked him about the religious moorings of marriage alliances among Muslims and he opted to elaborate by referring to the scriptures. I was thus taught a small section of an Arabic jurisprudential text, namely, *Fath-ul Mueen*, where the author discusses the conditions for marriage compatibility among Muslims. This text is said to be written in the sixteenth century by Zainuddin Makhdum II, who conducted dars in the Ponnani Mosque for several years. Dars is a higher form of religious training, which is conducted at the mosques where the religious scholar and his students live, and they receive their food from the community members. Since Muslims in Malabar follow the Shafi'i school of Islamic jurisprudence, the author of the text draws on the jurisprudential texts of the Shafi'i school. Though I focus on a single text, it should be highlighted that the ideas delineated in the text have wider currency in Malabar and are cited in other scholarly works and madrassa textbooks. Since madrassas are primary institutions of religious training for children and abridged versions of *Fath-ul Mueen* are taught in various grades, one can safely say that the ideas expressed in the text have wider relevance for Muslim lives in Malabar.

Saleem read a sentence in Arabic and then explained it to me in Malayalam. He said that the foremost condition for marriage among Muslims is *kafā'a* or *kufuv*, which can be roughly translated as marital compatibility. Muslims in Malabar usually use the word *kufuv* and they may say, for instance, two potential partners' kufuv do not match. The idea of kafā'a, marital compatibility, is widely used among Muslims across the world. Muslims, however, use this concept to suggest several ideas at once that may vary from society to society. Nadav Samin (2012, 110) suggests that kafā'a as a legal concept first emerged in the early Islamic town of Kūfa (in present-day

Iraq) where Arabs and non-Arabs intermingled and social distinctions were clearly demarcated. It was also the city where the Hanafi school of Islamic law originated and in which the conditions of kafā'a were first outlined. In Saudi Arabia and other parts of the Arab world, one of the most prominent social distinctions was between tribals and non-tribals (Al-Azri 2010; Samin 2012; Ziadeh 1957). Saudis who can avow descent from major Arabian tribes are considered tribals and this distinction is predominantly used in the choice of marriage partners today. By and large, tribal women are not permitted to marry down—that is, to marry non-tribals. Men are not bound by the same restrictions, and they can pursue hypergamous marriages—that is, marriages with non-tribal women.

Saleem explained the idea of kufuv as the right of a woman to choose her life partner. In theory, kufuv bestows authority to women; in practice, however, it is the male members of the family, such as fathers or brothers (guardians), who determine the marriage alliance for a woman. If a girl demands to be married to a man whom the guardian finds noncompatible, the guardian can stop the marriage. The Arabic text enumerates the range of people who are compatible with each other for marriage alliances. A free woman is not compatible with an enslaved man because they are unlike each other. Saleem explained this as "it may be demeaning in front of society for the woman to say or acknowledge that my husband, or his father or grandfather was a slave." A good woman and a Sunni woman are not compatible with a hypocrite or a reformist. A woman belonging to a taravād (high-status family lineage) is not compatible with a man who does not have taravād; an Arab woman is not compatible with a non-Arab; a Quresh, or woman belonging to the tribe of Hāshim or Mutthalib,[7] is not compatible with a man who does not belong to these groups. A man who became Muslim is not compatible with a woman whose father was also a Muslim. Saleem further explained this as, "If a woman is told that she is married to someone who just accepted Islam, it is demeaning for her in society. That is the nature of our society." The aim of these conditions, according to Saleem, is to forestall any mānak-kæd (dishonor) that may occur to a woman by being married to someone who is lower to her. Saleem further told me, "Suppose a father finds a groom who is rich but not compatible. If the daughter declines the proposal, the father cannot marry her to this rich person. This is because wealth may be a desired aspect but still an insufficient criterion to be solely considered for kufuv." Saleem continued, "The wealth can come today and be lost tomorrow. It is such an ephemeral thing." The jurisprudential injunctions provide

Muslims with a range of ideas to categorize social groups on the basis of marital qualifications.

The conditions of kufuv outlined in the text provide much fillip to the endogamous marriage practices among Muslims (cf. Kasim 2022). There is clearly a demarcation in terms of lineage in the case of Arab and non-Arab as well as among various tribes. So, ethnic and status consideration carried a heavier weight than wealth. There is also a preference for early converts to Islam. One can safely say that, in terms of marriage, there is no equality among Muslims. The potential misalliances are discouraged and framed in terms of a woman's honor,[8] which is attached to her family and lineage. Islamic concepts provide the moral register of actions and codes of honor to Muslims in which hierarchical social relations should be organized. The discussion on taravād here, which pertains directly to the context of Malabar will be picked up for analysis below. I just want to emphasize that it is Islamic concepts that are used to justify hierarchical choices and, as such, they are considered virtuous and good for the person and the family. As we will see below, the stigma attached to a family is more far-reaching in terms of ascriptive status and it seeps into one's occupational identity.

The Arabic text is relevant here. A woman whose family has extricated itself from a lowly profession will not be compatible with someone whose family has not escaped such an occupation because engaging in such work indicates decreasing a man's respectability and honor in society. So, someone who is or whose father is engaged in cupping or as a rag-picker or a shepherd will not be compatible with a woman whose father is a weaver. A weaver's son will not be compatible with a businessman's daughter. A weaver's son will not be compatible with a textile owner's daughter. The sons of both these businessmen are not compatible with a daughter of a religious scholar. Saleem explained that "the most important thing here is the authority. A father has the right to force his virgin daughter to marry someone he has found for her. He can marry her off to anyone he likes, but they should be compatible. If a religious scholar decides to send his daughter in marriage to the son of a businessman, if the daughter declines the proposal, the religious scholar cannot conduct the marriage." Once again, wealth is not a primary consideration, illustrating that morality is conceptualized along the lines of heredity, occupation, and family history.

These Islamic jurisprudential injunctions advocate and support endogamous marriage relations among Muslims based on ethnicity, occupation, and length of time of being a Muslim. In my discussions with Muslims in Malabar, other ideas that are taken into consideration also emerged. Even if most Muslims were unaware of the nuances of jurisprudential discussions, they often recited the following hadith reported by Imam Bukhari (810–870 AD) in *Sahih al-Bukhari* (5090), which gives another take on the social interactions and relationships among Muslims. The hadith goes like this: "A woman is married for four reasons, i.e., her wealth, her family status, her beauty, and her piety. So, you should marry the pious woman (otherwise) you will be losers." This hadith is often explained in religious sermons while describing ideal marriages, spousal relations, and family values. Such sermons may be conducted in madrassas or in public spaces in order to educate Muslims of Islamic religious values and they are quite common across Malabar. Most of the madrassas in Malabar have monthly programs to impart religious knowledge to the believers in the neighborhood. These injunctions are quite vague, unlike the jurisprudential proclamations outlined earlier. Rather than a prescriptive utterance, this is phrased as an observation on the everyday practices of Muslims. There is also a hint that in deciding a spousal relation, the ideal of piety should be preferred to other factors. Yet, Muslims in Malabar consider other factors as key to choosing a partner. Their hierarchical discourses with reference to barbers also suggest that factors like wealth and family status are often considered a prerequisite to embody piety. In the next section, I will look at how these jurisprudential concepts and injunctions have been operationalized and practiced among Muslims in Malabar.

Endogamy in Practice

Muslims in Malabar use the concept of kufuv as a catch-all term to signify elements that need to be factored into considerations of marital alliances. For instance, it is common to hear Muslims dismissing a marriage alliance by simply saying that "their kufuv do not match." They use the idea of kufuv to relate four ideas: wealth, status, beauty, and piety. These ideas may be unevenly weighted when considering a match and may depend on circumstances, but they remain relevant to any marital arrangements. Among these, the idea of status is loosely translated as taravād in Malayalam. In the past, the term taravād referred to a matrilineal ancestral household but now refer to both patrilineal and matrilineal ancestral house. In matrilineal taravād, the patrimony was bequeathed through the female line. The affairs of the family were managed by the senior male member of the family who was called *kāranavar.* Muslims along the coast followed matriliny; in the inland areas, however, patriliny was the form of social organization. In patrilineal taravād, the descent was traced through a male ancestor. The patrimony was distributed according to the principles of sharia, which gave women half the quantity of what men were given. A few Muslim families could trace their genealogy beyond one and a half centuries, and it gave them much prestige in the locality. The status of a taravād was determined by the past it could unearth through its genealogy (Arafath 2016). Since most of the Muslims were agricultural labor and did not own property, they did not have the documentation to trace their genealogies beyond one or two grandfathers. In the land records, the names of the buyer's and seller's parents are also written down, and if one had records of the land going back at least a hundred years, one could learn the names of at least three or four generations. In such contexts, some Muslim families were privileged to make a case for high status in the locality based on genealogical information that could be asserted and verified.

While the idea of taravād was the first principle of evaluation in marriage alliances, others such as *bhakti* (piety), *chorukk* (beauty), and *muthal* (wealth) were also considered. In most cases, however, the first principle restricted marriage to a limited number of potential alliances. For a Mappila, Sayyids were out of reach, as they preferred to keep it mostly an endogamous affair owing to their high status that was based on descent from the prophet Muhammad. Barbers were simply ruled out in the first instance because they were considered lacking in taravād due to their lowly occupation. For a Mappila, the first principle itself reduced the marriage circle to their own. As a second step, the concept of taravād is further used to distill potential alliances among Mappilas along with other factors. If piety is fused with a taravād, that family lineage will hold the higher status than a taravād, which has great wealth. If a taravād has historically produced great religious scholars over generations and wielded an immense amount of wealth in a locality, their family genealogy will be held in high esteem. Unlike other family lineages with wealth, their hold on knowledge might also give them greater advantage to establish their genealogy far beyond other families. Many such Mappila lineages in Malabar even insist on being recognized as descendants of religious scholars who have arrived on the southwest coast for the propagation of Islam at various times since the ninth century. If someone from a well-regarded taravād rises to be a great religious scholar, his family will be held in high esteem in the locality. Yet, if a person considered to be lacking in taravād becomes a religious scholar, his acquired piety will rarely be sufficient to override the status of his family lineage in securing a marriage alliance. In common parlance, piety is associated more with acquiring training in normative religious texts and procuring a degree than with individual devotion to Allah. In that sense, it is closely related to being accepted within the authoritative frame of the established religious groups in Malabar.

Among all social groups, marriages might be restricted within one's own taravād. Such marriages were quite common until the 1980s. So, for each taravād, there could be endogamous and exogamous marriages. Different reasons are given for these types of marriages, some emphasize the lack of wealth while others emphasize strategies to safeguard wealth, prohibiting transactions beyond the lineages. In any case, if lineage is considered to be a key factor in determining alliances, barbers would be automatically avoided because of their socially inferior status, therefore lacking an honorable lineage.

Pierre Bourdieu (1962, 11), the French sociologist whose early work was in Algeria examined, among other things, the systems of values shaping their social world, particularly how the concept of patrilineal patrimony mediates their practices. He argues that patrimony is the basis of endogamous marriages. In a context where agricultural lands and resources are scarce, families tended to engage in endogamous marriages to forestall the possibility of property moving out of the group. It was further ensured by the fact that women were not allowed to inherit to avoid the division of property. The members of the clan were "obliged to defend its patrimony (women, lands and dwellings) and above all its honor, the supreme value, more precious than life itself" (33). But in the case of Muslims in Malabar, I suggest that genealogy is the basis of marriage strategies. It works with the logic that one does not want to demote the status of one's family by getting into an unsuitable alliance.

The other two factors of kufuv, beauty and piety, may also work as overlapping ideas along with taravād and wealth. Beauty is a key concept for marriage alliances, but it is taken into consideration only after the two primary concerns, taravād and wealth, are estimated. Beauty can be defined, following George Hagman (2002, 662), "as an aspect of the experience of idealization in which an object(s), sound(s) or concept(s) is believed to possess qualities of formal perfection." In Islam, the concept of beauty is closely associated with the nature or natural world (Fahm 2020, 217). In the Quran (6:99), Allah says that He has created the world in its best forms and human beings are asked to reflect upon it to draw divine messages inherent in them. As such, conception of beauty is a foundational aspect of creation, and it also applies to human beings. Again, in the Quran (95:4), Allah says, "We have indeed created man in the best of molds" (Nasr et al. 2015). Physical attractiveness may be seen as an initial criterion for evaluating one's beauty, but Muslims in Malabar associate other principles, such as personality, modesty, habits, and behavior, as key ingredients for making a truly beautiful person: It is, one could say, an "aesthetic ecology." Put differently, there are multiple considerations that render someone alluring, and those considerations extend beyond external factors. A barber or fisher may be seen as not embodying the range of values associated with this aesthetic ecology and therefore not suitable for a potential marriage alliance. Sometimes, marriages do occur between bride-giving poor and rich families within a social group if the girl is considered beautiful. Here the notion of beauty is generally associated with fair skin and a chaste or modest demeanor. Such marriages, as and when they occur, are mostly arranged love marriages or are when the groom insists on marrying the girl. Similar to the idea of beauty, piety is also often used to hierarchize social groups among Muslims in Malabar. I will discuss this issue in detail in Chapter 7.

There is a hierarchy between the four concepts among Muslims in Malabar; taravād is the primary consideration, followed by concepts of wealth, piety, and beauty, all of which might be considered at a similar level. Whereas the relative standing of these ideas may vary for every family, depending on their circumstances, taravād is an inviolable mechanism when it comes to evaluating a marriage proposal. My point is that value relations are not a priori, marking social actions into the rigidity of rules and regulations. In each context, what mattered to Muslims was to choose from available values to justify, negotiate, and contest social relations. To this extent then, as the highest concept among these, the taravād trumps all other factors in determining a marriage alliance. Those who had wealth and land in the past can capitalize on it and are considered to have better taravād than those who were poor and dependent on wealthy families in the locality. An Islamic jurisprudential category, kufuv, is here translated into a hierarchical concept that differentiates between groups of people based on the idea of marital compliance.

I have already noted that, among Hindus, endogamous marriages are the norm across India. Even when marriage is sought within the caste, it can be further restricted based on marriage compatibility in horoscopes (jātakam), and to say that it does not match in the case of two potential partners is common (Osella and Osella 2000b, 99). Along with horoscope, wealth, status, and beauty are further considerations for marriage alliances among Hindus in Malabar. Arguably then, we can say that both Hindus and Muslims follow endogamous marriage relations, but these practices are understood, negotiated, and employed using two different value systems.

Intergroup and Love Marriages Among Muslims

Arranged marriages, in which parents or guardians assume the authority to give the final consent, have been the norm among various communities and castes in India. Shameem Black (2017, 345) writes that "Indians often defined themselves through an opposition to love marriage, which was sometimes portrayed as a fundamentally Western practice." Love marriages have the power to challenge the existing endogamous relations. Since they occur without prior knowledge and consent of the families involved, most of the time, the couple resorts to elopement. This becomes a crucial issue in the case of marriages between an upper-caste female and a lower-caste male among Hindus (Dhar 2013, 9). In the case of Muslims, too, love marriages between different status groups are a difficult affair.

Unlike arranged marriages organized under the control of patrons, love marriages were one possibility through which barber men and women could be engaged in marriage relations with Mappilas and fishers. Even in such cases, the elite Mappilas in the locality of the barber would intervene to stop the marriages. Sulaimān, a Mappila dramatist recollected an incident that happened in his locality in Calicut in the early 1970s. The barber had fallen in love with a girl in a different locality where he had gone to learn the martial arts. When the elite Mappila who was controlling the main mosque learned about the issue, he intervened and told the barber, "It is not good for us; we will find a better girl." The barber could not go against the directions of the person. Otherwise, he would be socially boycotted in the locality and forced to move out and find a job to sustain his livelihood. So, he complied with the command of the elite patron. I have heard similar stories about a few barbers and fishers in Malabar who had to break up a relationship of love and comply with the local authority of Mappilas.

I do not want to give the impression that barbers are always looking for marriage alliances with Mappilas. That is far from true. Many barber families marry among themselves, saying that Mappilas are not suitable allies for them because of the barbers' descent from an original Muslim, while the Mappilas are converts from various Hindu castes. Many also expressed their worry regarding a marriage alliance with Mappilas due to the possible humiliation they may undergo after the marriage in Mappila families. One of the barbers suggested that I should read the novel *Ossātthi* written by Beena (2017) to understand the horrors of such a scenario. The novel depicts a Mappila boy acting against the wishes of his wealthy family in the locality and marrying their barber's daughter. While she faces lots of trouble, such as boycott within the husband's family, she finds refuge in her husband who stands by her always. After the birth of a baby girl, the husband goes to the Gulf seeking a livelihood and dies there from an unforeseen disease. His widow's troubles at home intensify and she has to eventually leave for her maternal house where she opens a beauty salon to be able to raise her child. While this is fictional, many barbers in Malabar related similar incidents. A few, in particular, talked about the novel and expressed similar concerns if they were to involve their girl children in marriage alliances with Mappila families. With the spread of secular education and employment opportunities, educated barber women are now sought after for marriage alliances by Mappilas. Such marriages do occur these days, though they are rare. I look at the changing landscape of marriages in Malabar in detail in Chapter 7.

Conclusion

It is true that most Muslims in Malabar profess that there is no caste in Islam. At the same time, they engage in categorizing social groups based on their descent and occupation. The social distinctions thus obtained also shore up their long-standing social interactions between groups through marriage alliances. To justify such social distinctions, they draw upon Quranic and prophetic traditions. While, according to the Quran (49:13), Allah proclaims that human beings are categorized into tribes and clans so that people can recognize each other, Muslims stretch this injunction further to reflect upon and guide their moral behavior. As we have seen, marriage alliances have been restricted between various social groups among Muslims, be it based on tribe, descent, occupation, or wealth. Muslims in Malabar draw heavily from Islamic ideas to understand, sustain, and propagate asymmetrical social relations. The Islamic jurisprudential ideas clearly distinguish between social groups based on descent, occupation, wealth, piety, and length of being a Muslim. These ideas are disseminated to the wider population through various means, including in madrassas to young children, by religious scholars in their institutions of learning, and to commoners through religious sermons. These ideas shape hierarchical interactions and social relations. They contribute to restricting marriage alliances within the stipulated groups by providing much-needed justifications and rationalizations for continuing these practices.

A much-rehearsed contention in South Asian anthropology for the prevalence of hierarchical practices has been that Muslims have not done away with their earlier cultural practices of Hinduism. I have shown that, rather than searching for elements of caste in Muslim lives, a more fruitful way of approaching the question of hierarchy is to explore how Muslims make sense of, operationalize, and justify the hierarchical relations. On the face of it, both Hindus and Muslims share endogamy, and certain ideas, beliefs, and practices underlying the two communities might seem similar. However, the value systems undergirding endogamy in both of these communities are quite distinct and draw upon their respective religious traditions.

The hierarchical practices of endogamy are predicated on jurisprudential ideas from Islam. In any society, there are hierarchical relations. While they may be expressed in terms of tribal identity in the Arab region, in other places, they may take the form of ethnicity and caste. The idea of caste on the Indian subcontinent gives a strong anchoring point for thinking of and ordering social relations among Muslims. At the same time, in a context such as Malabar and India in general where caste was thought of and understood as a religiously sanctioned social institution among Hindus, Muslims had to mark their religion as more virtuous and egalitarian. It was their distinction from the other that always attracted the lower castes toward acceptance of Islam. However, as we saw, the multiplicity and complexity of views and opinions in Islam provide much leeway for Muslims to alter conventions, to negotiate, and to configure hierarchical social relations. There is no single, normative Islam; rather, Muslims draw upon various ideas from normative Islam to make sense of everyday life. It is because of this complexity that one finds Muslims in Malabar ordering their social life by drawing upon Islamic beliefs and jurisprudential concepts (among other ideas) to enable and support ideas of hierarchy.

CHAPTER 6

Securing *Antassu*

Some loose hair clung to the borders of Hamza's mundu and danced like waves on the carpeted floor as he moved around the barber chair in his shop. Hamza was focused on cutting the hair of a child. These scattered pieces of hair were the remnants of previous haircuts, of earlier customers. Still, each time, as soon as the job was over, Hamza was careful to sweep the hair into a corner beyond the view of the next person. I watched him at work as I waited outside his shop. It was early January 2019, around noon. As soon as he was done, Hamza came to the entrance of the shop and asked me what I was looking for. He was tall, well-built, and looked about forty years old. He wore a white-striped, yellow cotton shirt over a white mundu. When I shared my credentials and expressed my interest in learning about barbers, he invited me into the shop. He and I sat on a wooden bench inside, behind two barber chairs.

These chairs faced a large wood-framed mirror nailed to the wall at the same height as the barber chairs. There was a shelf fitted beneath the mirror on which Hamza placed his barber paraphernalia, such as scissors, combs, talcum powder, blades, and several kinds of hair dyes and face creams. Opposite the main wall, just above the wooden bench where we sat, there was another large wood-framed mirror fixed to the wall. Any customer sitting on the barber chair would be able to see the back of his own head reflected in the front mirror and would be able to evaluate the work of the barber. The room was divided into two sections: the main area where chairs and mirrors were situated and a smaller space separated by a plywood board. When I peeked into that smaller area, I found a washbasin and a heap of hair collected for disposal later. The partitioning in two parts, common in barbershops in Malabar, hid the waste from the customers' open view.

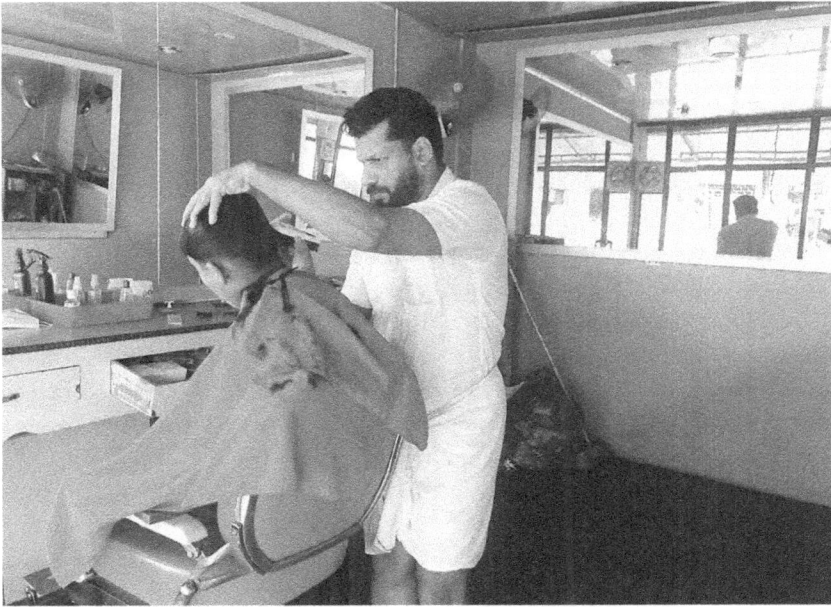

Figure 4. A barber cutting the hair of a child © P. C. Saidalavi.

Hamza's barbershop is in a small neighborhood called Puthuparamb, located two kilometers to the east of the national highway (NH-17) in south Malabar. Such localities, characterized by a cluster of shops, dot the road roughly two kilometers apart all across Kerala, serving what is a highly populated state with a density of 859 people per square kilometer. The shops include a grocery store, a teashop, a barbershop, and sometimes even a stall selling poultry and a bakery. People depend on these shops for their daily needs, and they venture to the nearby small towns only when they require more expensive consumer or household goods, furniture, or food items like red meat or large fish.

The relationships formed between a barbershop, such as the one owned by Hamza, and the locality can be traced back to the early 1970s. That was the time that barbers started opening shops at the behest of unionization movements, despite resistance from their patrons. Barbers subsequently moved away from the hierarchical intimacy of the patronage system toward that of dignified labor within the strictures of capitalism. Barbers often characterized this move as one that gained *antassu* (dignity) for them. This chapter describes the trajectory of this transformation by conceptualizing barbers' work as dignified labor. To understand the newer conceptions of the body and the work imagined by barbers, even within the strictures of subordination, inequality, and suffering, I use the term *dignified labor* to understand labor as mediated by ideas of antassu, achieved through the ownership of labor and the means of production, both of which are held by workers themselves. Gaining dignity calls for purposive, creative, and considered efforts on the part of workers. Through various processes and activities, such as moving their work from the domestic to the public space, refusing to do certain work, deciding the terms of their working hours, and instituting money as the only form of compensation, Muslim barbers effectively constructed autonomy, independence, and integrity as key components of their labor. Through these ideas, barbers sought to attach antassu to their work.

Following upon the Marxian formulation that there is a move from concrete to abstract labor within capitalism, I locate the idea of antassu as a key component in barbers' conception of the transformation of their work into dignified labor. It is by claiming their work as dignified—to be recognized, appreciated, and duly compensated—that barbers destabilized the patronage system. In what follows, I shall begin by outlining what I mean by antassu as it is related to dignified labor. I will then describe the efforts that went into making of a Muslim barber in Malabar. The political mobilization of agricultural labor in Kerala and the unionization movements among industrial labor were the backdrop that stirred this transformation. Barbers learned from these movements and devised political strategies to progressively extricate themselves from the patronage system in which they were embedded. I then examine more specifically, the history of barbers' unionization movements in Malabar and the construction of dignified labor through antassu.

Understanding Antassu

The kind of services offered by barbers can be understood within the framework of bodywork. Initially proposed by Chris Shilling (1993) while discussing Goffman's ideas of work involved in the presentation of self in social interactions, bodywork has generally been used to refer to actions undertaken by people on themselves or to meet the expectations of employers and peers (Bird 2021; Kerfoot 2000; Coffey 2013; Keyser-Verreault 2022). Yet, this is too narrow a definition and obscures many of the important features of bodywork in contemporary society. The conceptualization provided by Carol Wolkowitz (2002; 2006) helps us understand bodywork in its multifarious forms and sites. She defines bodywork as "employment that takes the body as its immediate site of labor, involving intimate, messy contact with the (frequently supine or naked) body, its orifices or products through touch or close proximity" (2006, 147). These may include services to the customers to keep up their bodies and to provide pleasure, leisure, and care. Much has been written on the relationships between body and work, focusing on varied types of service providers, such as nurses, fitness instructors and coaches, beauticians, dentists, doctors, physiotherapists, maids, and sex workers (Black 2004; Casanova 2013; Twigg et al. 2011). There also has been a general understanding that a transformation has occurred in the conception of the body with reference to bodywork. Carol Wolkowitz (2006, 151) notes that the "transition from relations defined by forms of personal servility (slavery, domestic service, women's conjugal obligations as wives or their religious duty as nuns) to waged labor relations mediated by the market has important implications for the definitions of the body that guide and emerge from body work occupations." While many scholars have analyzed newer conceptions of the body that have emerged through the institutionalized spaces where bodywork is conducted, particularly at the realm of health (Jones et al. 2023), less attention has been paid to how the workers themselves have reconfigured their work historically. Barbers laid more emphasis on achieving social dignity by reworking social relations that rendered them subservient within a "traditional" patronage network.

The term *dignity* is usually used in several senses across a range of disciplines and institutional contexts. I find the definition offered by Shultziner and Rabinovici (2012, 107) quite instructive in thinking about the situatedness of the concept of human dignity. They define it as "the universal human need for and pursuit of positive self-worth" aimed to create harmony between cultural understandings regarding human moral worth and the social relations with fellow human beings. The idea of dignity is locally understood and explained in varying ways in Kerala, using the Malayalam term *antassu*. Yet, antassu is quite more than what dignity can signify. First, it designates an acquired quality associated with one's station in life. It is a category of self-understanding. Second, it can be used as a tool of social commentary to assess the moral quality and personality of an individual. Even if you have high ranking in society in terms of genealogy and caste, you may be said to be lacking in antassu if you are not living up to the standard of life expected of your social position. I find it useful to think about this quality using what Evans-Pritchard (1976, 13) says about witchcraft among Azande. He notes that the concept of "witchcraft is not that of an impersonal force that may become attached to persons but of a personal force that is generalized in speech, for if Azande do not particularize, they are bound to generalize." While witchcraft is a personal force, it is not directed at specific individuals. It is a tool for understanding misfortune. In the same manner, antassu should be seen as a category for understanding one's own social position and as a tool for social commentary on another's position in life.

Everyone knows that there is something called antassu. I asked a number of Muslims in Malabar what they understood of antassu and I received a range of responses. What all these responses indicated was the archived character of this quality; it was not understood as an ascribed feature of any individual. Following are some of these definitions:

> A Muslim's first sign of antassu is his dīn (religion). A rich person
> should lead a life of luxury that is suitable to her economic standing;
> she cannot lead a life of penury. If a person does not possess enough
> money to eke out his living and has to depend on others, we may say
> that he does not have antassu. A good family, good parents, good
> relatives, all these could be signs of antassu. A sick person will say
> that he has gained antassu after becoming healthy. A person walks
> in polished dress and good manners, we would say that he walks in
> antassu. He hides his poverty and walks in style, then we say that he
> doesn't have antassu.

What emerged through these responses was the personalized quality of an individual, which people in general associate with one's socioeconomic and religious standing in society. In this generalized schema, where does a barber fit in? As I already mentioned, barbers were dependent on their patrons for their livelihood. They had to maintain proper behavior of deference and subordination in front of their patrons to ensure a continuing flow of generosity from their patrons. Moreover, their occupation was considered in an ambiguous manner. On the one hand, they were fulfilling an indispensable role in the community, and it was their moral obligation to do so. On the other hand, since they were dealing with various kinds of impurities in Islamic jurisprudential terms, their social standing was low. Many Muslim barbers told me that their forefathers did not live in antassu because they were subservient to other Muslims in the neighborhood and dependent on their mercy for their subsistence. If we analyze how Muslims looked at the idea of antassu, we can enumerate a few key elements of this idea. They are independence, autonomy, and integrity. If people were dependent on others, they seemed to lose their antassu. If people could not act according to their social standing, they tended to lose antassu. In the same manner, it was also considered to be a quality of personality whereby one stood for one's opinions and choices. Such assertions have been observed in other contexts and expressed through mediums other than political mobilization. For instance, Paik (2022, 1), studying the traveling public theater—Tamasha—of lower castes in Maharashtra notes that women performing in this theater were looked down upon as "immoral, lowly, dishonorable, and lacking *manuski* (human dignity, humanity)." They try to challenge the moral hierarchy of society through their performance and the supposed "Dalit women's sexual availability into a site of Dalit women's resistance, into a performativity of Dalit femininity and sexuality rooted in an improper caste politics" (295). The subordinates, it seems, always try to launch struggles for dignity even through iniquitous conditions and in multifarious forms.

An important issue as far as Muslim barbers have been concerned had to do with the alleged Islamic ideas about the low status of Muslims. First, they had to reconstitute their work as an honorable profession within the normative strictures of Islam. Efforts to reconstitute these ideas were only possible if barbers could gain antassu by embracing the qualities I have outlined above. In a sense, this reconstitution was made possible only after they achieved antassu. Yet, it is important to highlight it before I go into describing how barbers achieved antassu. Barbers allege that caricaturing barbering work as low status is the handiwork of certain religious scholars, and it cannot be found in any scriptures within Islam. When I pointed out that there are verses in Islamic jurisprudential texts such as *Fat-hul Mueen*, a few barber scholars noted two things. First, the passage within this text talks about barbers who conduct bloodletting. And second, religious scholars have often misinterpreted these texts and told the public that these verses referred to barbers, as we see in Malabar. Barbers now often contest and challenge religious scholars in Malabar whenever they try to denigrate the barbering profession and barbers as a community by confronting them and asking for proof from established Islamic scholars of the past to establish their claims. Such assertions have emerged recently and are tied to how barbers have been successful in gaining antassu for their profession within society. In the following sections,

I am going to describe how barbers achieved the qualities associated with antassu, such as independence, autonomy, and integrity, and how they reconstituted their work within the strictures of market relations.

Only if we attend to the construction of dignity will we be able to understand why Muslim barbers in Malabar were detesting their older social identity and harping on a new, anglicized identity. This story is distinct from two kinds of trends that we see in India. First, the opportunities opened by liberalization have empowered certain social groups from the lower rungs of the middle classes to seek new opportunities, but they tend to reproduce existing inequalities and power relations (De Neve 2006; Gidwani and Sivaramakrishnan 2003). Second, the economic liberalization and the decline of agricultural income has further worsened the condition of Dalits[1] and tribal groups in India (Shah et al. 2018). The story of barbers in the context of Kerala, is not unique, however. In fact, this story tells one strand of the Kerala model of development that has brought about significant changes in the socioeconomic standards of people in Kerala (Lukose 2009). The Kerala model of development has been hailed as a unique phenomenon of socioeconomic development in which public action, decreasing mortality, and increasing standards of living have been noted as characterizing this development, despite the state being a consumer state. The barbers' story, in effect, portrays how a subordinated community transformed itself and society by following a cultural script of public action.

The Making of a Political Community

Political mobilizations by the lower classes in Kerala can be traced to the initial decades of the twentieth century. The union activities that began among agricultural landless labor in southern Kerala since the 1940s gained force in the mid-1960s. They were heavily concentrated in the wetland region of southern Kerala and supported by the coir factory workers' union. Most of these movements were the fronts for communist parties in Kerala since the 1940s (Kannan 1999; Tharamangalam 1981). The demands of agricultural tenants and labor to enact structural reforms to end the unequal work arrangements in Kerala had taken a new valence when it became a dominant motive of electoral politics in the 1960s. The Communist party, which, in 1957, formed in Kerala the first ever democratically elected Communist government in the world, promised to end landlordism and distribute excess land to the agricultural laborers.

Figure 5. Barbers conducting a *dharna* © Aharika Baskar.

While the communist unions in industries and factories helped and supported unionization movements in other sectors, they were not interested in organizing barbers due to the scattered nature of the barber population and its low numbers. Many barbers, however, were quite active in organizing and mobilizing workers in other sectors. They drew energy and inspiration from these movements and their own experiences and sought to organize their own occupational community, which was divided into various castes and religious communities. They formed many local unions in various districts of southern Kerala in the 1950s and 1960s but could not bring them under a single umbrella to generate any political clout (Soloman 1972). The barber case was quite distinct from agricultural labor, which had demanded an end to the patronage system and sought land to live on and cultivate. Since barbers were engaged in service work, their aim was to rework and negotiate their social interactions and relationships with their established patrons. They sought, like agricultural labor, to establish cash as the mode of payment for their labor. This transformation corroborates a point made by Dipesh Chakrabarty (2001, 54) in explaining the notion of abstract labor put forth by Marx, that organizing "life under the sign of capital is to act *as if* labor could indeed be abstracted from all the social tissues in which it is always embedded and which make any particular labor—even the labor of abstracting—concrete." He suggests that abstract labor should be understood as a performative and practical category. This process of abstraction is visible in the construction of barbers' labor.

It was a group of barber communist activists who began organizational activities in their occupational community. They were not, in many cases, considered elites in their community in any sense of the term: neither economically prosperous nor well-educated. They had, however, the political capital required to mobilize their own community members. It is the political capital formulated within the structures and discourses of the communist parties, that gave them capacity to think beyond caste and community lines. As I said in Chapter 3, each caste and religious community in Kerala had its own barbers. Transgressing these caste and community boundaries was a challenge, with potential social and economic ramifications. Fearing social boycott, barbers were initially averse to the idea. But barbers working in union movements had already observed political action transforming labor relations of coir factory workers. Barbers envisioned that if such political mobilization and construction of community were to become possible, they had to escape the social subordination they routinely suffered through the patronage system. When I asked Abu, whom we met earlier, about the nature of this transformation, he observed that in the past only the communists believed that there should be strong unions for workers belonging to various professions. He added that one had to be especially committed to the cause at the time, as it entailed full devotion to the organization, often at the expense of family life. Since there were no social-media platforms like there are today, the union activists had to walk long distances to meet and possibly recruit potential barbers. To undertake such an initiative, one had to sacrifice one's earnings and, in many cases, shut their shops for a day. In a sense, as one of my barber interlocutors put it, one needed a "sacrificial mentality" to build an organization, and the communists had inculcated such convictions. On December 25, 1968, nineteen barbers from across Kerala congregated in a small hotel in Thrissur on the invitation of a local union of barbers in the district. Abu recollected seeing an advertisement about the meeting in a local daily newspaper but did not pay much attention to it. They formed the organization Kerala State Barbers' Association (KSBA) and decided to extend its activities across Kerala by organizing district committees. While Abu was working at his barbershop in Nilambur, a small hilly town in east Malabar, in early 1969, a few people came to his shop to invite him to participate in a proposed Malappuram district committee meeting of the KSBA. They approached Abu because he was already known as a spirited activist of the Communist Party in the area at that time. He participated in the meeting and decided to devote much of his time and energy to spread the message of the organization among barbers and urge them to become members of the organization. He viewed the organization as a key medium to raise the awareness of barbers' social subordination and as a means of gaining social dignity.

At the first meeting to form the Malappuram district committee of the KSBA on January 16, 1970, Abu was elected as the block secretary of the Nilambur area. Like Abu, many barbers were working on the ground across the district to build up the KSBA in the early 1970s. Abu recollected that there were several barbers who were afraid to join the KSBA fearing a backlash from other Muslims, while many expressed concern that the union was trying to finish off the barbers by trying to stop even the meager rewards they were earning. Many also told Abu, "We are poor, and you should not bring up difficulties for our families by the activities of your organization." Abu walked long distances to every part of Nilambur taluk (an administrative unit just below the district) to talk to barbers. Sometimes he would rent a bicycle for eight annas (16 annas make up one rupee) to facilitate his movement. When he went to his maternal uncles to encourage them to join the KSBA, they chided him, "Your parents are in lots of trouble due to your communism." But Abu did not relent. After talking at length about many of the challenges during that time, Abu sighed and smiled, and then added, "The houses of many barbers who dismissed me at that time have been, in later times, thatched by the money collected by the KSBA taluk committee." Abu continued, "Some of their girls have been given 40 or 50 grams of gold during their marriage, and some others have been helped with medical bills." There was elation in his voice when he spoke, and I could sense that he was proud of his work for the barber community in Malabar.

There were times when Abu failed to locate a barber despite hours of walking because barbers were always on the move, providing services in the homes of patrons. Even when they were found and spoken to, they were not easily convinced about opening shops and charging uniform prices; they feared that putting a price on their services would deter customers. But, once the unionization took root, confidence rose, and many saw the benefits: both the financial and the political gains of belonging to a union. Barbers could now both refuse to undertake demeaning aspects of their earlier jobs, such as shaving the armpits, and demand cash (rather than kind) for their labor. With the general increase in prices of commodities, the maintenance of households by simply receiving rewards in kind was increasingly untenable for barbers. Since they only received grain and occasionally vegetables and fruits, consuming them required other materials, such as oil and spices, which they could procure only with hard cash.

In this context, one could see why demanding cash for their labor was thus very attractive for barbers across Kerala in the 1970s. At times, activist barbers drew the ire of other Muslim communities, displeased with the former's newfound confidence. According to Chandran, a sixty-year-old Hindu barber, slogans such as the following were usually hollered during KSBA conferences or during confrontations between barbers and Mappilas over the opening of barbershops or over some unsavory practice of the Mappilas.

KSBA zindabad; barbershops we will open
Who is there to block us? KSBA zindabad!

Barbers' work was conceived in the past as undignified, the contours of which were defined by the prescriptions of Islam, economic dependence and discourses of disgust and humiliation. An important method for unhinging their work from its cultural moorings was radical, political action through unionization and the attendant reformulation of their work as labor. To appreciate some of the driving forces behind such social change in Kerala, it is worth reflecting on a parallel discussion in literature, emphasizing expansion of democracy and political action and changing economic orders as central to contemporary social transformations in India (Gorringe 2017; Jodhka 2015

Manor [1970] 2010). According to Jodhka (2015 50), many social groups have moved out of a caste-based economy, or caste-based occupations have become redundant with the growth of markets and capitalism. Moreover, the lower-caste groups mobilize around their identities using democratic means to assert their rights, to secure government benefits of positive discrimination, and to contest traditional power hierarchies, often resulting in atrocities by the dominant castes. One can see a similar shift in the case of barbers in Malabar where the community sought to rework its traditional occupation and acquire wealth and increase income. Rather than attaining education and a change of occupation, the barber community in general persisted with its occupation because barbers had both a guaranteed clientele and a reliable source of income. They mainly wanted to reformulate earlier conceptions of work and reconstitute it as labor. I now turn to describing the gradual movement of barbers from patronage work to that of labor.

Constructing a New Space

One of the key actions barbers undertook was to own a permanent space for their work in the public and disentangle it from the domesticity of the patrons. Yet, this change did not occur all of a sudden. I once asked Abu if he could describe to me the changes that have occurred in the mode of work done by barbers. He spoke of how his father used to work on wooden benches that were placed in specific spots in the town, usually on the veranda of some shop. On these benches, the barber and the customer would sit face to face and the customer would lower his head to facilitate shaving. Initially, they became part of the general chaos of small towns during a fair when petty traders lined the open streets, adjacent to one another, and displayed their wares. A different form of this operation of barbershops can still be seen on north Indian street corners. This is a feature, Tim Edensor (1998) has submitted, that was seen as a characteristic feature of Indian streets. He observed that Indian streets defy an order that adheres to Western aesthetics, making it appear as if simply haphazard and disorienting activities are placed alongside more formal and regulated experiences. The barbers in Malabar, initially formed part of this mix of heterogeneity of the streets with the impermanence and lack of ownership of the spaces. During these times, Abu noted, many customers would refuse to give any payment after the work was finished. As per the local patronage system, many customers would inform

Abu's father that they were just not carrying any money and that they would reward him later. In some cases, barbers would never receive their due. Abu's father could not insist on immediate payment because he did not have any kind of political support behind him to enforce such a system. This irregularity of street-vendor-type barbers was progressively replaced, over time, by the appearance of permanent establishments where a barber could formalize his work on the basis of time, wage, and labor.

In the inland regions of Malabar, the use of public space was the first step in unhinging the barbers' work from the domestic sphere. The observation made by Sudipta Kaviraj (1997, 86, 89) in the context of understanding filth and the public sphere in Calcutta is relevant here to help us think about this transformation. He posits that "public is a particular configuration of commonness," which signifies the "idea that the activity is open to all, irrespective of their social attributes." The movement from the domestic to the public space resulted in creating a permanent spot for the barbers at the weekly fairs and production centers. This shift from the domestic to the public helped barbers escape the embeddedness of their work within the rhythm of domestic agricultural production and weekly demands for services. With the opening of the shops, barbers installed barber chairs, which gave permanence to their labor. Unlike wooden benches, the chairs signified professionalism and could not be easily moved given their weight. In some instances, I was told, chairs were imported from Chennai, with some featuring a 360-degree swivel that helped ease the work of the barber. This attracted new customers and afforded a new aesthetic to barbers' work. Similarly, a shop signified a permanence to the barber's services. The mobile nature of their work arrangements in the past progressively disappeared in favor of the more stable dwellings of shops. Even if they were invited by some customers to their houses, barbers began holding their ground, refusing to visit houses to provide barbering services. An exception was made and is still made in the case of the sick and the homebound. Barbers have repeatedly emphasized to me that they will make home visits to provide services, sometime for free. Through this arrangement, barbers demonstrate their moral commitment to the sick and the frail and a more general contribution to the welfare of the community. In that way, they can both assert their professionalism and, at the same time, highlight the value and commitment of their craft.

The attempts by barbers to overcome the patronage system were fraught endeavors that needed to overcome prejudice, enmity, and interreligious tensions. The opening of the shops meant that barbers were progressively rejecting the patronage mechanism, which had been their mainstay until then. Such subversions of an age-old system were not received well by those who had vested interest in maintaining it. The actions of barbers often met with punitive consequences. I was often told that, at the time, many barbershops were attacked, property was damaged, and shopfronts were demolished. In 1970, when a barber opened a shop in a small locality in Malappuram, the barber allowed a Cheruman—a person from Dalit background—to sit on the barber chair at the shop and groomed him. According to Abdurahman, a sixty-eight-year-old barber in south Malabar who told me of this incident, some Mappilas saw this as an affront to their standing, despite his being Muslim. It enraged Mappilas as a Cheruman was always meant to stand respectfully and at some distance from the wealthy Mappilas, let alone sit in public places where they will also sit.

The Mappilas could not stomach that an untouchable Hindu was sitting on the barber's chair, and a Muslim barber was cutting his hair and shaving him. They abused the barber for violating the customs of the locality. He was accused of disgracing the Muslim community by providing services to untouchables. It is important to remember that until barbershops were set up for the public, barbers among Hindus and Muslims were only serving their own communities and respective castes, to avoid ritual pollution. In the past, even Hindu barbers were barred from serving the untouchables, who were required to cut their own hair and beards. A scuffle arose at the shop between the "wayward" barber and the Mappilas and the shop was subsequently shut down. Such incidents were quite common across Malabar when shops initially opened, inter-community services were discouraged and prohibited.

Abu himself recollected a similar incident in Nilambur that involved his father when he first opened a shop in the 1950s. "My father cut the hair of a Hindu Nair named Potiyādan Sami. He was a janmi and an elite in the locality. My father made a *kuduma* [keeping a tuft of hair on head by upper caste Hindus] for him." Seeing this event unfolding at the shop, some Mappilas at the locality got agitated. "My father was accused of flouting social norms. Cutting the hair of a non-Muslim itself was problematic. Here, my father had also made a kuduma for him, that was beyond their belief. They indicted my father for colluding with the *kāfirs* [non-believers] and receiving their money." Abu continued, "Even before this incident, some Mappilas in the locality had a rancour against my father because he was a communist. My father did not believe in the inter-community restrictions of barbering, and he was ready to serve anyone who was willing to pay." The matter

escalated, and eventually, the Mappila elites in the locality called for a boycott of his shop. After a month or so, he closed the shop due to the lack
of customers because most of his customers were Muslims and they were
afraid to go against the elite decision. "All three of us siblings were quite
small at that time and my father found it difficult to eke out a living. So, he
sent us along with our mother to her maternal house and the maternal family
were agriculturists-cum-barbers. Then my father went for bamboo work in
the river, called *poyambani*." The work was to fell the bamboo in the forest and transport them through the river to Calicut. The work was irregular
and illegal. "Each bundle of bamboo, called *mulappāndi* consisted of around
thousand bamboos and someone had to stand on top of them and manoeu-
vre their movements through the river." Abu recollected that this must have
happened when he was ten or eleven years old. His father did this job for
some time, and it was during the monsoons that there was much work of this
kind. "During the dry season, my father turned to selling tea powder, which
he went and bought from Chembal estate in Goodalloor. He would walk in
the neighbourhoods of Nilambur and sell them to households. He did this
for almost two years." He returned to barbering profession after two years
when there was a slackness in the boycott and many Mappilas assured him
that they would come for his services. He then opened a new shop few hundred meters away from the old shop. Abu recollected that "My father rented
it for four rupees per month." Abu noted that even as things were beginning
to change, Mappilas would carefully scrutinize my father's customers and
would only come in if an untouchable or a lower-caste Hindu was not present. In Abu's story, we see a gradual shift from barbering work tied to the
community to that of market-oriented relations. That transformation was
key to the construction of self-identity for barbers.

Producing a Barber

A key aspect of wresting their services from their earlier cultural moorings
was the production of a new identity by reconstituting the barber community's
occupational name. Since names are an important signifier of one's identity
and constitution of self-worth, people attach much weight and importance to
them (Asempasah and Sam 2016; Brewer 1981; Pandian 1983; Patel 2017). I
have already noted that many castes and religious communities had their own
barbers to serve them. These barbers also had unique names. While Muslim

barbers were called *ossān*, there were many barber castes among Hindus with similar names. Barbers serving Ezhavas (an OBC caste in the governmental categorization today) were called adutthōn. These nomenclatures—precisely because they implied social subordination and disgust—were deemed derogatory by barbers. They carried the emotional and social content accumulated through generations. Unlike groups occupying high status who take pride in their names, the lower groups were uncomfortable with titles such as ossān, which they rarely use to refer to themselves. The Sayyids, for example, proudly deploy the title "Sayyid" as a prefix to their names to emphasize their high status among Muslims. I have met many barbers who were dissatisfied with the earlier term ossān and sought to avoid mentioning it publicly. When they opened shops, names such as barber and hairdresser were used by them. Once again, this can be seen as evidence of the shift from "occupation" to "profession." A similar tendency has been documented by Suseendirarajah (1978) in Sri Lanka where a young barber preferred to be addressed by the English term rather than by the earlier caste name *pariyaariyaar*. He suggests that "perhaps these alien forms are looked upon by them as free from the traditional social stigma that usually accompanies the native forms" (313). In many instances, Muslim barbers in Malabar also preferred to use the English terms rather than the old ones, which signified social subordination. A shop's nameplate, for instance, may be read as "Hamza Hairdresser" or "Hamza Barbershop." A key aspect of these names is that they are all in English. They do not carry the baggage that local names bear and even offer a degree of distinction associated with anglicized terms.

The resignification of their profession with an English word helps escape any local, cultural attributes. These changes could also be reframed using the terms "laborer" and "customer," which denote a fixed wage for the jobs they were doing. Now the term *beautician* is increasingly used, as barbers have also started providing services such as facials, bleaching, and coloring. These changes also signify changes in the nature of their profession. When they were called ossān, they conducted tonsure, head-shaving, circumcision, and ear-piercing. When they became barbers, their domain of work shifted from the domestic realm to public spaces where their services were clearly defined in relation to a market-based economy. For instance, consider the term *beautician*, which means barbers engaged in massaging and providing facials, as well as all other modes of beautification. It also speaks of the experience that the clientele expects in these establishments, one that is dignified and is not simply about the "maintenance" of the self (as discussed in Chapter 3) but rather, as Ahmed (2006) has argued, an upgrade of the body for both personal and public consumption.

Institutionalizing Money

The construction of antassu as self-worth by barbers can be observed if we analyze the social transformations accomplished by barbers through the shops. They constructed their own space, implemented their own rules and regulations, and established money as the only mode of payment for their services. The most important aspect of the social transformation was the disentangling of barbers' compensation from rewards in the patronage system to that of money. As soon as the service provided by barbers is divested of its cultural moorings, it becomes aligned along the lines of a market economy and cash transactions are normalized in the work relations of the barbers. Money became the index in which the importance of barbers' labor became real in the world. The barbers' institutionalization of money as the mode of compensation for their labor illustrates what Parry and Bloch (1989, 12) identify as "our own cultural discourse about money—that it represents an intrinsically revolutionary power which inexorably subverts the moral economy of 'traditional' societies." Simmel (2004, 445) also observes the revolutionary impulses of money in social life when he writes that "the mathematical character of money imbues the relationship of the elements of life with a precision, a reliability in the determination of parity and disparity, an unambiguousness in agreements and arrangements." By setting up shops and bringing their service from the domestic sphere to the public, barbers demanded money for their services. To establish its validity and dismantle any doubt about the precision of wages, the KSBA produced and revised price charts since the 1970s, which barbers confidently and prominently displayed at their shops and fixed their wages accordingly.

The wider circulation of money in Kerala since the late 1970s onward was brought about by migration to the Persian Gulf countries. Kerala is the third-largest remittance receiving state in India, preceded by the states of Punjab and Gujarat. As of 2020, Kerala emigrants abroad are estimated to be 2.12 million out of which almost 90 percent are working in the Gulf countries. While the remittance from abroad equaled "23% of the state income and exceeded the total government expenditure as well as the value added in agriculture and industry," since 2011, the percentage of remittance has started

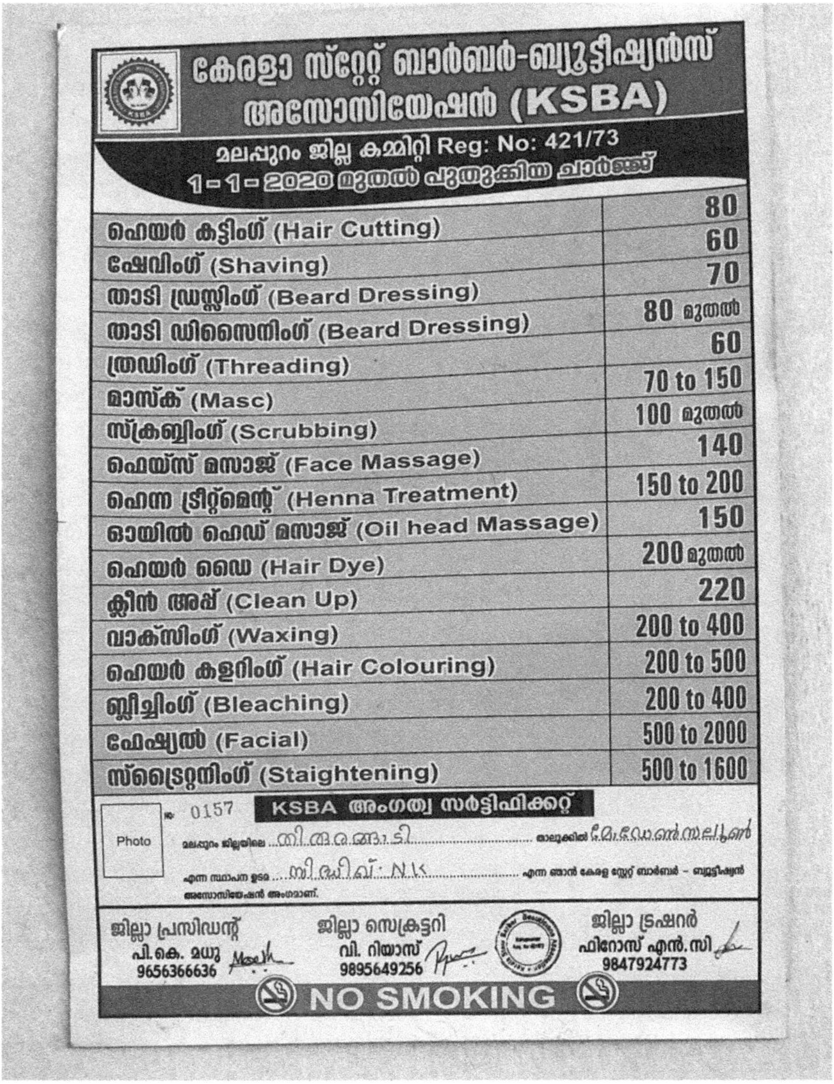

കേരളാ സ്റ്റേറ്റ് ബാർബർ-ബ്യൂട്ടീഷ്യൻസ് അസോസിയേഷൻ (KSBA)	
മലപ്പുറം ജില്ല കമ്മിറ്റി Reg: No: 421/73	
1-1-2020 മുതൽ പുതുക്കിയ ചാർജ്ജ്	
ഹെയർ കട്ടിംഗ് (Hair Cutting)	80
ഷേവിംഗ് (Shaving)	60
താടി ഡ്രസ്സിംഗ് (Beard Dressing)	70
താടി ഡിസൈനിംഗ് (Beard Dressing)	80 മുതൽ
ത്രഡിംഗ് (Threading)	60
മാസ്ക് (Masc)	70 to 150
സ്ക്രബ്ബിംഗ് (Scrubbing)	100 മുതൽ
ഫെയ്സ് മസാജ് (Face Massage)	140
ഹെന്ന ട്രീറ്റ്മെന്റ് (Henna Treatment)	150 to 200
ഓയിൽ ഹെഡ് മസാജ് (Oil head Massage)	150
ഹെയർ ഡൈ (Hair Dye)	200 മുതൽ
ക്ലീൻ അപ്പ് (Clean Up)	220
വാക്സിംഗ് (Waxing)	200 to 400
ഹെയർ കളറിംഗ് (Hair Colouring)	200 to 500
ബ്ലീച്ചിംഗ് (Bleaching)	200 to 400
ഫേഷ്യൽ (Facial)	500 to 2000
സ്ട്രൈട്ടനിംഗ് (Staightening)	500 to 1600

No. 0157   KSBA അംഗത്വ സർട്ടിഫിക്കറ്റ്

Photo   മലപ്പുറം ജില്ലയിലെ തിരുരങ്ങാടി .... താലൂക്കിൽ കെ.എം.ഓൺ.പി.പ്പൻ

എന്ന സ്ഥാപനം ഉടെ .... വി.മ്.ഫി.ത്: N.K .... എന്ന ഞാൻ കേരള സ്റ്റേറ്റ് ബാർബർ – ബ്യൂട്ടീഷ്യൻ അസോസിയേഷൻ അംഗമാണ്.

ജില്ലാ പ്രസിഡന്റ്	ജില്ലാ സെക്രട്ടറി	ജില്ലാ ട്രഷറർ
പി.കെ. മധു	വി. റിയാസ്	ഫിറോസ് എൻ.സി
9656366636	9895649256	9847924773

Figure 6. Price chart prepared by the KSBA © P. C. Saidalavi.

declining as a percentage of the state's income (Kannan and Hari 2020, 956). Most Gulf migrants in Kerala originated from the Malabar region, consisting of mostly unskilled labor and often having studied only up to grade four. The success of the initial migrants to the Gulf countries was weighed according to the amount of cash that they could remit to parents and relatives. Conspicuous consumption was often the visible expression of this type of success (Karinkurayil 2020, 2024). As anthropologists Filippo Osella and Caroline Osella (2000a, 128) have succinctly argued: "Money is the basis of the migrant's success, and he should display an almost careless attitude to it." It was as if the migrant's behavior almost suggested that wealth was at his disposal and there were "endless possibilities of making more." If he fails to indulge in lavish consumption, he instantly puts his financial position in doubt and may lose his claim to status. Many barbers also migrated to the Gulf countries, starting in the 1980s, and worked as barbers there (Haneefa 2021). Migration also helped barbers to set up better shops, provide comfortable sitting and work arrangements, and introduce new technologies to enhance their services. Barbers could now spend their disposable income or invest in things they could not beforehand, as when they only had grains and gifts as their rewards. Now barbers could participate in the economy as equal citizens, as consumers.

Monetary transactions irked many older patrons, who believed that barbers should continue to accept rewards in kind. Some older barbers narrated conflicts and remonstrations between barbers and their earlier patrons in different parts of Malabar. Pokkar Haji, a barber in the coastal area of Malappuram district whom we met earlier, recollected that he was abused for putting up the board of the KSBA displaying rates. Many got into arguments with him, saying that a barber should never demand money for his services and should be satisfied with whatever was given to him. He reminded them that those days have passed and without timely payment he would not be willing to provide any service. Some also tried to humiliate him by belittling the community and their efforts to form an organization for themselves. Until the unionization, barbers were seen as politically docile, whose only function was to submissively serve their patrons. By displaying the sign and the board of the KSBA, barbers were viewed as striving above their station, which constituted a threat to some Muslims in Malabar. Some taunted him saying "barbers have become great leaders" and it was taken by Haji as a great testament to his success as a barber: a badge of honor. In fact, later in his life, Haji contested local elections and became a panchayat member. This in itself was quite significant for a barber because, as I was often told by barber activists, they have been both systematically denied any powerful positions in mainstream organizations and have been sidelined from contesting for any meaningful democratic positions.

By shifting their work from the domestic to the public space, barbers effectively rejected their patrons' power and authority to control them. The patrons could no longer control the timing of the barbers. In the past, barbers had to wait in their patron's houses to provide their services. This was a revolutionary step as far as barbers were concerned. Patrons could no longer control the timing of the service; barbers could now decide the working hours, and they instituted a queue system, which challenged the existing hierarchies of wealth and power in the locality. Waiting became a key form of regulating the work rhythm within the shops, and barbers provided appropriate seating arrangements and a regular supply of magazines and newspapers to occupy their customers while they waited for their turn. It also meant that the customers are also now considered shorn of their own identities, such as family, age, and wealth in accessing services at barbershops.

Service as Choice

Another key resolution passed by the union was that barbers would decide the services they would be providing to customers at their shops. Touching another person's body secretions was seen as further reinforcing the stigma of barbers as undignified and bordering on the immoral. The decision by the KSBA to stop shaving the armpits of customers should be seen as a key step to divesting all notions of filth and immorality that could be associated with barbers' services. When barbers tried to enforce this resolution in the shops, it resulted in verbal insults and a range of body plays at the shops. Abu remembers that in many shops customers would repeatedly show their armpits and barbers would demand they put their arms down. Sometimes, if the barber was young and muscular, he would force down the arm of the customer. Such assertion by barbers was difficult to sustain, and incidents like this could lead to heated arguments, and even physical altercations with customers. Barbers maintained that it was a decision taken by their union and no one could force them to do anything they did not feel comfortable doing. If barbers were manhandled, they often contacted local officials of the KSBA and sought their help. The local KSBA committee would then contact higher-ups and immediately swing into action by personally visiting the barber and offering full support. The support from the union further triggered such assertive action by barbers. The assistance took various forms, as detailed below.

A communist Hindu barber in south Malabar narrated an incident in which a barber was beaten up and his shop vandalized for refusing to shave an armpit. The barber sought help from the local KSBA committee, and they decided to hold a march in the town in the evening. Shouting slogans like "KSBA zindabad; we will open the shops; we will decide what to do" and "Even if given lakhs of rupees; we will not shave the armpits," the barbers, holding KSBA flags, marched behind a banner of the union. They marched from the town center to the barber's shop where they planted a KSBA flag in front of the shop. The barber opened his shop, and the local committee offered him a chair, mirror, and other paraphernalia that was damaged in the vandalism. While just a few barbers were the targets of such violence, in many places, barbers faced verbal abuse and threats. But they took on the challenges with grit and determination. Such political action and organized social action were key to building confidence and self-worth, which helped further reinforce the notion that dignity of labor was within their reach.

Another way in which barbers asserted their self-worth was by declaring holidays. There was no concept of a holiday for barbers until the KSBA assigned Tuesday as barbers' holiday. Many Mappilas resented the decision and told barbers that they should not arbitrarily decide on a weekly day off; rather, they should work according to the convenience of their patrons. One barber told me that he was asked, "Haven't we followed certain customs till this time, why should we make efforts to change them?" Many people used to mock barbers, saying, "It is the day of the ossāns." The introduction of the weekly day off meant that times had indeed changed, and the barbers had started calling the shots in deciding the relationships between their clients and themselves. It was a declaration that their time was worthwhile, and the division between leisure and work afforded to others was now something they could also have.[2] In barbers' lives under the patronage system, there was no fixed time for work or life (also leisure). With the professionalization and implementation of a holiday, barbers achieved this "modern" division in their life, and they could now use their "leisure time" for other activities, they could participate in the public space independently, and they could engage in pursuits unbound by patronage.

Seeking Antassu Within the Household

Although the KSBA was conceived as a union for all barbers, women did not partake in its activities for a long time. However, women became familiar with the changes happening in barbering services at the behest of their husbands or brothers. They were often instructed to align their work in accordance with the resolutions passed by the union. Since the services provided by women were limited to women, the domestic/public distinction brought about by barber men through unionization did not apply to them. Women had to fight the discrimination and social subordination in the domestic sphere to clinch antassu for their labor, as their services included various skills like nail-cutting, hair removal, and other ritual tasks that were all conducted inside the homes of their patrons. In the wake of barbers' decision to stop certain jobs, Ayisha recollected, barber women refused to cut nails and shave intimate parts of their patrons' bodies. If they were abused and humiliated for not per-forming these tasks, barber women thereafter stopped going to the patron's house. If they were asked by women what they should do to get these services, barber women instructed them to buy razors and shaving blades, which were becoming increasingly available for purchase in the market. Barber women thus sought to change the conceptions of the body by reconfiguring their deci-sion not to offer certain services as a collective one taken by barbers. Some-times, barber women also schooled these Mappila women by resorting to the prescriptive tenets of Islam, which prohibited engagement with the private parts of other persons' bodies.

A few of these barber women have, in fact, participated in the activities of the KSBA indirectly. Ayisha, a female activist of the KSBA, told me that when the government of India launched a program in the early 1990s to integrate barber women as assistants to gynecologists in hospitals in rural areas, the KSBA launched a women's organization to facilitate the training of barber women and to help their entry into the hospital system. Accordingly, many barber women gained certificates of training and got jobs as assistants to doctors. Though the program was later ended by the government when the number of doctors and private hospitals increased in rural areas, or due to some other reason I was unable to ascertain, many barber women contin-ued to collect pensions from the government as former employees until their death. Ayisha also observed that the KSBA gave women barbers confidence to negotiate their own social relationships and the cash they will be paid for each service. These days, barber women are invited to bathe the newborn for

a minimum of seven and a maximum of forty days. While there is a particular amount that is to be given for each service, it is not specified. However,
barbers allude to the amount they expect to receive for their services from the
clients. This allusion may take the form of mentioning the amount that was
given to them by a particular client a few days ago. Such allusions let their
clients know the fare that will have to be given for a tonsure or a bathing. Such
terms of negotiation were unimaginable in earlier times. Barber women also
challenged the hierarchical practices at their clients' houses by calling them
out and sometimes retorting verbally to particularly humiliating comments.
They suggested, and in some cases threatened, that if cash was not given, they
would not be coming to attend to their clients.

Barber women also acted as mediators in the transition from delivery
done at home to delivery done in the hospital. When Ayisha started working
as a midwife in the 1970s, women going to the hospitals for giving birth was
still an uncommon practice. As birthing units were gradually set up in hospitals, she often directed her clients to the hospital. When I asked her why, she
said, "It is a lot of pain to watch women undergoing birth-pains; you lose a
part of yourself seeing it." I asked her how women responded to her suggestion of going to the hospital. She replied, "Women feared going to the hospital
for delivery at that time, but nowadays they are afraid to give birth at home."
There were lots of stories making the rounds about the mishaps that had
happened to unnamed women in this or that hospital. It was also rumored
that many doctors preferred to make money by performing C-sections—a
practice that is quite pervasive in Malabar now. Barbers assured women in
emergency cases that they would be better off in the hospital for giving birth
and sometimes a barber woman would accompany the expectant woman to
the hospital to boost her confidence. For these services, barber women were
paid in cash. Ultimately, as private hospitals boomed in Malabar from the
1980s onward owing to the flow of remittance and the general increase in
living standards, people became more aware of the facilities provided by the
hospitals, including medication, natal care, and other amenities. Over time,
women preferred to go to the hospitals rather than giving birth at home under
the care of barber women. While women's work arrangements did not move
from the domestic to the public space as in the case of men, monetization of
their labor helped erase many of the cultural attributes attached to their earlier services and they could now negotiate the terms and wages for their labor.

So far, I have examined how unionization and associated activities
have diluted the patronage system that subordinated barbers in Malabar

for generations. In this transformation, radical political action initiated by barbers has been a key factor. Through their unionization activities, barbers established shops, refused to serve their earlier patrons at home, demanded cash for their services, and organized their labor according to time and money. These transformations brought in a sense of social change and dignity for their labor among Muslims. In the next section, I examine how a barber is viewed by his customers at the barbershops nowadays.

Indexing Antassu

On a Monday evening in December 2019, while I waited on a plastic chair to talk to Hassan, who runs a barbershop near a coastal town in Malabar, I piqued the interest of one of Hassan's customers, who was having a haircut at the time. I was carrying my backpack and was sipping water from my water bottle. He surmised that I was not a customer and asked Hassan who I was. When the customer learned that I was waiting to talk to Hassan about his life, the customer exclaimed, "He is amazing!" When I inquired further, he said that he has been a regular customer of Hassan's since he graduated from high school. "If I do not cut my hair from him, I do not feel satisfied," he added. Another customer who was sitting in an adjacent chair chipped in, saying, "Once I had a haircut at Rāmanāttukara [a town a few kilometers away] and I did not feel alright about it. It was not that there was anything wrong about the haircut." When I asked him what he did about the bad haircut, he said, "I did not venture out of my house for a week. When I realized that my hair had grown enough not to be embarrassing, I came here and had a second cut." After the second haircut, he said he felt confident. I have quoted bits of these conversations just to give an idea of how valued a barber and his craft might be for customers nowadays. He is seen as owning a special set of skills and is capable of understanding the needs of his established customer base, as part of maintaining long-standing social interactions. I heard many barbers priding themselves on their customers. As Hassan put it during our conversation, "A barber is an artist." After all, another person said, "a customer hands over his head to a barber as soon as he sits on the chair." Then it is the barber's skills that allow him to groom and create a unique style that is satisfying to the customer.

According to barbers I spoke with, the transition from a standardized cutting style in the community to one that they developed as barbers in the shops was one of trial and error. Many older barbers recollected that as they opened the shops in their localities, young men and children began to visit the shops on their own. Sometimes these customers would carry a small piece of paper from the male head of the family informing the barber how their hair should be cut. In other cases, youngsters took liberty with their heads at the barbershop, but only to be later forced by the male family head to revisit the barbershop and cut the hair again to fit the "normal" Muslim style—that is, plain, short hair. Over time and for many reasons, the authority of the male heads in the family has diminished—driven, in part, by gulf migration and by the remittance economy (Osella and Osella 2000a). Such changes were also expressed in consumer choices and personal style. For instance, youngsters began styling their hair differently, as they deemed fit. Barbers learned the new styles of haircuts from the latest movies or soccer and cricket players and worked on them to meet the demands of their young customers. As Ummar, a fifty-year-old barber explained to me, such new demands meant that barbers had to learn various styles of cutting hair through trial and error, and many customers were willing to offer their heads for experimentation. In short, this self-conception of a barber as an artist is the culmination of a long process of political struggle and changing consumer habits set in motion since the 1970s. This idea of barber as an artist is a key aspect of barbers' self-identity today and it was voiced by many barbers and customers across Kerala.

Barbershops have now become an important aspect of grooming rather than simply the maintaining of an Islamic comportment. For youngsters, it is a place to set their individual styles, mostly according to the fad of the day, imitating sportspersons, soccer players, and film stars. Many young barbers remarked that several of their young customers would come with an image downloaded from the internet of one of their heroes and ask the barbers whether they can cut their hair in the same style. With the availability of trimmers, heaters, straighteners, and a host of new tools and techniques, such requests have become easier for barbers to fulfill. Many barbers recollected that their first razor-blade shavers or trimmers were gifted to them by customers who brought them from Gulf countries. The upgrading of their skills with new tools and techniques has meant the rates barber charges for each service have risen correspondingly. Barbershops have become sites where the terms of services are negotiated between barbers and clients. Barbers have secured dignity as skilled artists owing to their labor and time. Certain barbers can now charge according to their experience and expertise gained, with some having a reputation for certain styles. It was through cultivating skills and expertise on their own that certain barbers distinguished them-selves from others. This has been a common experience of barbers, as Ahmed (2006, 173) shows in his study of male workers in beauty parlors in Delhi and Bihar. He notes that some barbers became popular and known in the locality by "experimenting with different hairstyles by looking at pictures and post-ers." Rather than simply operating as functionalists in a community, some barbers took pride in their trade and sought to highlight the shift from occu-pation to profession and even to craft.

How do we understand the new conception of labor formulated by bar-bers? The relationship between labor and capital is usually portrayed as con-flictual. While the capitalists tend to maximize their profits, the laborers are geared toward resisting it by demanding higher wages for their labor. In the Marxian frame, the ultimate aim for the labor is to demolish the capitalist system and to reformulate means of production. This kind of neat binary of confrontation between capital and labor has been found to be wanting. Two things have happened. One, labor has found various means and avenues to negotiate with capital. Such mobilizations could only work within the ambit of industrial time where labor is done in blocks of time in fixed places. The south Indian state of Kerala has been hailed as a state where the lower-class mobilizations combined with state interventions to create one of the most successful cases of redistributive and social-development programs in the developing world (Heller 1999). Two, a reformulation of capital and labor has occurred. From an industry-based capitalism, we have moved increasingly toward service-oriented capitalism (Standing 2014). What has often been emphasized is how the classic category of labor itself is being done away with in the newer forms of economic activities.

In the Indian context, the trajectory of capital is also intertwined with the life of caste and community. Dalits are found to be at a disadvantage to avail themselves of the opportunities of capitalism within the prescriptions and proscriptions of social prejudice associated with caste. Even when they are able to become capitalists, their enterprises are often limited to activities of their traditional occupations (Mosse 2018; Jodhka 2010; Prakash 2015). Like Dalits, lower class Muslims also face severe economic hardships and discrim-ination not only on the basis of caste but also on the basis of their religious identity (Gayer and Jaffrelot 2012).[3] Since all the work was imbricated in the caste framework on the Indian subcontinent, it will be useful to look at not only the disadvantaged sections, such as Dalits who mostly took to manual and menial labor, but also the service castes, such as barbers, washermen, and priests. Service work is different from traditional manufacturing work in terms of its output. Service work is not geared to producing tangible objects. It necessitates interpersonal interaction and engagement, and the idea of labor in its classical sense is inadequate to understanding what is involved in labor now. For example, feminist scholarship has long characterized domestic labor as a form of service work requiring *emotional labor* (Hochschild 2012) as its key constituent. In transforming their work from patronage to labor, barbers successfully created a new sense of self and identity for themselves.

Conclusion

The value of antassu as self-worth was constructed through several of these practices. Since values are often implicit in practices, it is the analyst who maps the underlying essence of the actions. The value becomes explicit when people come together to do certain things with common ideas and perceptions. A radical, political force triggered by the union and a range of actions undertaken by barbers in Kerala helped barbers extricate themselves from what they increasingly came to see as a dominating and humiliating social relation, which could no longer be justified and sustained in changing social milieu. The caste and community definition of barbers' occupation was transformed into a profession, with their labor commoditized as part of a wider market-based transaction in public spaces. As for Muslims, the conception of barbers' services moved from a notion of moral-religious duty upheld intergenerationally toward that of a more secular idea of labor negotiated at the shops. The delimitation of labor to the shop, the regulated time spent on each service, the restricted time for opening and closing, and the fixed holiday (Tuesday) all instigated far-reaching changes, both at the community level and on an individual level, where barbers came to draw their own clientele based on experience and reputation.

By delineating the social change in Malabar, I have illustrated the transformation of a moral worker tied to his patrons into that of a laborer who transacts his time and labor for money. In money, where labor is abstracted as value, one could make a demand based on the cost of labor, and it could be easily tied to broader market implications, such as inflationary pressures, and a broader increase in wages in other sectors. Money helped the rational calculation of social life and encouraged the reordering of moral values. It accorded importance for abstraction and calculation, rather than giving primacy to interpersonal interactions, behavior, and customs implicit in the transactions in kind. The rewards in kind, as they were part of the production of the household, could be seen as embodying the part of the person. In this sense, rewards in kind are gifts in the Maussian sense. They generate a feeling of indebtedness in the receiver, primarily because of the entanglements the rewards in kind have with the patron. The abstraction of services into labor severely diminished such commitments and money anonymized the moorings of the patronage work. Money converted the work into the calculations of market exchange and into labor that can be sold to anyone willing to buy it. The bonds of personal dependence were superseded in the contractual relationships obtained through money.

In understanding the transformation from work to labor, the idea of dignified labor is quite relevant. Unlike traditional forms of capitalist enterprises in which material products are the final outcome of labor, service domains such as barbering produce an aesthetic experience for the customers. It is the experience of being spruced up and the intersubjective appreciation that is being paid for at the barbershops. Barbers are able to provide such an experience because they have extricated themselves from the patronage system and modeled their work now according to the capitalistic modulations of abstract labor.

With the socioeconomic improvements and transformation of work arrangements engendered by barbers, caste relations are altered and contested by barbers—an issue I take up for analysis in the next chapter. Caste sensibilities are nowadays often implied through gestures, insinuations, and trading in gossip. It is the barbers' attempts to challenge the visible aspects of hierarchical practices that have pushed such sensibilities to the "backstage," although marriage alliances are still prohibited between barbers and other Muslim groups.

CHAPTER 7

Seeking Egalitarianism

Muslim barbers in Malabar have now become more assertive and collectively organized. This is a result of five decades of unionization efforts, gulf migration, religious and secular education, and nonbarbering employment opportunities. Some of these issues were discussed in Chapter 6. This chapter probes the impact of these changes on negotiating caste relations among Muslims in Malabar. At least two models of social change have been advanced to explain the impetus emerging from the lower classes among Muslims: one, in terms of socioeconomic improvements and, the other, in terms of ideology. Both of these models are also related to each other at one level: socioeconomic improvements can help one achieve cultural attributes and thereby engender ideological change. However, to use Bourdieu's (1986) formulation, transforming social and economic capital into cultural capital is not an easy process. It needs sustained effort and resources. In the socioeconomic model, which can be termed "ashrafization," the lower groups are conceived to be imitating the cultural repertoire of the higher groups with the intention of raising their social status (Levesque and Niazi 2023). Features like the purdah system and assuming higher-caste identities have been enumerated as examples of such tendencies among lower-caste Muslim groups. Statements like "Next year, if grain is dear, I shall be a Sayyid" have tended to color the discourse of social mobility among Muslims, with reference to caste. It seems, on the face of it, to be quite easy to change one's social identity among Muslims on the basis of economic mobility. As Filippo Osella and Caroline Osella (2000b, 12) have noted, actors could be seen as agents making choices for upward social mobility, which makes "good sense in view of their historical and social locations and represents a set of options from a set of possibilities which itself is not limitless." However, the social histories of the groups to which someone belongs, as well

as the personal trajectory of individuals, suggest specific responses to circumstances and "predisposes them towards certain responses or strategies"
(12). Since an individual is always already identified by one's caste membership, mobility had to also take place in terms of the group. Individual mobility does not usually bring about a change in social status within the local
caste structure.

In the second model, which can be termed "Islamization," the urban, literate Muslims are seen as embodying the real, authentic Islam and look down
upon lower classes/castes as not being "real" Muslims. This has also been one
of the dominant cleavages through which reformist Muslim organizations
have tried mobilizing and institutionalizing themselves against the traditionalist Muslim organizations that are seen as sympathetic to the "lower"
forms of Islam (Robinson 2008; Osella and Osella 2013). The lower class/
caste practices and beliefs are often portrayed as falling under the ambit of
the non-Islamic, and they are called upon to learn and follow correct teachings of Islam. Such a process in South Asia has been referred to as "pattern
of perfection" by Francis Robinson (1983). Robinson notes that if we take
a *longue-durée* approach, we can see Muslims moving toward a pattern of
perfection, from a folk, popular Islam toward that of scriptural Islam. Such
a logic is transposed to understand Muslim caste in the following way. The
beliefs and practices of caste among Muslims are deemed as the sole domain
of the experience of lower-caste Muslims because they are still influenced by
Hinduism; as and when they learn and internalize correct teachings of Islam,
they should be able to eradicate caste practices and mentalities.

I find that the models of social change advocated for understanding
lower-caste Muslims are unhelpful for comprehending the complexity, diver-
sity, and depth of meanings of their beliefs, practices, and strategies. Extending the argument posed by some studies on Muslim hierarchy in South Asia
that certain Islamic ideas and categories have been used to buttress and
challenge hierarchy in interpersonal relations (Mines 1975; Levesque 2020;
Lee 2021b), I argue that in the negotiation, contestation, and resistance to
caste from the social groups on the lower rung of hierarchy among Muslims,
Islam has become a key analytic and a site. To appreciate the strength of this
argument, it should be remembered that various Islamic notions have been
employed by Muslims in Malabar to justify and rationalize hierarchical relations. So, my suggestion of Islam becoming a more central ground emphasizes the domain of "normative Islam" becoming a terrain of contestation of
hierarchy. In a sense, unlike many contemporary anthropologists, I suggest

that the challenge to normative Islam does not simply or exclusively reside in the domain of the everyday (Schielke 2009; Schielke and Debevec 2012; Fadil and Fernando 2015); rather, it also lies in the potentialities in the normative Islam itself for alternative readings, interpretations, and meanings. However, the question of when such potentialities become realized alerts us to pay close attention to the idea of "context" as I outlined in Chapter 1, following upon the arguments of Shahab Ahmed (2016).

As barbers have become economically mobile and acquired both religious and secular education, they have increasingly become assertive in charting a distinct trajectory for Islam, which is rooted in egalitarianism—a universal capability to embody piety. This rereading and enlivening of Islam drawing from multiple subject positionalities, which I have called a *lived tradition*, enable barbers to contest and challenge the established and authoritative readings sustained by religious organizations. At the same time, these assertions do not work in a vacuum; they connect with other discourses of social mobility, dignity, and egalitarian tendencies in Malabar. All these narratives are, however, drawn from men. I could not interview a lot of barber women, particularly none who have gained secular education and employment. Yet, the discourses of egalitarianism were lively in the narratives of older barber women and how they renegotiated their earlier patronage relations into that of money relations. Though the narratives in this chapter are drawn from men, the discourse of egalitarianism is not an exclusive purview of barber men. Women also partake in these discourses and use them to negotiate and reformulate their relationships within the domestic spheres of their earlier patrons.

What is Egalitarianism?

Delineating the strategies of mobility used by Muslim barbers in Malabar, I want to show how Islam has become a key site of conflict and negotiation of caste. One should not forget that barbers do not detest hierarchy; they acknowledge and value hierarchy in terms of the religious principle of piety. Their bone of contention lies in the fact that Muslims attempt to operationalize caste practices and sensibilities based on other principles, such as genealogy, wealth, and occupation, the spirit of which they deem to be un-Islamic.

To think about the contours of the formulation of barbers' arguments, I find the idea of egalitarianism quite useful. Egalitarianism is usually seen as the view that people are equal and should be treated as such. Equality may be conceived either in terms of liberal traditions of freedoms or equal rights or in terms of socialist traditions of opportunities and wealth. In either case, as Megan Laws (2022) notes, these traditions seem to converge on the point that egalitarianism expresses a form of social, economic, and political organization that is free from tyranny. That is, people are free from seeing their opportunities and freedoms subjugated by others and their rights to opportunities and wealth are not circumscribed by status or rank.

Anthropology has made significant contributions to this debate by looking at, empirically, what it is like to live in an egalitarian society (Haynes and Hickel 2016; Parry 1974; Rio 2014). It has been shown that such societies keep mechanisms in place to reconcile problems of redistribution and problems of freedom, maintaining ideas about humans and nonhumans as key actors in social relationships and by inculcating practices of sharing and ways of relating to each other. In many African societies, we observe social leveling mechanisms either through mandatory gift-exchange relationships or through making demands on others who have better means of accumulating or accessing wealth and power. In these societies, the benefits of sharing or maintaining autonomy outweigh the benefits of accumulating prestige, wealth, or power (Dawson 2021; Di Nunzio 2017; Wiessner 2002). Terms like distribution and sharing should not be understood simply as relating to goods and objects—as we usually understand them by notions of egalitarianism. Rather, they also describe potentialities to act—properties inculcated in individuals through social processes. It helps us understand a range of discourses and practices where human beings are engaged in embodying, activating, and negotiating interpersonal relationships. We produce these potentialities much the same way that we produce goods or objects, through labor or by caring for or attending to one another.

Building on these ideas, I use the term egalitarianism to refer to discourses that posit moral equality among believers and that are widely held among Muslims. My point is that Muslim barbers could be seen as activating a discourse of egalitarianism where individuals should be categorized based on their abilities to embody piety, rather than through status, rank, or wealth that one possesses. Most Muslims in Malabar would assert that Islam is an egalitarian religion in which all human beings are seen as equal before Allah.[1] The relationship envisioned here is an unmediated one between the creator and his subject. The social inequalities existing among Muslims challenge the equal moral worth presupposed before Allah. The ideas of egalitarianism are often implicit in the individual strategies of mobility, but they take publicly recognizable forms in the case of collective mobilizations to contest hierarchy and to demand space for egalitarian social relations.

While experiencing social subordination at the hands of various Muslim groups, Muslim barbers also seek to activate egalitarianism as a value among Muslims through their strategies of mobility and by contesting hierarchical sensibilities. They regard egalitarianism as a core principle of social life envisioned by normative Islam. The conceptions of egalitarianism espoused by barbers are broadly shaped by statements in the Quran and based on stories and events in the lives of the prophet Muhammad or his immediate companions. It is useful to reflect on the categorization of these discourses as religious and social, as undertaken by Louis Marlow (1997, 2–5), to understand the complexity and nuances of egalitarian influences in Muslim social lives. He suggests that there may be a logical connection between the proclamation of the oneness of Allah and the upholding of the principle of equality among the human beings created by him. A famous statement cited from the Quran (49:13) in support is: "O mankind! Truly We created you from a male and a female, and we made you peoples and tribes that you may come to know one another. Surely the most noble of you before God are the most reverent of you. Truly God is knowing, Aware." (Nasr et al. 2015). The thrust of this statement is that the division into "peoples and tribes" made by Allah does not have any bearing on the personal merit of the individual. At the same time, while the Quran frequently emphasizes the meaninglessness of distinctions in rank in terms of afterlife, it certainly does not try to abolish them in the present world. On the social plane, Marlow (1997, 5) observes, "Egalitarian ideology co-existed with observable inequalities in the actual distribution of power, wealth and social esteem." Religious egalitarianism, however, provided a strong foundation for the subordinated to contest social hierarchies or at least to make claims for equality. The disadvantaged in a society will often turn to available discourses of egalitarianism and unmediated connections to God—as is often said of the Bhakti traditions (Lorenzen 2004). Those in power, however, will often be less inclined to admit such discourses and apply them in practice.

The division into social and religious planes with reference to egalitarianism, I suggest, is often untenable if we analyze the social world of barbers in Malabar. The critique that barbers make of the binary of social and religious planes among Muslims emanates from their experiences of everyday life in Malabar. They assert that egalitarianism of Islam needs to be materialized in this world if we are to live as Muslims following the spirit of the Quran. Dilley (2004) has used the social-religious division as an analytical device to study the social organization of Muslim groups in Senegal. He suggests that the hierarchy existing between Muslim social groups in Senegal is often evaluated and justified on the basis of the distinct kinds of knowledge and power that each social group oversees in pursuit of its respective occupations. The bodies of knowledge and power drawn upon by artisans, praise-singers, and musicians bring them into a "contested relationship with Muslim clerics, who have variously denigrated and devalued the occupations caste members practice" (Dilley 2004, 6). Such a position would imply that the social groups belonging to the lower castes can overcome the barriers as and when they acquire the knowledge and power held by Muslim clerics. If it is simply a matter of acquisition, hierarchy could be superseded if individuals leave their traditional occupations and acquire religious knowledge. In practice, however, acquiring religious knowledge does not necessarily facilitate one's ability to secure power and escape subordination. Even after leaving traditional occupations, individuals are often constrained by the limitations attached to their original, collective identity.

In the following sections, I probe the complexities of the operationalization of the principle of egalitarianism by looking at three case studies: first, a case of individual mobility supported by secular education and employment; second, an instance of seeking individual mobility through religious education and piety; and, finally, the recent strategies of working barbers to contest their subordination. To be sure, individual mobility allowed some barbers to pursue secular education and employment, overcoming the hierarchical boundaries, with some even marrying "above" their station into non-barber families. But such cases are outliers and can help us understand the broader social constraints faced by most of the community. In the second case study, barbers who acquire religious education and assume religious roles, such as leading the prayer in a mosque or teaching in a religious institution, seek egalitarian treatment and deference from everyone through piety, as it is the norm among Muslims in Malabar. Ironically, I find that formal religious education often forms one of the key impediments to social mobility for these barbers. This is curious because, in theory at least, one's ability to display the moral qualities championed by normative Islam—in particular, the value of piety—should be regarded in high esteem. Religious scholars should ideally be desirable candidates for long-term social relations, including marriage. In practice, however, this is far from reality because the social plane presents a set of other

demands that make it very difficult for barbers to escape their ascribed occupational status, as powerful as piety ought to be, in theory (Marlow 1997).
The value of piety may apply to particular individuals but rarely to the collective, which remains bound to enduring prejudices associated with its ascribed
occupational designation. In addition, there is little to suggest, I maintain,
that social mobility encompasses the entire group, largely because barbers, as
a collective, continue to practice their community occupation, which leaves
them in a position of social disadvantage despite economic improvements.
In the third case study, I look at how barbers who continue with their traditional occupation seek to challenge hierarchical relations. Apart from cham-
pioning the discourses of egalitarianism available in Islam, barbers also follow
the dominant cultural scripts of establishing status in the locality. In addition, they seek to project and identify themselves as descendants of an Arab
Muslim. Seeking to establish and revive kinship networks, producing family
histories, publishing yearly calendars, and organizing various kinds of family-
oriented philanthropic initiatives, they attempt to construct and establish a
distinct and elevated taravād for themselves.

Individual Mobility and Frames of Egalitarianism

Individuals are often motivated and constrained by their circumstances to
pursue what they consider to be valuable to their lives. The idea of "projects"
put forward by Sherry Ortner (2006, 147) is useful to understanding the individual initiative. Individuals seek to fulfill what she calls "projects," which
are "about people having desires that grow out of their own structures of life,
including very centrally their own structures of inequality; it is, in short, about
people playing, trying to play, their own serious games even as more powerful
parties seek to devalue and even destroy them to overcome the restrictions
of social order as 'projects.'" Following Ortner, we should view individuals as
embedded in social relationships, living and arranging their lives in accordance with cultural scripts that prompt social action in line with the pursuit of
their own desires and intentions. At the same time, these individual actions do
not operate in a vacuum; simultaneously, other actors are organizing their own
actions, which may oppose or align with the actions of the others. Hakeem's
story, which I discuss below, reveals how individual projects of overcoming
hierarchy are successful to a degree where secular education and employment
are key aspects of this endeavor. It also unravels the tensions between offering

religious arguments for informing moral behavior and finding opportunities in what secular education and employment can offer. It should be remembered that these choices and projects of mobility are always shaped by specific circumstances that affect one's life, as detailed below. While education and employment are sometimes key to social mobility, overcoming hierarchy and achieving social mobility is undertaken within a complex network of exchanges and connections, as instances of marriage exemplify. In part, because it is a social affair and brings together several stakeholders, marrying outside the endogamous circle can pose a great challenge to those involved and the support structures generally available are withheld, leaving the couple to contend with these challenges alone or isolated. I consider two concepts—projects and constraints—key to understanding the individual initiatives of two Muslim barbers I discuss below. They help us understand the severe social constraints in which even educated and employed barbers find themselves when they attempt to change their social circumstances and achieve mobility.

Hakeem, one of the highly educated barbers I met, viewed marriage arrangements as a type of project whereby one could advance one's social standing. He looked at it as an undertaking to overcome the social hierarchy and the stigma attached to the barber community, which is a common strategy of upwardly moving groups among Muslims (Ahmad 1976). Hakeem was introduced to me as someone I must interview for my research project because "he was educated and could talk about the history of the barber community in detail." On a clear morning in the summer of 2019, I rode my motorbike to a concrete, two-story house. The house was encircled by a high wall, with a gate facing the road. The floor was paved with interlocking tiles. These were all signs of affluence in Malabar. We sat in the living room on the sofa and started talking. As soon as I started recording, he switched to English, indicating his educational credentials. This was quite odd for me because I had never interviewed someone in Malabar in English. While most educated people in Kerala will understand English, conducting the conversation in English is out of the ordinary. Because I am from the same region and we both speak the same language, moving to another language seemed "unnatural" and one could "lose" much in translation, especially the nuances of language. But moving to English signaled the similar educational backgrounds we share. Hakeem has studied in prominent Indian universities and has earned an MBA and PhD in management. I believe that by switching the language, Hakeem was doing at least two things. Most barbers I talked to were not as highly educated as Hakeem, and he had his own vision of emancipation for barbers. He was distinguishing himself from them. In addition, I felt that he conceived himself to be better than I or at least equal to me (a Mappila) and was emphasizing and showcasing this through his medium of communication.

The element of education as the steppingstone to social mobility is one that many across India share. Education is often viewed as the basis for individual empowerment and as a resource for social and political transformations. This enthusiasm, however, sits uneasily with the widespread unemployment experienced by the educated (Jeffrey et al. 2008). Along with education, the welfare programs implemented by the state and central governments in India for the benefit of various castes and communities are taken to be the model that should be followed for uplifting marginalized groups, such as barbers, among Muslims.[2] In southern Kerala, for example, an organization has been created by educated and government-employed barber-community members called the Muslim Socialist Association (MSA), which advocates education and employment as the method to overcome the social inferiority of the barber community. Such projects, however, did not appeal to the barber community in general since it meant leaving their profession and investing in education. Such investments cannot guarantee a job, let alone convert into a lucrative government job in what is a competitive employment market. These efforts are far removed from the grassroots-level demands of barbers seeking more fundamental recognition of and respect for the services they provide to the community.

When we met, Hakeem talked about the social divisions that exist among Muslims, and he held barbers partly responsible for their predicament. He saw his individual project of overcoming hierarchy as a response to the long-standing ideas of hierarchy that were pervasive among Muslims. Hakeem envisioned his project (to use Ortner's term) as based on a specific aspect of the history of barbers that he had learned. His father and grandfather were traditional physicians along with being barbers. His grandfather had learned medicine from an itinerant scholar from Lakshadweep and Hakeem's father took over the practice after his death. Because of their specific expertise, they had forged extensive social connections across different strata of society, including Sayyids and wealthy Mappilas.[3] He opined that, in the past, barbers were well-off compared to the majority of Mappilas who were quite poor. Most of the Mappila houses in their locality did not have a steady means of livelihood. A few wealthy Mappilas owned most of the land in the area and others worked as labor or as fishers. Barbers, because of their patronage relationships, had a steady and reliable occupation that afforded them subsistence living in the form of paddy and other seasonal produce. Many barbers helped the neighboring Mappilas, observed Hakeem, as they often struggled to eke out a living.

If subsistence living and the ability to support their impoverished neighbors was one way in which barbers could display their generosity and economic standing, they also sought to create a superior position by reference to the past. As detailed in Chapter 2, barbers considered themselves superior because of their mythical origins from an Arab Muslim who came to the Malabar coast in the seventh century. Hakeem repeated this origin story but offered an additional fascinating interpretation. According to him, this belief in mythical origin, coupled with barbers' relatively stable economic condition, were key reasons for the reluctance of people in the barber community to form marital relations with poor Mappilas. Hakeem was talking about pre-1970s Malabar.

According to Hakeem, the major transformation in hierarchical relations took place as a result of the Gulf migration in Kerala, around the 1980s and 1990s. It was because of the Gulf boom that poor Mappilas managed to raise their socioeconomic standards and subsequently come to look down upon their barber neighbors. Such was Hakeem's interpretation of the shifting power relations, couched in economic terms. At the same time, Hakeem also offered some critical reflections with regard to his own community, which he saw as lacking a vision for an egalitarian society and making efforts to that end. Accordingly, he had ideas about how to change the plight of the barber community: largely through the institution of marriage or, more specifically, intermarriage between barbers and Mappilas.

Marriage is viewed as a site of long-standing social interaction between two families, which is maintained through mutual recognition; exchanges of pleasantries and customary gifts; constant re-creation of ties through phone calls and visits; and, importantly, access to wider social networks. For a member of a subordinated group, marrying within the group limits further possibilities of bridging connections with broader social networks. As Hakeem put it, "If I marry a barber girl, I am connected to that barber family only; we are all limited by our own occupation and identity." Marrying outside one's group opens up the possibilities of forging connections with a wider group of Muslims who can provide resources and connections for one's further social improvement. Hakeem tried this path and faced some challenges from Mappilas. Moreover, to work out such a marriage connection for himself,

Hakeem had to undermine established structures of authority within his own community. He spoke of how the lack of vision in the barber community came to the fore during his own marriage. Though his father had wider social connections because of his services in traditional medicine, he did not think of arranging a marriage from a non-barber family for his son. Hakeem further reasoned that even if his father tried on his own to find a Mappila alliance for his son, it is doubtful that he would have been successful. Nevertheless, while Hakeem was trying to find himself a marriage partner from a Mappila family, with limited success, his father once asked him, "Why do we seek marriage from outside the barber community? We are equally good." Hakeem characterized this statement as "a most dangerous one," as it indicated an exclusive and defeatist vision, where communities are fixed into positions, forestalling any possibility of social mobility for the barber community in Malabar.

Hakeem consciously sought to transcend the social boundaries that have been drawn between barbers and Mappilas. His educational credentials, as an MBA and a PhD from prominent Indian universities helped him overcome these boundaries. While Hakeem's ambition may be seen as part of an individual project rarely afforded to others in the community, his socioeconomic standing does suggest wider considerations were at play. He spoke of how, once he completed his MBA and began work as a marketing executive in a company that produced soaps and detergents, his marriage prospects increased. He recalled how Mappilas working in the company began offering marriage alliances. As one of the most successful marketing professionals in the company, he was held in high esteem and projected as the ideal candidate to be emulated by others in the company. Most of the marriage proposals that were suggested came from the top layer of the management in the company. In a few cases, the fathers of potential spouses visited Hakeem's house and inquired in the neighborhood about his family background. As soon as families learned of his barber identity, most proposals fell through. Hakeem was well aware of these "background checks" and saw them as humiliating, for they not only denigrated his community but also failed to see his achievements as an individual. Hakeem explained that it was especially frustrating, as such humiliation was because of his social background, and he could do little to change it. The success he achieved as an individual was placed against the broader community of Muslims where ascribed status was more valuable than achieved status. While his achieved status was considered a product of his efforts and hard work in his community of barbers, individual achievements could not offset the lineage credentials that accrued legitimacy in the broader community of Muslims.

Nonetheless, over the years, Hakeem had cultivated a wide network of friends, many of whom belonged to the Mappila community. So, when Hakeem decided to marry a non-barber, many of his Mappila friends tried to arrange an alliance for him. Despite many such attempts, none succeeded. At one point, Hakeem recalled that during one of their get-togethers, one of his friends admitted that, given his background, it seemed nearly impossible to arrange a marriage alliance, and that Hakeem should marry one of his own. Hakeem responded sharply, "If someone is handicapped, will you suggest that he should marry a handicapped girl?" Listening to this retort, his friends became silent. Such frustrations were common at the time, he recalls. Another instance Hakeem told me about was when another of his friends brought an alliance from a newly converted Muslim, who was a physician. Hakeem threw the same question at his friends again. When he related this story, he offered an interesting insight into the motivations behind the marriage alliance from a non-barber family. He told his friends that he was looking for someone to expand his social network and connections. And the new converts are themselves alone in the world. He was referring to how converts are often outcasted by their previous Hindu community and stripped of their prior social networks. Hakeem, however, saw himself as someone who had extensive familial connections and social networks, which should have been seen as an asset to his marital potential. Hakeem viewed marriage as very much a strategic alliance, designed to expand and enhance his standing rather than constrain it.

Hakeem was eventually able to arrange a marriage alliance with a Mappila girl through one of his Mappila friends. He married a girl from an influential Mappila family from Malappuram. The father of the girl came along with his brother to inquire about Hakeem and his family background. Hakeem recalled: "When my father-in-law came, along with his brother who was a retired police constable, to inquire about me, they learned that I belong to barber community. The brother expressed concern, asking, 'Should we have a marriage alliance with such a family?' My father-in-law replied, 'He is educated and let us ask about his values and behavior and if they are good, we need not worry about other things.'" The education and the potential employment opportunities that were evident in Hakeem's profile helped him gain such an alliance. However, as Hakeem noted, the most important aspect was the progressive approach of his in-laws. His father-in-law had worked in the railways and traveled far and wide in India, something that Hakeem suspects helped him develop a view that was unconstrained by prejudice. Hakeem believed that such an experience was crucial in seeing other modes of being in the world, where education and one's values as a human being override other imperatives deemed important in marriage. He added that his wife's family members were supporters of a Marxist party and therefore had a vision of society not constrained by religious notions of community based on lineage and purity of blood. Since Communists had been quite active in forming trade unions and organizing the peasantry in Kerala and successfully wielded state power for several years, people in Kerala have been familiar with their attempts at changing the social structure of Kerala. Within the changing political hardscape of Kerala, the communist parties have been able to bring about significant changes through legislation and by introducing new policies, which have undermined the feudal relations that existed in Kerala (Heller 1999). The idea that public action and initiative can bring about social change is a general repertoire of Kerala given these political histories (Jeffrey 2001). Since Mappila Muslims often used ideas and practices of Islam to justify and perpetuate hierarchical practices, Hakeem observed, it will be difficult to change these practices using Islamic ideas. Hakeem himself was well aware that, due to his upbringing, he was less familiar with Islamic traditions and so less able to venture an argument for equality on the basis of religion. At any rate, he saw such assertions as far less effective than "secular" ones. For Hakeem, it is the history of communism that should prevail as a vision of society that is not constrained by oppressive social structures.

Hakeem believed that his in-laws were conscious of the social evils plaguing the community and thought that organizing marriage alliances to overcome the strict endogamy was the right way to proceed. However, such marriages are rare. Hakeem was quite successful in his initiative and hopes for a better future. He noted that if marriages were to take place between barber families and Mappilas more extensively, these social distinctions would disappear in a matter of a few years. He was proud that he set a precedent and recounted that an increasing number of intercommunity marriages were taking place across his extended family. Later, when I was in Australia following fieldwork, he called me to share the happy news of his cousin's marriage and emphasized that he, too, had married from a non-barber family. All the marriages he recounted from both his maternal and paternal families had one thing in common: Every family member had a secular education and employment; some were doctors and others were management professionals or accountants. Their parents have not engaged in the traditional profession of barbering for some time. They were financially well off and were slated to pursue successful careers. To this end, the "cultural scripts" that shaped their lives were in tune with their agentic capacities and projects of social mobility.

It is important to mention here that Hakeem was not alone in seeking a marriage alliance from a Mappila family. Overcoming his social background should not be understood as an individual project alone; rather, his vision of a society helped him persevere despite the repeated humiliation that he suffered. Hakeem represents a small but wealthy section of the barber population. One chief avenue for those who held employment outside the strictures of their traditional occupation was through intermarriage, largely based on one's educational credentials and career prospects. Arguably, then, intermarriages can be said to be realizing the value of egalitarianism on the social plane. Yet, this was possible only because like-minded families were willing to consider these factors as significant for marriage alliances and educated barbers as social equals for long-standing social interactions. Such inter-community marriage alliances were still relatively rare in Malabar and were largely the preserve of successful men. The post-marriage arrangements also present many ongoing challenges and frustrations for barbers. I have heard many educated barbers recounting the troubles and humiliation they faced from non-barber families after marriage. Latheef, a fifty-year-old barber from southern Kerala told me of an incident that occurred in his family to justify such concerns among barbers. The girl belonged to a barber family who had already moved out of the barbering profession for other pursuits. The girl acquired an engineering degree from a college in Malabar, where she fell in love with a Mappila boy. The marriage went through, and the boy's family learned of the girl's family history and background only on the day of the marriage when they saw many barber families around. Upon marriage, the boy's family did not visit any of the girl's relatives—a custom prevalent among Muslims. Eventually, the pressure from the boy's family forced the girl's family to become estranged from their own barber relatives. Many barbers told of such incidents that have occurred in recent times and were worried that their own families might face similar challenges if they married their daughters to Mappilas.

As I have mentioned, detaching oneself from the community-based occupation of hairdressing was key, something that was not afforded to most barbers. This strategy of occupational detachment, however, is an important aspect of social mobility for barbers in Malabar. According to Hakeem, the religious-based arguments were, in fact, reproducing such hierarchies. He argued that Islam helped develop in Malabar deep and persisting social structures, providing moral rationale, support, and justification for hierarchical relations. Waging a fight within the structure to change moral behavior and reshape thinking and practices itself was surely predestined to fail. He, therefore, emphasized the need to pursue other avenues and opportunities to challenge and destabilize the hierarchical structures, which would be achieved through secular education and employment. This may appear as an individual approach, unlike the union-based one. Nevertheless, Hakeem saw such a "secular" model as empowering both individuals and community and achieved through the key institution of marriage and extended networks forged therein. Then, there is the way some Muslim barbers sought to change the social structure from within—to varying degrees of success—which is the subject of the next section.

Individual Initiatives and Social Constraints

In the previous section, I described the case of Hakeem, who offers an instance of a successful individual initiative to overcome the strictures of social hierarchy. However, not everyone becomes successful in one's attempts to move out of the social constraints into which one is born. I now turn to the case of Basheer to illustrate a failed project, which also illuminates tension in materializing the egalitarian principle in everyday life. He teaches Arabic at a high school in a coastal town in Malabar. During our conversation, he noted that he tried to arrange a marriage alliance from a non-barber family for himself but was unsuccessful. As a reason for his failure, he observed that Muslims are not living the ideals of Islam, which endorse egalitarian social relations. They still seek to live, according to him, by the hierarchical practices that are similar to the pillars of the Hindu social structure. I was amused by his response because it was barbers who often characterized Muslims as following Hindu caste practices, yet, at the same time, denied any possibility of considering caste as existing in Islam. It is the construction of a distinction between Muslims and Islam that helps barbers to claim that Muslims still follow Hindu caste practices. When I asked Basheer if he could explain his observation further, he said, "Among Hindus, Brahmins marry only Brahmins and Nairs only marry their ilk. What is the difference between them and Muslims? We do the same, Mappilas marry among themselves, and barbers are constrained to marry amongst themselves." Basheer was finding similarities between Hindu and Muslim practices on the basis of endogamy without attributing any role to Islam in sustaining such structures, which I have detailed in Chapter 4. Islam, according to Basheer, instituted the ideal of piety for distinction among Muslims, and other considerations should not shape marriage practices among Muslims. By anchoring the axis of sociality on piety, he was challenging the hegemonic roles other factors play in Muslim sociality. Since the axis of normative Islam is piety, which oriented one's life toward the hereafter, he was alluding to the inability of Muslims to realize the principles of sociality ordained by Allah. If that axis were to be actualized in real life, his religious knowledge should trump other factors, such as genealogy, which Muslims in Malabar consider key to organizing social relationships.

Along with being a teacher, Basheer is one of the top leaders of a Muslim reformist religious organization in Kerala. He recollected that even while he was doing his undergraduate degree in Arabic teaching (Afzalul Ulema) at a prestigious college in Malabar, he was already well-known for his oratory skills in the organization. He traveled across Kerala to impart religious teachings to Muslims and, by the time he finished his undergraduate education, he came to occupy an important position in the organization. As he became famous, many Mappilas sought marriage alliances with him through the organizational networks. As he observed, "As soon as they came to my locality and inquired, they realized that I belonged to the barber community; they returned as fast as a rubber ball thrown on to a stone wall." The metaphor in his description is quite revealing and suggests an instinct-based response to knowing his community background, effectively canceling his formidable educational credentials and personal traits. After all, the initial proposal came because they were attracted by his charm, personality, oratory skills, and religious knowledge. The fact that he was born to barber parents was enough to discredit all his achievements in the religious field and secular employment. Ascribed status once again trumps achieved status. To this end, Basheer's observation about emulating Hindu society in spirit (if not in substance) is highly insightful.

In studies in South Asia, the reformist organizations among Muslims have been considered socially progressive in contradistinction to the traditionalist groups (Osella and Osella 2013; Robinson 2008). The latter are often deemed backward, shackled by tradition, and their practices are caricatured as influenced by Hinduism. The reformist projects seek to wean Muslims from these practices and turn them into "perfect Islam." Following these standards, one would be tempted to look for active projects of social transcendence initiated by the reformist organizations to overcome the social boundaries of hierarchy and prejudice. But what we observe in Malabar is that there is no distinction between the traditional and the reformist religious organizations as far as the issue of barbers is concerned. Both work to sustain the traditional hierarchical relations by limiting social mobility, as the case of intermarriages between barbers and other Muslims illustrates.

In contrast to Hakeem, Basheer had a different vision about the history of barbers among Muslims. His father was a barber who went from home to home in the locality, serving his patrons. His maternal grandmother was brought from a nearby neighborhood to their present locality by a wealthy Mappila family to provide services for them. So, he grew up in an environment defined by patron-client relationships between barbers and Mappilas and Sayyids. He noted that barbers in the past were dependent on their patrons for their livelihoods. Indeed, their life chances were determined by the relationships they had with wealthy patrons in the locality. The plot of land on which his parents lived was, for example, freely given to them by the wealthy Mappila family whom they served. They were required to be present at the patron's house whenever the patron needed services for pregnant women of the household or regular barbering services. According to Basheer, his father was quite social and well-versed in local affairs from his avid reading of local newspapers. Perhaps that was the reason, he mused, that his father was insistent that all his children should acquire secular education and, if possible, move away from the traditional profession of barbering. For Basheer, marrying out of the barber family was another step in moving away from the traditional network of barbers in which his parents were involved. It was motivated by a sense that barbers deserve more; they deserve to be equal members of society.

In the case of Basheer, too, Mappila friends tried to arrange a marriage alliance but all failed. The important difference between Basheer and Hakeem is that while Hakeem was working in the sector of secular education and employment, Basheer found his main sphere of activity in the religious field as an orator and a scholar. This is an important distinction in understanding the success and failure of respective individual projects. Basheer's search for a suitable alliance was restricted to the religious circle he was enmeshed in that projected itself as a socially progressive organization. Ultimately, Basheer married a new convert to Islam. While he deemed this act a protest against the socially regressive mindset of his fellow religious members, his act closed off any possibilities of socially overcoming the boundaries between barbers and Mappilas. I have met a few religious scholars who belonged to the barber community and not one has been able to marry outside the community. I have chosen Basheer's case because the reformist organization to which he belonged was often touted to be role models of social progress among Muslims. And yet, there, too, the "invisible" ties binding and distinguishing communities proved impossible to break.

The two cases, of Hakeem and Basheer, show the intricacies of individual projects of social mobility. Though the projects had different outcomes, they should be seen as representing individual efforts enabled by socioeconomic improvements and bound by social constraints. They were motivated by different strands in the struggles of barbers to realize egalitarianism as a value of social relations among Muslims. What is striking about the case of Basheer is that despite his being an acclaimed religious scholar—the symbol of piety, which is considered the supreme virtue of egalitarianism—he was unable to break the barriers of social hierarchy. In one sense, if piety has been the sole value of social distinction in Islam, he should have been considered the most desirable candidate for a respectable marriage alliance among Muslims. But the ideal of piety is fused with principles of lineage and wealth in determining the social status among Muslims. It is against this complex interplay of ideals, values, and principles rubbing against the realities of everyday life that individuals like Basheer find themselves frustrated. I should mention that wealth is achievable, and, in fact, Basheer belongs to what we might call the affluent middle class.[4] But the idea of lineage, which binds an individual to preceding generations, is an ascribed category and rarely amenable to change. Unlike in Hinduism, it is not anchored in scripture (e.g., Law of Manu), and values of purity and pollution. But there is an overlap in the social sphere insofar as individuals are often evaluated by their relation to the whole—whether caste (with occupational designation) or community based. To this end, one might understand the oft repeated declaration that caste exists in Islam.

If we look at the barber community as a collective, individual strategies have not been feasible because they want to continue with the community occupation. While avenues of social mobility are available, barbers, as a social group, seldom attempt to deviate from their community occupation. We see different strategies among the community members to realize the ideals of egalitarianism in everyday life. They undertake collective projects to obtain social dignity and respect among Muslims and thereby normalize their profession and identity.

Collective Strategies

Obtaining secular education or seeking religious qualifications have not been very attractive modes of livelihood for most barbers in Malabar. Given the reliable wages for their jobs nowadays, most barbers want to persist with barbering and, at the same time, gain dignity and respect in the Muslim community. Without changing their profession, barbers seek to devise other strategies for acquiring social dignity and respect among Muslims. They try to achieve this by collective projects of protests and memorandums to religious officials and by reconfiguring their lineage, casting themselves as distinguished and equal to other Muslim groups in Malabar.

Unlike Hakeem and Basheer, who viewed intermarriage as a feasible vehicle for acquiring social dignity, the barber community as a collective seeks to gain dignity by activating discourses of egalitarianism, afforded to them in several registers in Islam. For instance, we have seen that barbers hold religious scholars and leaders of religious organizations responsible for the plight of the community. Barbers accuse the religious institutions of failing to live up to the egalitarian ethos of Islam. Even more so, they castigate religious leaders and scholars who, instead of upholding the egalitarian values and aspirations of Islam, act against those principles. So, the collective strategies utilized by barbers were primarily criticizing such misdeeds and demanding that religious scholars take a public stand against discrimination toward the barber community.

The engagements with religious scholars by barbers have often taken public forms. They can range from publicly questioning religious scholars, submitting memorandums, writing letters to them, to even writing opinion pieces for daily newspapers. To illustrate the nature of these engagements, I return to the ethnographic vignette introduced in Chapter 1. We saw an incident in 2019 at a mosque where a religious scholar proclaimed in his sermon that barbers were unsuitable to lead communal prayers for Muslims. The incident took place in a gathering in the month of Ramadan where more than five hundred people congregated to participate in the special prayer at night (*tarāvīh*) and to listen to the religious scholar's sermon afterward. In one of the sermons, as an answer to a query by a Mappila, the religious scholar equated barbers with children born in adultery. There was a barber in the audience who was agonized by the statement. After returning home, he vented his feelings on the family WhatsApp group. He was encouraged to challenge the religious scholar during the session on the following day. The next day, he asked the religious

Figure 7. Men praying at the mosque in a single row © Aharika Baskar.

scholar during the question-and-answer session, "I am a barber. I listened to your talk yesterday. You said that barbers are comparable to children born in adultery. That they can never take on the role of imams [one who leads the prayer in a mosque] for the prayers. Does Islam indeed say that? If yes, please give me some evidence supporting your claims." The scholar was caught unaware, as he did not expect such a challenge, particularly from someone who he had maligned the previous day. According to Shafeeq, a fifty-year-old barber who related this incident to me, the scholar tried to extricate himself from a direct answer by saying that he was, in fact, talking about children born in adultery and whether they can be followed in prayers. He was not talking about barbers and was simply making a comparison to emphasize his point. Nevertheless, the religious scholar did not retract his words or offer an apology for his earlier remarks. He even tried to justify himself, saying that he had seen such statements in various Islamic texts, but he did not provide any direct evidence for his statements.

The barber who challenged the scholar recorded the whole conversation as he was advised to do by his family members. He then circulated the voice clip to the family group, and it went viral in the community through social-media platforms. I, too, heard of this incident and got hold of the audio recordings from Shafeeq, who stays a few kilometers from my home. I was told that the barbers were greatly agitated by this incident, and a few confronted the religious scholar over the phone, seeking proof to support his utterances. Others threatened to manhandle him if he did not produce evidence for his statements from the Quran or the prophet's sayings.

Sensing the brewing ire against him, the religious scholar apologized for his statements in an audio recording, which was also widely circulated among barbers. He said that he was mistaken in equating the barbers with children born in adultery.[5] He admitted that he had no evidence to back the claims he had made. This represents a much larger issue of the use of or allusion to available textual evidence by religious scholars that those with no access to the texts cannot confirm or deny. Knowledge (or pretending to know) is a powerful instrument! When pressed, the religious scholar made the case to be a mistake on his part and apologized for hurting barbers' sentiments. The barbers, in turn, recognized it as long-standing prejudice that they faced time and again and decided to seek a more comprehensive redress.

Many volunteer organizations and family trusts among barbers deliberated on the issue at numerous meetings, decided to form a separate committee and decided upon a religious intervention. To stem such denigrating averments against their community, they asked religious scholars to issue fatwas against such tendencies in society. Fatwas are legal pronouncements made by religious scholars on pressing issues of personal and social matters, in accordance with Islamic religious tenets and principles (Hossain 2002). Most of the Muslim-majority states across the world have legally appointed state fatwa committees, or councils, that pronounce these judgments. It is on the basis of fatwas' derivation from the shariah that they are able to procure legitimacy and authority (Agrama 2010). These legal pronouncements are given to any Muslim who seeks such help. For instance, in her ethnography on divorce among Muslims in North India, Katherine Lemons (2019) observes the ease and flexibility through which both Muslim men and women approach muftis for legal opinions pertaining to their married life. In a place like India, fatwa committees are maintained by various religious organizations among Muslims, and they issue fatwas when Muslims seek Islamic legal opinion on matters concerning their daily lives. By resorting to the options within the legal frame of Islam, barbers were asserting an understanding of legal procedures and their right to be involved in the process available to them as members of the Muslim community.

Barbers realized that unless and until religious scholars made public statements against the social subordination and stigmatization of barbers, the community would continue to suffer, with little prospect of overcoming enduring prejudice among Muslims. When the committee members presented memorandums to the leaders of various Muslim religious organizations in the state, I was informed that, many dismissed such incidents as things of the past and characterized them as one-off incidents arising out of the ignorance of religious scholars to understand the real essence of Islam, which they proclaimed was egalitarianism. The religious leaders, however, assured the barber representatives that they would look into the matter and discuss the issue at the next sitting of their respective organizational committees. It has been more than five years since the event, and not one of the religious organizations has taken a public stand or brought out a fatwa as demanded by the barbers against the social subordination of barbers.

The experience of humiliation and subordination administered by religious scholars against barbers is not an uncommon phenomenon. I have heard many such incidents happening across Kerala. In each case, barbers have sought to challenge these narratives by seeking evidence for prejudice in the Quran and the sayings of the prophet Muhammed. In the several cases I have been able to document, which occurred since 2008, religious scholars have repeatedly failed to provide evidence. Once they were confronted by the barber community, these scholars pleaded for forgiveness for their mistake and insensitivity. It may well be that in postponing their pronouncements, religious scholars are trying to sidestep the thorny issue of prejudice and oppression in Islam. This is a difficult issue in the context of India where Islam's egalitarianism was historically pitted against the unequal practices associated with the caste system. Recognizing the plight of barbers in the form of an apology or a fatwa is, in effect, an admission of complicity.

The beginning of such religious confrontations should be traced to organizational activities instigated by educated Muslim barbers to change their condition among Muslims. Muslim barbers have formed various organizations, such as the MSA and family unions to push intra-community reforms. These organizational forms drew on wider programs taking place in Malabar at the time. Mappilas had begun to conduct family unions, establish family associations, and engage in producing family histories and calendars from the early 2000s. Barbers were following these established cultural scripts to create a sense of community, elevate their social status, and boost the

confidence of community members. What is important to understand about
these incidents and initiatives is the conviction of barbers that the subordination faced by them is an unwarranted prejudice that stems from a misin-
terpretation of Islam. This is, therefore, a religious matter, and it cannot be
solved simply by intergroup marriages or by discarding their profession but
rather by a more systemic intervention that would purge such religiously
justified claims. To this end, they sought fatwas as potential redress, but
none could be attained. Perhaps this is also an indication of their relative
power in religious circles. That is, barbers seem to have little clout in the
broader Muslim community so as to force the issue of prejudice on to the
forefront of religious matters. Nevertheless, persistence might pay off, as
such actions by their social organizations may incrementally work in their
favor as they amass more evidence of prejudice. Such actions mean that they
are refusing to occupy a subordinate position and want to take center stage
as actors seeking redress in public discourse. It also means challenging Muslim complacency in professing lofty egalitarian ideals, claims barbers show
to be empty.

Apart from confronting religious authorities, barbers also collectively
resort to innovative projects and programs to elevate their social identity and
secure social dignity among Muslims. To augment the claims of high status for their lineage, barbers have recently also resorted to organizing family
gatherings in Malabar. In this, they have followed an already well-established
cultural script of claiming status among Muslims in Malabar. While barbers
have only organized family gatherings and produced calendars, many other
lineages among Muslims have produced family histories, directories, and
magazines, along with conducting family gatherings and producing calendars. There is a common design and aspiration behind these calendars. In
family calendars, the lineage name of the family is written in bold letters at
the top, in either English or Malayalam. If the lineage has already registered
their family as a trust with the concerned body of the state government, the
registration number is also displayed. A family logo is also given in the calendars. Apart from these, there are quotations from the Quran or the hadith, emphasizing the importance of family bonds among Muslims. Important
Arabic dates, such as the prophet's or saints' birth or death anniversaries, are
also marked in these calendars. The names and phone numbers of officials
of the family trust may also be given on the calendars. Such calendars are
distributed among family members and are often nailed on the front walls of
houses in Malabar. Barbers showcase these calendars at their homes as well as

Figure 8. Calendar prepared by a Mappila family © P. C. Saidalavi.

at their shops. The calendar is visible to all the customers who visit the shops for barbering services.

It is instructive to compare the status claims among Muslims with those among Hindus and Christians. The lineage is usually referred to by the term *taravād* in the local language, Malayalam. As already discussed, the idea of taravād refers to the line of descent, which should be marked through a single ancestor. It was initially used to refer to the matrilineal households of Nairs in Kerala (Schneider and Gough 1961). Many Muslim family histories vouch for high status, asserting that the original ancestor who began their family was a convert from a Hindu upper-caste family. Such anchoring of the family in a higher caste among Muslims is sought to distinguish the older Muslim elites from the newly rich families who cannot put forth such socially elevated status. This is similar to the case among Syrian Christians in Kerala who are said to have written family histories since the early twentieth century (Varghese 2004; Donald 2022). Donald (2022, 57) notes that "The content of these family histories includes the reconstructions of popular beliefs; family and church genealogies that claim Brahminic and apostolic origins; the biographies of prominent family members. . . . They operate as social and historical commentaries from the perspective of the kin network." Muslim family histories follow similar tendencies. Moreover, these older Mappila elites will have documents, such as land deeds, beginning at least from the late nineteenth century to prove the legitimacy of their family. Sometimes, they even showcase some privileges granted to their family by the local rulers. The land documents emphasize the longevity and distinctions of the family line. While these are not very old, only a maximum of 150 years, the lack of such documents in the hands of the nouveau-riche (e.g., Gulf migrants) creates all the difference. Since most barbers were traditionally attached to each mosque community and were offered a plot of land free of cost on which to construct a house, they did not often hold the title to these properties until the 1970s.

Barbers follow the dominant script of producing family histories and an elevated genealogical status by recourse to "invented histories."[6] By affirming high status based on their mythical descent from an original Muslim, barbers try to instill confidence among themselves and recognition by others. But, in some cases, such claim-making also risks exclusivity that binds them to their community and thereby potentially hampering efforts at overcoming the social subordination through intermarriages. This is an argument made by Hakeem at the beginning of this chapter. If they consider themselves "equally good," there is no need to think of social mobility in terms of intermarriages, he observed. In a sense, there is a disconnect observable in the strategies undertaken by those who pursue barbering and those who seek other professions as a means of livelihood. The proclamations of high status in terms of lineage declared by barbers also augment the already well-established culture of status considerations in Malabar. Since belonging to Hindu high castes in Kerala is a mark of distinction, many Mappila families who maintain such origins accrue much prestige and respect among Muslims. The mythical origins, in contrast, do not fare much in favor of barbers.

A key historiographic project in South Asia that dealt with the engagements and interactions between the subordinated and the dominant group has indeed been Subaltern studies. The project was conceived to bring to light what the historian Ranajit Guha (1997) called subalterns in Indian history and how they have been systematically neglected, sidelined, or appropriated by the nationalist historiography. Guha observed that subalterns may often find themselves in a double bind with their projects, as their narratives are often already trapped in the accounts dominated by elites by following the already well-established cultural scripts. However, it is also their embeddedness in those cultural scripts that gives them an edge in their counternarratives. The collective strategies of barbers point to yet another possibility of activating egalitarian social relations among Muslims. Highlighting Islam's inherent potential of egalitarianism gives both much strength to the assertions of barbers and chances for bargaining for commitment and empathy from religious scholars. These collective strategies, however, follow many of the established cultural frames of family, lineage, and status among Muslims in their attempts to challenge established hierarchy and carve out a dignified identity for barbers. Therefore, their success in reconfiguring and undermining hierarchical tendencies are always of limited effect.

Conclusion

I have illustrated three tendencies of seeking egalitarianism by barbers in their social relations with other Muslims in Malabar. In the case of individual strategies, they are often motivated by discarding the traditional profession of barbering. Many barbers who sought secular education and employment tried to overcome hierarchy by contracting marriage alliances with non-barbers. They looked at endogamy as the most important institution of hierarchical reproduction. They thought that an increasing number of intermarriages would eventually dissolve the social distinctions based on hierarchy. However, few have been successful in gaining social dignity by pursuing non-barbering professions. Those who pursued religious knowledge and livelihoods have not been successful in gaining marriage alliances from non-barbers even if they wished. According to the precepts of normative Islam, often espoused by barbers, to argue for status claims, piety should be regarded as the ultimate value that overrides prejudice about one's background. Hence, religion becomes a vehicle for asserting one's self-worth and an ideological ground for the contestation of hierarchy among Muslims.

Yet, as I have argued, individual mobilities cannot be taken as the marker of change, as hierarchy is inherently a social system where the primary unit of reference remains that of a particular group or community. Herein lies the parallel with the Hindu caste system. To be sure, hierarchical systems are ever-changing and always contested, but they are also reproduced in practice in the course of everyday life. At the level of the individual, educated persons like Hakeem could transcend the boundaries of hierarchy through projects of marrying outside the traditional endogamous circle. Such individual experiences of overcoming hierarchy should be tempered with the individual projects that are less successful, as the case of Basheer illustrates. The economic improvements attained by a group may not lead to superseding the hierarchical relations that existed in a locality. They may lead to individual social mobility if they are undertaken as projects of social aspiration. In some situations, these individual cases might fail, leading to contrarian personal decisions to actively withdraw from the project itself.

The fact that Islam is the ideological battleground over values such as egalitarianism becomes quite evident in the collective strategies of Muslim barbers who persist with their traditional profession. They seek to gain dignity and respect as social equals among Muslims along with continuing their profession, which earns them a reliable income. Barbers consider their jobs voluntary and important for the upkeep of the Muslim religious community. At the same time, they challenge any suggestion of social distinction in Islam, enumerating several incidents from the history of Islam where social egalitarianism was upheld as the mode of social organization. Most of the incidents cited are from the time of the prophet Muhammad or his four caliphs. Barbers bring up these references to challenge the social subordination directed against them by other Muslims. While Muslims in Malabar infuse hierarchical sensibilities to order their relations using concepts and categories in Islamic jurisprudence, barbers anchor themselves on the conception of an ideal Muslim society, drawing from the normative textual traditions in Islam.

While challenging hierarchical social relations on the ideas of egalitarianism of Islam, they are also engaged in the already well-established cultural script of family gatherings to elevate their own lineage of claiming descent from an original Muslim from Arabia. The contemporary collective projects undertaken by barbers to organize family gatherings, produce calendars, and write family histories have given a sense of identity and confidence to assert the distinctions of their lineage and history and to confront the issues facing the family and the community. Nevertheless, an important underside of these conscious collective projects is to establish the legitimacy of Islamic categories that purport to sustain the hierarchies. The family gatherings, the writing of histories and booklets, and the production of calendars have originally been projects undertaken by non-barber Muslims in Malabar. It can be argued that by conducting the same programs and being engaged in the same games, they are already at a disadvantage owing to their long-standing social subordination. Moreover, by participating in these programs, barbers tend to contribute to legitimizing the processes of highlighting one's family lineage as a suitable and harmless category of social distinction. Since marriage is already predicated on the notion of lineage among Muslims in Malabar, projecting the mythical lineage in the case of barbers may not be fruitful for the political project of overcoming social hierarchy.

Comparing the contemporary struggles of Muslim barbers with Hindus offers revealing insights about the differences in the workings of caste between these communities. There are obvious parallels with Hinduism and notions of ascribed versus achieved status familiar from the caste system. The calls for egalitarian social relations undertaken by the lower castes among Hindus in postcolonial India have been directed against the state. They seek state intervention to prevent humiliation and atrocities directed against them and seek education and employment benefits from the state to overcome the historical discrimination they have faced in the caste system. In short, Hinduism is viewed by the lower castes as forestalling any possibility of endowing social equality to them. In contrast, in the instances I examine here, Muslim barbers seek to actualize an egalitarian ethos by reference to Islamic traditions and thereby to contest and reconfigure caste. Many scholars have observed this tendency in examining upward-mobility attempts among Muslim social groups in North India (Ahmad 1976; Madan 2001; Mehta 1997). This has been particularly visible in the case of efforts to reconfigure the names of social groups among Muslims that function to "erase" traditional markers that render them as backward and/or subordinate (Lee 2018b). Once again, one could argue that similar strategies have long been employed by the Hindu caste, especially during the British rule (Doron 2013). Yet, the social processes I examined here in the context of Muslim barbers is deeply rooted in Islamic traditions, rather than drawing on the discourses of the state and democracy. I suggest that there is no equivalence between Muslim and Hindu caste if we analyze Muslim social relations in terms of their values, their ideological underpinnings, and the fields of contestations.

AFTERWORD

This book has explored the transformation of a patronage and status system among Muslims in Malabar, South India, with a particular focus on barbers, an essential but low-status occupational group. Muslims in Malabar drew upon several values, including lineage, wealth, piety, and dignity to order their social relations in a hierarchical manner. These values were supported, constructed, and maintained by socioeconomic inequalities and structures, differential access to wealth and resources, and constructions of moral personhood. In the resultant caste system, we might see parallels between practices of both Muslims and Hindus in India. Yet, Muslims often made these values relevant and meaningful in their everyday lives by attributing, redefining, and evaluating them using Islamic historical narratives as well as jurisprudential concepts and categories. Barbers have been able to severely disrupt such narratives and categories by reconfiguring them to their own ends. They undermined the patronage system and strived for more egalitarian labor relations in Malabar, which happened in the wake of unionization, monetization of labor, secular education and employment, attaining religious knowledge, and the general socioeconomic improvements in the region.

A minor event, driven by the covid pandemic, reveals the ambit of social transformations in the region. I met Hamza in December 2021 at his shop when barbershops were reopened in Kerala after a long hiatus. He was sitting on his barber chair when I reached the shop. As soon as he saw me, he got out of the chair and came to the entrance to greet me. After exchanging pleasantries, I asked him how covid had treated him. He sighed and said, "It was very difficult initially." He paused and then continued, "It was fun for the first few days. I did not need to go to the shop. I could sleep as long as I wanted. But reality struck after a week." He then spoke of how after a week or so, he began to feel a void, as if there was nothing to do. He told me that he was at a loss as to what he should do with so much free time at his disposal. The government of India imposed a nationwide lockdown on March 30, 2020. Everyone had to shut their shops, except those who provided essential goods and services. Clearly, the repeated lockdowns had severely affected the livelihood of barbers (see Haneefa 2021).

The damage suffered by barbers was ongoing through the pandemic. Even when general shops were allowed to open as the daily number of covid cases began to decrease, barbershops were barred from operating. The rationale was that barbers worked closely with a range of people and their shops were seen as potentially contagious zones, conducive for the spread of the virus. The shutdown of barbershops meant that people were unable to care for their bodies, and their hair, moustaches, and beards grew naturally, in an unruly manner. At first, there was a novelty to it, when youngsters sporting long beards and hair began circulating their images across social-media platforms. Some began to cut and trim their hair and beards using shaving sets, trimmers, and scissors easily available at the market or through online stores. But this also reveals a generation gap. As Hamza observed, older people found dealing with their long hair a real hassle. They could hardly use the trimmer or new gadgets, and they were unwilling to take such risks. Neither did they want to use, on their own, a razor on their faces. Most of Hamza's older customers were used to keeping their faces and heads neat and clean by regularly visiting Hamza at the shop. But with his shop remaining closed, they began visiting Hamza at his house, where he started accepting his old clientele. The arrangement was such that Hamza cut his customers' hair and trimmed their beards in the front yard of his own house. The seating arrangement was far from ideal: Customers would sit on the ground without any back support and Hamza had to crouch to serve them. After a while, he said, a few of the older people suggested that they should venture to the shop to retrieve some basic instruments and bring home the barber chair. They arranged for a small pick-up van and transported the chair to Hamza's house. He placed it in the front yard and served his customers.

This vignette highlights the changes that have occurred in the relationships between barbers and other Muslim groups in Malabar. Such arrangements were unimaginable for a barber in the past, at least until the 1970s. Indeed, before that time, we can imagine that, as a barber, Hamza would have been forced to visit his patrons' homes to offer services, with significant risk to himself and his family. As I have shown in Chapter 3, both barber men and barber women were involved in a dominating patronage system, under which they had to visit the houses of their patrons. They catered to all Muslims of the locality by providing barbering services on a weekly or fortnightly basis. During those times, barbers received a fixed amount of rice twice a year and other seasonal produce, such as vegetables and yams. Barbers had to bring sacks to carry these rewards home. They did not receive any monetary compensation from patrons for the routine work they performed; monetary compensation in the form of a few rupees was provided only for service during special occasions, such as for midwifery, tonsure, and circumcision. Since barbers were dependent on their patrons' mercy for their livelihood, they were also compelled to engage in what were considered demeaning practices of hair removal from armpits and crotch. The barbering services thus involved coming in close contact with the refuse and dirt of patrons, which, according to dominant interpretations of Islam, was seen as immoral and open for divine punishment. Though such interactions created intimacy between barbers and their patrons, they were always mediated through hierarchy and subordination. Such relations of subordination, alongside their undignified occupation, meant that barbers were seen as "outcastes" and unsuitable for long-standing social relationships such as marriage alliances. I use the term *outcastes* to denote some of the overlaps with caste-Hindu society, although, as I have argued, the reference points and justifications for such hierarchical relations are very different among Muslims in Malabar.

Though the relationships between barbers and their patrons were mediated through patronage and thus dependency, the patrons needed the barbers just as much as the barbers needed their patrons. The comportment of an ideal Muslim in Malabar—initially, that of shaven head and ordered beard—was produced and maintained by barbers for everyone. The notion of what makes for a Muslim ideal in terms of bodily comportment has changed over time, as has the nature of the occupation, for most of the twentieth century. In the past, with the skewed economic relations, patrons could demand and force the services from barbers whenever they wished, even when a barber was unwilling. Patrons could impose measures such as a social boycott to make barbers comply with the norms of the locality. Muslims in Malabar generally believed that barbers were fulfilling a moral duty by maintaining the deportment of the community. Being attached to the mosque community in each mahallu, barbers had the appearance of semireligious officials, offering essential services for the community. Their services were conceived within the ambit of rewards set by their Muslim patrons and sanctioned by ideas of Islam in Malabar. While an essential service aimed at preserving the sanctity

of Muslims, the act of barbering was considered undignified in terms of juristic ideas of purity/impurity and halal/harām in Islam, effectively rendering
barbers' social status as lowly and degraded (see Chapters 3 and 5).

Recounting the lives and experiences of their ancestors or themselves,
many barbers identified humiliation as a key aspect of their identity among
Muslims. Their personal worth as human beings and individuals was often
questioned in mundane activities, such as on the playground and in schools
and madrassas. Many barbers expected that schools and madrassas would be
free from the grasp of hierarchy (see Chapter 4). They envisioned that since
schools were recognized as producing tomorrow's model citizens of the state,
the discourse of civility would inform relations in these spaces. Similarly, religious spaces and institutions such as madrassas were thought to embody the
ideals of Islam where personal identity and social distinctions were immaterial to piety as enshrined in the Quran by Allah. However, not only were
these expectations unrealized, but these spaces also facilitated and supported
social distinctions. Since humiliation is an experiential event, barbers often
recognized its weight both in their bodies and as an affront to their lifestyle
choices. But they could rarely challenge the long-entrenched social structures
that perpetuate their social subordination.

I used the concept of caste as a critical starting point for the book because
this concept is used widely to refer to non-Hindu social structures in South
Asia. I created a working definition, characterizing caste as "a regime of hierarchical inequality based on birth." I have tussled with the idea of caste in various ways, showing how it works in the everyday life of Muslims in Malabar. If
we consider hierarchy to be a religious conception, in the manner of Dumont,
we can see that both Islam and Hinduism have distinctive characterizations
of hierarchy that lie deep in their own theological frameworks. I must profess
that Muslims are a deeply hierarchical society like Hindus in India. To follow
a dominant tradition of conceptualizing caste in South Asia, which sees it as
a structural phenomenon, not as a cultural phenomenon unique to Hindus,
then we can say that Muslims, too, have caste. Even the debates among Muslims in India fall along this division. Those who want to contest hierarchical
relations among Muslims, particularly those in the lower rung of society in
Malabar, would find it politically most potent to term Muslim hierarchy as
caste because it immediately speaks to a long tradition of anti-caste politics in
India. They would like to define caste as a structural principle. However, most
Muslims in Malabar assert that caste is a cultural phenomenon specific to
Hindus and that Muslims do not have caste. They would dismiss the existence

of hierarchical practices either as a thing of the past or as a residue and trace of ignorance among Muslims to fully imbibe and internalize the egalitarian principles of Islam. This claim, however, always falls flat because "caste" does not rest on knowledge; it rests on power.

Caste relations among Muslims in Malabar were constructed along several lines. A long-standing factor of distinction and signal of ranking among Muslims had been genealogy, locally translated as *taravād*. Genealogy does for Muslims what caste does for Hindus. It divides groups of people by assigning value on the basis of birth. For Muslims, birth is not considered within the ritual domain of a caste, but within a much smaller, kinship group based on taravād and family lineage. The term taravād originated from the matrilineal household of Nairs, a Hindu caste, but, over time, Muslims also used the term to refer to their ancestral household. Two factors contributed to the status of a taravād among Muslims: land and lineage. Those who held land in the past, employed outside agricultural labor, and enjoyed customary services from clients, were said to have high status. The longevity of a taravād was another sign of distinction. High-status taravāds could produce documents, such as land records stretching back to the latter part of the nineteenth century, to establish the distinction of their lineage. Within this framework, barbers were clearly disadvantaged. Barbers were a service-based community, dependent on their patrons. They did not traditionally own land, nor could they avow and establish a high status for their lineage through accepted means.

Another key marker of distinction among Muslims in Malabar is piety. It is the disposition and mode of being that is generally thought to be close to Allah. Muslims try to activate this state of being through a range of practices—namely, routine prayers, devotion, and focused ritual action. It is said that a person should try to follow the prescriptions and proscriptions of Islam, conveyed through the words of Allah in the Quran, and the traditions and actions of the prophet Muhammad and his companions. According to Muslim clerics in Malabar, Allah has proclaimed that those who are held in high esteem in front of Him are the most pious. This view fits well with Sayyids, who trace direct descent from the prophet Muhammad, and, as such, are said to have the greatest promise to achieve piety. It is thought by Muslims in Malabar that some aspects and traces of the prophet's behavior are manifest in Sayyids, and they are therefore naturally disposed to achieve piety. They can increase their potential by pursuing religious knowledge and practices. Mappilas are said to achieve piety by acquiring it through religious scholarship and actions alone. Those families who have traditionally produced religious scholars and have controlled land are held in high esteem among Mappilas. Hence, both wealth/power and religious disposition place these communities in good standing. With barbers' work bordering on impurity and harām, his livelihood was thought to be entangled in a style of life that jeopardized proximity to Allah. Barbers were considered unsuited and unable to cultivate and embody piety, and they were therefore deemed low in caste hierarchy.

From the 1970s, barbers of all religious communities challenged the social subordination imposed on them in Kerala. Barbers were looked down upon by Hindus, Muslims, and Christians in Kerala, although the values and practices underpinning their subordination in each religious community were distinct. Some of the barbers in southern Kerala were active members of the Communist Party and involved themselves in the radical political activities organized by the coir factory workers and agricultural labor. These movements were making a significant impact in society and restructuring existing social relations by demanding higher wages, social dignity, and respect from the owners of the means of production. The election of the communist government in Kerala in 1957 was helped by union movements among factory workers and agricultural labor. A few barbers were greatly inspired by these changes and formed a union in the late 1960s and early 1970s—the KSBA. The unionization started taking root among Muslim barbers in Malabar by the mid-1970s. Barbers opened shops in their localities and refused to serve in the houses of their patrons, as elaborated in Chapter 6. They fixed the working hours of the shop and demanded specified rates for each type of service. The social distinctions between individuals and families in the locality were consciously superseded at the barbershop as barbers ventured to offer their services to anyone who visited them and they required customers to join a queue. The queue symbolized the erasure of existing distinctions, effectively rendering all customers the same. It is underscored by a moral imperative that refuses concessions based on caste, community, or ethnicity. Hence, barbers offered their services to anyone who would pay. Barbers had to face a lot of resistance and physical assaults from their earlier patrons, but they refused to budge. Over time, the new arrangements were accepted, and customers sought the services of barbers at the shops for fixed rates.

Let me return to Hamza, the barber whose customers brought the chair to his house during the pandemic. The willingness of his customers to visit his house for barber services during covid was an index of the change that has occurred in the relationships between barbers and other Muslims in Malabar.

Muslims still considered the services offered by barbers as essential and were ready to take steps to procure them when the shops were shut. A customer usually makes efforts to secure a product or service in a market environment. Muslims in Hamza's neighborhood required his services and were willing to do whatever was required to get those services. They even ventured into his household, which was unthinkable in the past.

This type of initiative was possible in a neighborhood such as the one in which Hamza operated, where he knew all his customers personally. Urban barbershops, in small and big towns, too, remained shut for long periods during the pandemic. However, their customers were often not regulars, and their relationships were not built on familiarity and long-standing personal interactions. However, nowhere did the association between barber and customer lapse into an earlier mode of subordination during the crisis. Many barbers were asked by Muslims as to what they should do to get a haircut. Barbers, including Hamza, told them to come to their homes to get barbering services. It may seem a minor request, but given the histories of social change that I have outlined in this book, the fact that barbers could now make such a suggestion, rather than adhere to the will of the wider Muslim community, is instructive. Even if barbers were requested or if a demand were made, barbers had the confidence to refuse such demands.

The social change engendered by barbers in Kerala since the 1970s was also greatly helped by the socioeconomic improvements the state witnessed owing to remittances from the Gulf countries. The Gulf brought more money into circulation in Kerala, injecting far more social mobility, better living standards, and disposable income to be spent on acquiring education and employment (Rajan and Zachariah 2019). Gulf-returned people needed barbers and had become accustomed to paying for their services in comfortable shops at Gulf countries. With the increasing remittance from the Gulf countries— which formed a quarter of Kerala's gross domestic product (GDP) in the late 1990s (Kannan and Hari 2020)—and strong union activities, imposing rates for each task and occasionally increasing such rates became easier for barbers. The standard of living in Kerala steadily improved from the 1970s, and some barbers also migrated to the Gulf countries to work as barbers where they earned better incomes. Owing to these socioeconomic improvements, by the early 2000s, barbers also started educating their children for employment in other sorts of work, like other Muslim groups in Malabar.

Discarding the traditional profession of barbering and pursuing secular education and employment has created opportunities for a few barbers.

They acquired wealth and permanent income through employment either in government services or through private means. A few of them have been able to marry outside the barber community. This posed a major challenge to endogamy, which has been the cornerstone of reproduction of social groups and hierarchy among Muslims. A few barbers pursued religious education and scholarship instead of following the barbering profession of their fathers (Chapter 7). Because piety was considered the axis of normative Islam, one might assume that becoming a religious scholar would improve a person's social status. A religious scholar had a great opportunity to imbibe and exemplify piety through his knowledge, devotion, and everyday practices. But such a possibility has not translated into the life of barbers. Despite some choosing the path of religious scholars, they have been denied status and marital alliances from outside the barber community because of their background. In contrast, those barbers who gained secular education and employment have been able to pursue marriage alliances from a wider social circle.

Abandoning the traditional profession has not been an option for most barbers since it was considered an essential service and promised a steady income. Barbers have, in recent times, sought to reconfigure their identity using the idea of taravād, which has been a legitimate criterion of status among Muslims. Barbers have found a culturally accepted idiom in which to assert the worth of their taravād. One such path was by claiming descent from an Arab Muslim who accompanied Mālik-ibn-Dīnār and is said to have arrived on the Malabar coast after the death of prophet Muhammad to propagate the faith of Islam (Chapters 2 and 7). The discovery of ancient roots that are "respectable" or even heroic has been a common phenomenon for claiming high status among various Hindu castes in India, a process scholars have termed "sanskritization" (Srinivas 1956). While a similar process has been defined as Ashrafization among North Indian Muslims (Ahmad 1967), in Malabar, we see that such claim-making is the common thread of all Muslim groups' sense of origin and expansion. In Malabar, such reconfiguring of genealogy is not restricted to barbers alone. All Muslim groups, except Sayyids, trace their origins and the dissemination of Islam to this Arab missionary, Mālik-ibn-Dīnār. Since this story is a common inheritance of almost all Muslims in Malabar, anchoring the origin of their family to such an Arab Muslim bestows a sense of identity and dignified lineage for barbers.

Delineating various arenas and practices of caste and its contestations among Muslims, I have posited that we can identify several values, such as

wealth, piety, genealogy, antassu, and egalitarianism, as ordering social relations between barbers and other Muslim groups in Malabar. While piety is
prized among Muslims, especially at an individual level, there is no single
value among Muslims that encompasses all other values. In cases of marriage, taravād often trumps piety. Some of these values are identified and
proclaimed by my interlocutors, and others are highlighted through the rendering of their lives and experiences. Values are created through social action
and, therefore, are amenable to change. I have illustrated in Chapter 6 that
barbers undermined the existing patronage system and constructed a new
value of "antassu" through radical political action and the establishment of
barbershops in public spaces (featuring fixed rates and wages). Barbers also
decided on their working hours, holidays, and proper conduct at the shops.
By modulating their work in accordance with capitalist market relations, they
constructed it as dignified labor, labor that is negotiated between an owner
and a customer in aesthetic terms.

To challenge and contest caste sensibilities and practices, Muslim barbers draw upon discourses of egalitarianism available in Islam, along with
an increasing number of broader projects of social mobility, such as recon-
structing the past, seeking secular education and employment. In my conversations, most Muslim barbers asserted that Islam puts forth the idea of
an egalitarian community of believers where one's genealogy, wealth, and
occupational specializations should not be the determinant markers of social
distinction. Instead, piety, which is envisioned by Allah as the true marker
of distinction among believers, should form the basis of social relations. The
egalitarian impulses of Islam provide the much-needed energy and power to
the barbers to challenge the established iniquitous social structures. Islam,
with its egalitarian ethos, provides a more radical antidote to the injustices of
caste among Muslims.

Using a value-based approach, this book has illustrated how Muslims
in Malabar organize their everyday lives within the strictures of iniquitous
socioeconomic structures, democratic articulations, and a vibrant Islamic discourse that both facilitates as well as offers a critique of caste. Past tendencies
of observers to identify features of Muslim hierarchy and then equate them to
aspects of the Hindu caste system in South Asia is an oversimplification that
this book has tried to address. The dominant conception of caste in South
Asia has been that it is primarily a Hindu religious conception, nevertheless
influencing domains of social activity across different religious communities.

Scholars working on Muslim communities in South Asia have, with few excep-
tions, largely followed this Dumontian line of reasoning and sought to find
caste in Muslim lives. Following scholars like A. M. Hocart, Nicholas Dirks,
Susan Bayly, and Sumit Guha, I have posited that caste should primarily be
understood as a regime of hierarchical inequality based on birth operating
on the Indian subcontinent. Yet, how it operates in various communities and
across economic, political, social, and cultural spheres is unique. Moreover,
as economic, political, and social affairs have already been registered through
caste sensibilities, Muslims had to negotiate with them while they modulated
their everyday lives according to the prescriptions and proscriptions of Islam.
So, an Islamic hierarchy based on piety and a now deemed Hindu caste had to
find means of negotiation, contestation, and destabilization. While hierarchy
is imagined and rendered through religious idioms, it is not imputed to social
groups through textual interventions. This gave Muslims a range of possibilities to organize their social relations, by using concepts and categories such
as taravād that implied hierarchy. Even in Arab society, social prestige and
honor were attributed to individuals on the basis of their memberships in
particular tribes and clans. In India, this became more complex because Muslims wanted to operationalize hierarchy, but it needed to be delineated and
practiced in a context where caste also existed as a legitimate mechanism of
hierarchy. Muslims creatively constructed a hierarchy that might sometimes
resemble Hindu caste, but the underlying values and meanings of Muslim
caste are predominantly Islamic. It will be interesting to see how caste operates in various religious communities and even within a single community
across regions of the subcontinent. It will be contextually determinant and
calls for interesting ethnographic explorations.

The close analysis of Muslim caste also brings up interesting questions for
anthropological understandings of Islam. Caste has often been deemed an
exogenous category that challenges the normative posturing of Islam. To render this problem into the contemporary anthropological discourses of Islam,
caste is located at the domain of the everyday, which challenges the contours
of the normative Islam. Yet, I have shown that caste operates among Muslims
using various jurisprudential and moral categories available within the normative Islam as well as by drawing upon the broader status considerations
available within the local cultural milieu. Even the challenge to the normative, contrary to the anthropological consensus, does not simply or exclusively reside in the location of the everyday. Rather, in practice, we often see
these two realms informing and shaping each other to such an extent that the

usual theoretical divisions into normative/everyday, text/practice, and great/ little traditions become untenable. The logic of the practice is also determined by local ideas of status and prestige rooted in lineage, occupation, morality, and—also associated with caste—at the same time, infused and shaped by Islamic understandings of piety, as well. In short, what forms caste assumes and allows for within a context needs to be established by specific historical and ethnographic analysis.

NOTES

Preface

1. Bourdieu (1990, 53) defines habitus as a system of attitudes and dispositions embodied and practiced "without presupposing a conscious aiming at ends or an express mastery of the operations necessary in order to attain them." In this sense, our actions take their form in accordance with the patterns of culture, and we do not need to often rationalize our actions to undertake them. These patterns of culture work both as "a model of and model for" actions in the world.

Chapter 1

1. The term *Mappila* is generally used in Malabar to refer to all the Muslims. The social distinctions we see among Muslims are not recognized in official records, even in the case of fishers and barbers. Everyone is denoted as Mappila. In this book, I follow the recognition of social hierarchy among Muslims and follow the respective terminologies. To refer to all the Muslims in Malabar, I simply use Muslims in Malabar; in other cases, I use the hierarchical names. I describe this term in detail later in Chapter 2 when I describe various social groups.

2. The idea of social sphere, as I use it throughout the book, maybe compared with Bourdieu's idea of the field. A field is defined as "a configuration of objective relations between positions" (Bourdieu and Wacquant 1992, 112). These positions are agential that are objectively defined, providing specific habitus and capital to be expended and acquired. To use an example from Bourdieu, in an artistic field, there will be artists, buyers, auctioneers, curators etc. All these agential positions embody specific habitus and capital. At the same time, all these agents will also be controlled, regulated, and dominated by what an art is. There will be multiple such fields in a society. While I find strong resonance between field and social spheres, I do feel uncomfortable with the possessive nature of capital as Bourdieu defines it. If field is about relationality, can capital simply be possessive? I find it difficult to convey the meanings of various values I describe in the book such as piety, genealogy, antassu, wealth, and egalitarianism by Bourdieu's concept of capital. Some of these values are divine, some are possessive, others are transitive and still others are, to use an apposite phrase from Evans-Pritchard (1976, 13) personalized force generalized in speech. Social actors will be utilizing various values to their advantage, sometimes even those that may not lie in the "field" in which the action takes place.

3. At the base of this comparative project is a distinction between individualistic and holistic conceptions of society. Dumont posited that western society valued the individual as an independent and autonomous actor, while Indian society looked at persons as dividual—a socially embedded, heteronomous actor performing a culturally written script of caste hierarchy.

4. R. S. Khare (1984) has shown that egalitarian ideologies were not foreign to Indian thought. As Khare shows, Lucknow Chamars, a Dalit group, resorts to egalitarian tendencies in Indic philosophies, such as those of Buddhism, to challenge the Brahminical ideas of hierarchical personhood. So, one's analysis in India has to look not only at how modern ideas of equality penetrated the subcontinent but also at how earlier ideas of equality reformulated, reconstructed, and negotiated with the modern.

5. One important strain of this critique has been that Dumont has posited that western societies are defined by equality and Indian society is shaped by hierarchy. While the West is seen as changing, India is seen as caught in a bind, perennially trapped in its hierarchy (Appadurai 1988; Béteille 1979).

6. I thank Muhammed Asaf for this input.

7. The history of Islam as narrated from a north Indian point of view does not do justice to its history on the Indian subcontinent. For instance, Islam arrived on the Malabar coast, riding on the waves and rhythms of the sea, at least two hundred years before Mahmud of Ghazni got to Punjab. See Abdulla Anchillath (2015). Moreover, Islam's history even in the north Indian region cannot be simply reduced to Mughal rulers, as they did not have any active role in proselytizing the masses. In fact, Islam did not grow in strength in the heartlands of the Mughal Empire. Rather, it was in the outlying regions of the empire that Islam took root, mainly through the activities of itinerant and adventurous Sufis and scholars. See Richard Eaton (2000).

8. This argument is also advanced by lower castes among Hindus. For an analysis of how boatmen in Banaras deploy such myths, see Assa Doron (2012).

Chapter 2

1. Whether such a self-ascription existed in the past is questionable. Peter van der Veer (1994, 19) observes that categorization and rigidification of Indian populations into religious communities such as Hindus and Muslims was a key aspect of colonial thought in India. "The division was not a colonial invention. But to count these communities and to have leaders represent them was a colonial novelty, and it was fundamental to the emergence of religious nationalism."

2. Such dream visions are part of an acceptable canon across the Muslim world for conviction of faith and as a medium of communion with God. For example, see works by Mittermaier (2010) and Alatas (2020).

3. Zainudheen Makhdum (1942) used this text as a reference for his book *Tuhfat-al-Mujāhidīn*, written to inspire Muslims to wage war against the Portuguese.

4. This is the barber caste among Nairs. The Malayalam term means "a person who beautifies a head."

5. The term is used with various spellings, including Moplah, Mappilla, Mapuler, and Mappila. I use "Mappila" and resort to other terms when I quote.

6. Engseng Ho (2006) maps the progeny of Sayyid immigrants from South Yemen to various places across the Indian Ocean and notes that children born out of the communion of these Sayyids and local women were notified by the term *muwallad*. It seems that such categorization of creole population using new epithets was a common phenomenon.

7. Similar practices were evident among Hindus, where people in low castes adopted upper-caste-sounding names to elevate or even erase their status.

8. Perumal (2025) has analyzed the boundary-making between the fishers and inland Muslims using the category of smell. One of the key cultural markers used to distinguish between the spatiality of the coast and inland has indeed been the olfactory registers. However, there are other factors too. See Saidalavi (forthcoming).

9. But it is also true that some of the converts who had been wealthy prior to their acceptance of Islam have been successful in quickly erasing their previous caste identities.

10. Such references are visible in *Correspondence on Moplah Outrages in Malabar, 1853–1859*; see pages 208, 236, and 245. I thank Safwan Amir for these references. These colonial records also suggest that many individuals were also identify by the occupations they undertook, without the terms necessarily signifying a social group. We can see prefixes like *pully mukri*, meaning a person who works in the mosque to call *azān*; see page 235 of the same document. Since such jobs were not often hereditary, it seems, the lowliness attached to their occupation, if at all there was, was not permanent and could be overcome. *Correspondence on Moplah Outrages in Malabar, 1853–59*, United Scottish Press, 1863, https://www.tamildigitallibrary.in /admin/assets/book/TVA_BOK_0046775/TVA_BOK_0046775_Correspondence_on_moplah _outrages_in_malabar.pdf.

Chapter 3

1. The term *yajamana*, which is often used in the Hindu context to refer to the patron who conducts the ritual, is not applicable among Muslims. As Heesterman (1985, 26) says, in the classic system of ritual, the pivotal point is the *yajamana*, "the patron at whose expense and for whose benefit the ritual is performed." Barbering services are not regarded as ritual and none of my interlocutors were aware of such a term. Instead, they referred to the wealthy patrons as *muthalāli*, one who owns a great amount of wealth and who refers to other clients by their respective names.

2. This in itself becomes a problematic starting point when there is no consensus on the analytical contours of caste.

3. For a useful analysis of such political mobilizations centering on *mohullas*, see Bailey 1983; Freitag 1989; and Pandey 2006. They argue that mohullas, with their ethnic, caste, and communitarian constellations, became pockets of communal mobilizations and violence during the British period and continue to be so.

4. Since the latter half of the twentieth century, rivalries between religious groups have spawned mahallus, thus leading to construction of many mosques in a single locality belonging to diverse groups.

5. For a global political economy of hair and its ritual significance, see Tarlo 2017.

6. Saqafi is a degree and a title provided by Markazu Saqafati Sunniyya in Calicut upon successful completion of a religious training program.

7. For a useful analysis of its use and circulation, see Kooria 2018.

8. The local *vaidyans* and *hakims* (Hindu and Muslim doctors, respectively) would be embroiled in negotiating and contesting with European medicine in India from the early twentieth century, regarding the scientific basis for their respective healing systems, practices, and medical procedures. See Arnold 1993.

9. Personal communication with O. B. Roopesh on March 26, 2022.

10. These texts are taught in madrassas in Kerala and various parts of India run by the Samastha Kerala Sunni Vidyabhyasa Board, which controls more than 8,000 madrassas.

11. This practice has now changed. Now those who slaughter an animal as part of the tonsure ceremony distribute the meat on their own.

Chapter 4

1. A similar argument has been made by Pandian (2022) while analysing how upper castes in India transcode caste in other terms. The ideas of vegetarianism, hygiene etc. are conceived as personal affair, as choice made by the upper castes. These modern inflections are then used by upper caste Hindus to construct an identity for themselves. This notion of individualization of hygiene was not possible for the lower castes because they were always already embroiled in filthy, dirty, and unclean stuff. Pandian's point is that caste was defined in India as the other of the modern. Ayisha seems to be occupying this kind of a modern positionality here to launch a critique of humiliation brought about by Mappilas. How barber women construct a self-identity for themselves needs to be further explored.

Chapter 5

1. The term *jāti* is often used interchangeably with *caste* to refer to varna hierarchy, but the term can also mean a subcaste, or even an exogamous section (clan) to which one belongs. See Dumont ([1980] 1998, 62).

2. What we predominantly see is a discourse around caste. See Ahmad (2023) and Rai (2018). A clear exception has been Lee's (2018b) work on the halalkhor. My point is that to understand how "caste" works among Muslims, we need to look more into lived Islam rather than the outside.

3. Robin Jeffrey (1976) has also remarked in his study of Nairs in Travancore that Christians were integrated into the local caste system. It is also important to note that while the Brahminical notion of the caste system in terms of purity and pollution was strongly implemented in Kerala, it has been observed that both Nairs and Ezhavas have been able since the British period to make considerable social mobility in Kerala, with a corresponding decline of Brahmin (Namboodiri) material dominance (See Jeffrey 2012; Osella and Osella 2000b).

4. One can observe two forms of kinship systems in Malabar: patrilineal and matrilineal. Matrilineal communities are concentrated along the coast and have been involved in Indian Ocean trade and commerce for centuries. Matriliny itself became a key political issue among Muslims in Malabar in the 1930s and, over time, a majority of Muslims have turned to patrilineal descent although various practices associated with matriliny, such as matrilocality, still exist in some parts of coastal Malabar. For further details, see Panakkal and Arif (2024); Kottakkunnummal (2014). As I mentioned earlier, my book is focused on inland Muslims and their social dynamics.

5. The term actually means brotherhood, but it is used among Muslims in North India to refer to lineage or caste groups. See Alavi (2001) for further details.

6. The term *Sunni* is used to refer to the traditionalists here in contrast to the reformists who are termed either *Wahabi* or *Salafi* in Kerala. See Osella and Osella (2013).

7. These two tribes originated from brothers who are implied by the titular name. The prophet was born in the tribe of Hāshim and these two tribes are compatible with each other for marriage.

8. Honor societies and honor cultures have been much studied and debated in anthropological literature. Honor, with its complementary opposite, shame, was said to be the foundation of societies that evaluate their members according to their adherence to a strict code of conduct,

requiring particular manifestations of pride, male independence, and assertiveness, whereas women needed to remain chaste and show modesty and sexual constraint. For an examination of these honor-based societies and the surrounding debates, see Kamir (2006).

Chapter 6

1. The term *Dalit* is used as a political category to refer to the scheduled castes among Hindus in India. They have been the former untouchable groups in India.

2. For this division of time conceptualized along the lines of task/labor and work/leisure, see E. P. Thompson's (1967) influential article.

3. This is a line of research is worth pursuing, particularly to understand how capital and global security discourses intertwine with communalism in India and how it affects different groups among Muslims. Scholars working on lower class Muslims neglect this aspect to locate communalism solely as a competing arena of power and representation within the realm of the state. See Ansari (2018).

Chapter 7

1. The Arabic term *Allah* is commonly used by Muslims in Malabar. There are also two other Malayalam terms: *padachavan* and *thamburān*. The former term means the creator and the latter term was used in the past as a respectful address to the Hindu Nayar landlords by their lower-caste servants.

2. Such claims have broader resonances with some north Indian Muslim groups. One important movement making such assertions emerged in Bihar in the 1990s, which came to be referred to as the Pasmanda movement. To understand the genealogy of such contentions, see Ansari (2009) and contemporary Pasmanda articulations in various contexts; see also Ahmad (2023), Ahmed (2023), and Bellamy (2021).

3. I explain the genealogy of these groups among Muslims in Chapter 2. Sayyids claim descent from the prophet Muhammad. Mappilas are mainly converts from lower-caste Hindus, but they also include converts from high castes.

4. Middle class has largely been understood as an income/economic category and therefore a matter of privilege, but, as Jodhka and Prakash (2016) have shown, it is not a homogeneous category; rather, it is differentiated by caste, class, and religion, which give different middle classes varied capacities and access to resources.

5. Such children are considered bastards and are never spoken of in relation to their fathers. If the child is a girl, the *qadi* acts as her guardian in the case of marriage. Personal communication, Rasheed Saqafi, April 5, 2022.

6. By invented history, I mean the stories initiated, discussed, and orally transmitted among barbers in Malabar that seek to construct a new identity and past for themselves. The term does not presuppose a judgement that the "invented history" is either false or true. For a similar phenomenon among Dalits, see Badri Narayan (2004). As an anthropologist, I am interested in the force of such phenomena and the works that are done by them.

BIBLIOGRAPHY

Abraham, Santhosh. "Constructing the 'Extraordinary Criminals': Mappila Muslims and Legal Encounters in Early British Colonial Malabar." *Journal of World History* 25, no. 2–3 (2014): 373–395.

Agrama, Hussain A. "Ethics, Tradition, Authority: Toward an Anthropology of the Fatwa." *American Ethnologist* 37, no. 1 (2010): 2–18.

Ahmad, Imtiaz. "The Ashraf and Ajlaf Categories in Indo-Muslim Society." *Economic and Political Weekly* 2, no. 19 (1967): 887, 889–891.

———, ed. *Family, Kinship and Marriage Among Muslims in India.* Manohar, 1976.

———, ed. *Caste and Social Stratification Among Muslims in India.* Manohar, 1978.

———, ed. *Ritual and Religion Among Muslims in India.* Manohar, 1981.

Ahmad, Tausif. "Politics of Recognition and Caste Among Muslims: A Study of Shekhra Biradari of Bihar, India." *Caste: A Global Journal on Social Exclusion* 4, no. 1 (2023): 92–108.

Ahmad, Zarin. *Delhi's Meatscapes: Muslim Butchers in a Transforming Mega-City.* Oxford University Press, 2018.

Ahmed, Azeem. "Social Mobility and Politicisation of Caste Among the Rayeens of Uttar Pradesh." *Contemporary South Asia* 31, no. 3 (2023): 442–457.

Ahmed, S. M. Faizan. "Making Beautiful: Male Workers in Beauty Parlours." *Men and Masculinities* 9, no. 2 (2006): 168–185.

Ahmed, Shahab. *What Is Islam?: The Importance of Being Islamic.* Princeton University Press, 2016.

Al-Azri, Khalid. "Change and Conflict in Contemporary Omani Society: The Case of Kafa'a in Marriage." *British Journal of Middle Eastern Studies* 37 (2010): 121–137.

Al Fiqhul Islami. Islamic Educational Board of India. (n.d.).

Alam, Arshad. "Challenging the Ashrafs: The Politics of Pasmanda Muslim Mahaz." *Journal of Muslim Minority Affairs* 29 (2009): 171–181.

Alatas, Ismail F. "Dreaming Saints: Exploratory Authority and Islamic Praxes of History in Central Java." *Journal of the Royal Anthropological Institute* 26, no. 1 (2020): 67–85.

Alavi, Hamza. "The Two Biraderis: Kinship in Rural West Punjab." In *Muslim Communities of South Asia: Culture, Society and Power,* edited by T. N. Madan. Manohar, 2001.

Ali, Syed. "Collective and Elective Ethnicity: Caste Among Urban Muslims in India." *Sociological Forum* 17, no. 4 (2002): 593–620.

Aloysius, G. *Religion as Emancipatory Identity: A Buddhist Movement Among the Tamils under Colonialism.* New Age Publishers, 1998.

Ambedkar, B. R. *Annihilation of Caste.* Dalit Sahitya Akademi, 1987.

———. *The Untouchables: Who Were They and Why They Became Untouchables.* Siddharth Books, (1948) 2008.

———. *The Buddha and His Dhamma: A Critical Edition*, edited by Akash Singh Rathore and Ajay Verma. Oxford University Press, 2011.

Amir, Safwan. "Contempt and Labour: An Exploration Through Muslim Barbers of South Asia." *Religions* 10, no. 616 (2019): 1–14.

———. "Temporary Sisterhoods: Thinking Ethics Through Postnatal Care Among South Asian Muslims." In *Care(ful) Relationships Between Mothers and the Caregivers They Hire*, edited by Katie B. Garner and Andrea O'Reilly. Demeter Press, 2024.

Ammerman, Nancy. *Studying Lived Religion: Contexts and Practices*. NYU Press, 2021.

Anchillath, Abdulla. *Malabārile Islāminte Ādhunika Pūrva Charithram* [*Pre-Modern History of Islam in Malabar*]. SPCS, 2015.

Anjum, Tanvir. "'Be Hell for Those Who Call Me Saiyyid': Social Stratification Among the South Asian Muslims and the Sufi Worldview." *Pakistan Journal of History and Culture* 32, no. 2 (2011): 43–64.

Ansari, Ghaus. *Muslim Caste in Uttar Pradesh: A Study of Culture Contact*. Ethnographic and Folk Culture Society, 1960.

Ansari, Khalid A. "Rethinking the Pasmanda Movement." *Economic and Political Weekly* 44, no. 13 (2009): 8–10.

———. "Contesting Communalism(s): Preliminary Reflections on Pasmanda Muslim Narratives from North India." *Prabuddha: Journal of Social Equality* 1, no. 1 (2018): 78–104.

———. "Revisiting the Minority Imagination: An Inquiry into the Anticaste Pasmanda-Muslim Discourse in India." *Critical Philosophy of Race* 11, no. 1 (2023): 120–147.

Ansari, M. T. "Refiguring the Fanatic, 1836–1922." In *Subaltern Studies, XII: Muslims, Dalits and the Fabrications of History*, edited by Shail Mayaram, M. S. S. Pandian, and Ajay Skaria. Permanent Black, 2005.

Appadurai, Arju. "Putting Hierarchy in Its Place." *Cultural Anthropology* 3, no. 1 (1988): 36–49.

Arafath, P. K. Yasser. "The Nadapuram Enigma: A History of Violence and Communalism in North Malabar (1957–2015)." *Economic and Political Weekly* 51, no. 15 (2016): 47–55.

Arnold, David. *Colonizing the Body: State Medicine and Epidemic Disease in Nineteenth-Century India*. University of California Press, 1993.

Asad, Talal. "The Idea of an Anthropology of Islam." *Qui Parle* 17, no. 2 (2009): 1–30.

Asempasah, Rogers, and Christabel Sam. "Reconstituting the Self: Of Names, Discourses and Agency in Amma Darko." *International Journal of Humanities and Cultural Studies* 2, no. 4 (2016): 154–168.

Aslam, E. S. M. "Caste, Conversion and Collective Resistance: Understanding Religious Conversion to Islam in South Malabar 1850–1930." MPhil diss., Jawaharlal Nehru University, 2013.

Ayyar, K. V. Krishna. *The Zamorins of Calicut: From the Earliest Times Down to A.D. 1806*. University of Calicut, 1999.

Azam, Shireen. "The Political Life of Muslim Caste: Articulations and Frictions Within a Pasmanda Identity." *Contemporary South Asia* 31, no. 3 (2023): 426–441.

Babb, Lawrence A. *The Divine Hierarchy: Popular Hinduism in Central India*. Columbia University Press, 1975.

———. "Destiny and Responsibility: Karma in Popular Hinduism." In *Karma: An Anthropological Inquiry*, edited by C. F. Keyes and V. E. Daniel. University of California Press, 1983a.

———. "The Physiology of Redemption." *History of Religions* 22, no. 4 (1983b): 293–312.

———. *Redemptive Encounters: Three Modern Styles in the Hindu Tradition.* University of California Press, 1986.

Balakrishnan, P. K. *Jathi Vyavasthithiyum Kerala Charithravum* [*Caste System and Kerala History*]. DC Books, 2004.

Barbosa, Duarte. *Description of the Coasts of East Africa and Malabar in the Beginning of the Sixteenth Century.* Cambridge University Press, 2009.

Bayly C. A. *Rulers, Townsmen and Bazaars: North Indian Society in the Age of British Expansion, 1770–1870.* Oxford University Press, (1983) 2002.

Bayly, Susan. *Saints, Goddesses and Kings: Muslims and Christians in South Indian Society, 1700–1900.* Cambridge University Press, 1989.

Beena. *Ossāthi* (a Muslim barber woman). DC Books, 2017.

Beidelman, Thomas. *A Comparative Analysis of the Jajmani System.* J. J. Augustin Incorporated Publisher, 1959.

Bell, Daniel, and Wang Pei. *Just Hierarchy: Why Social Hierarchies Matter in China and the Rest of the World.* Princeton University Press, 2020.

Bellamy, Carla. "Being Muslim the Chippa Way: Caste Identity as Islamic Identity in a Low-Caste Indian Muslim Community." *Contributions to Indian Sociology* 55, no. 2 (2021): 224–253.

Benson, Janet E. "Politics and Muslim Ethnicity in South India." *Journal of Anthropological Research* 39, no. 1 (1983): 42–59.

Béteille, André. "Homo Hierarchicus, Homo Equalis." *Modern Asian Studies* 13, no. 4 (1979): 529–548.

Bhatty, Zarina. "Social Stratification Among Muslims in India." In *Caste: Its Twentieth-Century Avatar*, edited by M. N. Srinivas. Viking, 1996.

Bird, Tess. "Being Alone Together: Yoga, Bodywork, and Intimate Sociality in American Households." *Anthropology & Medicine* 28, no. 3 (2021): 395–410.

Black, Paula. *The Beauty Industry: Gender, Culture, Pleasure.* Routledge, 2004.

Black, Shameem. "Love Marriage." *South Asia: Journal of South Asian Studies* 40, no. 2 (2017): 345–348.

Bourdieu, Pierre. *The Algerians.* Translated by A. C. M. Ross. Beacon Press, 1962.

———. *Outline of a Theory of Practice.* Translated by Richard Nice. Cambridge University Press, 1977.

———. "The Forms of Capital." In *Handbook of Theory and Research for the Sociology of Education*, edited by J. Richardson. Greenwood, 1986.

———. *The Logic of Practice.* Translated by Richard Nice. Stanford University Press, 1990.

———. "Pierre Bourdieu on Marriage Strategies." *Population and Development Review* 28, no. 3 (2002): 549–558.

Bourdieu, Pierre, and Loïc J. D. Wacquant. *An Invitation to Reflexive Sociology.* Polity Press, 1992.

Breman, Jan. *Beyond Patronage and Exploitation: Changing Agrarian Relations in South Gujarat.* Oxford University Press, 1993.

Brewer, Jeffrey D. "Bimanese Personal Names: Meaning and Use." *Ethnology* 20, no. 3 (1981): 203–215.

Casanova, Erynn M. De. "Embodied Inequality: The Experience of Domestic Work in Urban Ecuador." *Gender and Society* 27, no. 4 (2013): 561–585.

Chaitanya, K. M. "Sati is Passé. But What About Made Snana?" *BangaloreMirror* December 2, 2014. https://bangaloremirror.indiatimes.com/opinion/views/western-ghats-the-kukke -subramanya-sarpa-dosha-made-snana/articleshow/45351126.cms

Chakrabarty, Dipesh. *Provincializing Europe: Postcolonial Thought and Historical Difference.* Oxford University Press, 2001.

———. "The Dalit Body: A Reading for the Anthropocene." In *The Empire of Disgust: Prejudice, Discrimination, and Policy in India and the US*, edited by Zoya Hasan et al. Oxford University Press, 2018.

Chapple, Christopher. *Karma and Creativity.* State University of New York Press, 1986.

Clark-Decès, Isabelle. "Toward an Anthropology of Exchange in Tamil Nadu." *Hindu Studies* 22 (1018): 197–215.

Coffey, Julia. "Bodies, Body Work and Gender: Exploring a Deleuzian Approach." *Journal of Gender Studies* 22, no. 1 (2013): 3–16.

Cohn, Bernard S. *An Anthropologist Among the Historians and Other Essays.* Oxford University Press, 1987.

D'Souza, Victor S. "Social Organization and Marriage Customs of the Moplahs on the South-West Coast of India." *Anthropos* 54, no. 3/4 (1959): 487–516.

———. "A Unique Custom Regarding Mahr (Dowry) Observed by Certain Indian Muslims of South India." *Islamic Culture* 29, no. 4 (1965): 28–29.

———. "Status Groups Among the Moplahs on the South-West Coast of India." In *Caste and Social Stratification Among Muslims in India*, edited by Imtiaz Ahmad. Manohar, 1978.

Dale, Stephen F. *Islamic Society on the South Asian Frontier: The Mappilas of Malabar, 1498–1922.* Clarendon Press, 1980.

Das, Veena. *Life and Words: Violence and the Descent into the Everyday.* University of California Press, 2007.

———. "Engaging the Life of the Other: Love and Everyday Life." In *Ordinary Ethics: Anthropology, Language, and Action*, edited by Michael Lambek. Fordham University Press, 2010.

Dawson, Hannah. "'Making Plans through People': The Social Embeddedness of Entrepreneurship in Urban South Africa." *Social Dynamics* 47, no. 3 (2021): 389–402.

Deeb, Lara, and Mona Harb. *Leisurely Islam: Negotiating Geography and Morality in Shi'ite South Beirut.* Princeton University Press, 2014.

Deliege, Robert. "The Myths of Origin of the Indian Untouchables." *Man, New Series* 28, no. 3 (1993): 533–549.

Deshpande, Ashwini. *The Grammar of Caste: Economic Discrimination in Contemporary India.* Oxford University Press, 2011.

De Neve, Geert. "Economic Liberalisation, Class Restructuring and Social Space in Provincial South India." In *The Meaning of the Local: Politics of Place in Urban India*, edited by Geert De Neve and Henrike Donner. Routledge, 2006.

Dhar, Rajib L. "Intercaste Marriage: A Study from the Indian Context." *Marriage & Family Review* 49, no. 1 (2013): 1–25.

Di Nunzio, Marco. "Marginality as a Politics of Limited Entitlements: Street Life and the Dilemma of Inclusion in Urban Ethiopia." *American Ethnologist* 44, no. 1 (2017): 1–13.

Dilley, Roy. *Islamic Knowledge and Caste Knowledge Practices Among Haalpulaar'en in Senegal: Between Mosque and Termite Mound.* Edinburgh University Press for the International African Institute, 2004.

Dirks, Nicholas. *The Hollow Crown: Ethnohistory of an Indian Kingdom.* Cambridge University Press, 1987.

———. *Castes of Mind: Colonialism and the Making of Modern India.* Princeton University Press, 2001.

Donald, Nidhin. "Every Family Its Own Historian? The Case of Syrian Christian Family Histories." *Economic and Political Weekly* 57, no. 28 (2022): 57–64.

Doron, Assa. "The Needle and the Sword: Boatmen, Priests and the Ritual Economy of Varanasi." *South Asia: Journal of South Asian Studies* 29 no. 3 (2006): 345–367.

———. *Life on the Ganga: Boatmen and the Ritual Economy of Banaras.* Foundation Books, 2013.

———. "Unclean, Unseen: Social Media, Civic Action and Urban Hygiene in India." *South Asia: Journal of South Asian Studies* 39, no. 4 (2016): 715–739.

Doron, Assa, and Robin Jeffrey. "Mobile-izing: Democracy, Organization and India's First 'Mass Mobile Phone' Elections." *Journal of Asian Studies* 71, no. 1 (2012): 63–80.

———. *Cell Phone Nation: How Mobile Phones Have Revolutionised Business, Politics and Ordinary Life in India.* Hachette India, 2013.

Douglas, Mary. *Purity and Danger: An Analysis of the Concepts of Pollution and Taboo.* Routledge, (1966) 1988.

Dumont, Louis. *From Mandeville to Marx: The Genesis and Triumph of Economic Ideology.* University of Chicago Press, 1977.

———. *Homo Hierarchicus: The Caste System and Its Implications.* University of Chicago Press, (1980) 1998.

———. *Essays on Individualism: Modern Ideology in Anthropological Perspective.* University of Chicago Press, 1986.

Düwell, Marcus, et al., eds. *The Cambridge Handbook of Human Dignity: Interdisciplinary Perspectives.* Cambridge University Press, 2014.

Eaton, Richard. *Essays on Islam and Indian History.* Oxford University Press, 2000.

Edensor, Tim. "The Culture of the Indian Street." In *Images of the Street: Planning, Identity and Control in Public Space,* edited by Nicholas. R. Fyfe. Routledge, 1998.

Evans-Pritchard, E. E. *Witchcraft, Oracles and Magic Among the Azande.* Oxford University Press, 1976.

Fadil, Nadia, and Mayanthi Fernando. "Rediscovering the 'Everyday' Muslim: Notes on an Anthropological Divide." *HAU: Journal of Ethnographic Theory* 5 no. 2 (2015): 59–88.

Fahm, Abdulgafar O. "Everything Has Beauty but Not Everyone Sees It: An Islamic Alternative to Assessing Beauty." *Journal of Intercultural Communication Research* 49 no. 3 (2020): 211–226.

Fanselow, Frank S. "The Disinvention of Caste Among Tamil Muslims." In *Caste Today,* edited by C. J. Fuller. Oxford University Press, 1996.

Foucault, Michel. "The Subject and Power." *Critical Inquiry* 8, no. 4 (1982): 777–795.

Freitag, Sandria. B. *Collective Action and Community: Public Arenas and the Emergence of Communalism in North India.* University of California Press, 1989.

Frembgen, Jürgen Wasim. "Marginality, Sexuality and the Body: Professional Masseurs in Urban Muslim Punjab." *Asia Pacific Journal of Anthropology* 9, no. 1 (2008): 1–28.

———. "Itinerary Ear-Cleaners: Notes on a Marginal Profession in Urban Muslim Punjab." *Anthropos* 106, no. 1 (2011): 180–184.

Friedmann, Yohanan. "Qissat Shakarwatī Farmād: A Tradition Concerning the Introduction of Islam to Malabar." *Israel Oriental Studies* 5 (1975): 233–258.

Fuller, C. J. "Misconceiving the Grain Heap: A Critique of the Concept of the Indian Jajmani System." In *Money and the Morality of Exchange*, edited by Jonathan Parry and Maurice Bloch. Cambridge University Press, 1989.

Fuller, C. J. "Kerala Christians and the Caste System." *Man, New Series* 11, no. 1 (1976): 53–70.

———, ed. *Caste Today*. Oxford University Press, 1996.

Fuller, C. J., and Haripriya Narasimhan. "Companionate Marriage in India: The Changing Marriage System in a Middle-Class Brahman Subcaste." *Journal of the Royal Anthropological Institute* 14 (2008): 736–754.

Gautier, Laurence, and Julien Levesque. "Introduction: Historicizing Sayyid-ness: Social Status and Muslim Identity in South Asia." *Journal of the Royal Asiatic Society* 30, no. 3 (2020): 383–393.

Gayer, Laurent, and Christophe Jaffrelot, eds. *Muslims in Indian Cities: Trajectories of Marginalisation*. HarperCollins, 2012.

Geertz, Clifford. *The Interpretation of Cultures: Selected Essays*. Fontana Press, 1993.

Ghosh, Papia. "Partition's Biharis." *Comparative Studies of South Asia, Africa and the Middle East* 17, no. 2 (1997): 21–34.

Giddens, Anthony. *The Transformation of Intimacy: Sexuality, Love and Eroticism in Modern Societies*. Stanford University Press, 1992.

Gidwani, Vinay, and K. Sivaramakrishnan. "Circular Migration and Rural Cosmopolitanism in India." *Contributions to Indian Sociology* 37, no. 1–2 (2003): 339–367.

Gilmartin, David, and Bruce Lawrence, eds. *Beyond Turk and Hindu: Rethinking Religious Identities in Islamicate South Asia*. University Press of Florida, 2000.

Goodhart, Michael. "Constructing Dignity: Human Rights as a Praxis of Egalitarian Freedom." *Journal of Human Rights* 17, no. 4 (2018): 403–417.

Gorringe, Hugo. *Untouchable Citizens: Dalit Movements and Democratisation in Tamil Nadu*. Sage Publications, 2005.

———. *Panthers in Parliament: Dalits, Caste, and Political Power in South India*. Oxford University Press, 2017.

Gould, Harold A. "Priest and Contrapriest: A Structural Analysis of Jajmani Relationships in Hindu Plains and Nilgiri Hills." *Contributions to Indian Sociology* 1 (1967): 26–55.

Graeber, David. *Toward an Anthropological Theory of Value: The False Coing of Our Own Dreams*. Palgrave, 2001.

———. "It Is Value that Brings Universes into Being." *HAU: Journal of Ethnographic Theory* 3, no. 2 (2013): 219–243.

Guha, Ranajit. *Dominance Without Hegemony: History and Power in Colonial India*. Harvard University Press, 1997.

Guha, Sumit. *Beyond Caste: Identity and Power in South Asia*. Permanent Black, 2016.

Gundert, Hermann, ed. *A Malayalam and English Dictionary*. C. Stolz Basel Mission Book & Tract Depository, 1872.

Gupta, Dipankar. *Interrogating Caste: Understanding Hierarchy and Difference in Indian Society*. Penguin Books, 2000.

———, ed. *Anti-Utopia: Essential Writings of André Béteille*. Oxford University Press, 2005.

Guru, Gopal, ed. *Humiliation: Claims and Context*. Oxford University Press, 2009.

Hagman, George. "The Sense of Beauty." *International Journal of Psychoanalysis* 83 (2002): 661–674.

Haithami, Shuaibul. Samastha Wayanad Jilla Ulama Conference [Samastha Wayanad District Ulama Conference], September 13, 2023, video, 3:48:40-4:18:49. https://www.youtube.com /watch?v=NTyga3Sz_9A.

Hall, Stuart. "Foucault: Power, Knowledge and Discourse." In *Discourse Theory and Practice: A Reader*, edited by Margaret Wetherell, et al. Sage Publications, 2001.

Haneefa, Muhammed. "Muslim Barbers of South Malabar and Covid-19: Homogamy, Caste Occupation and Economic Hardship." *Anthropology Today* 37, no. 1 (2021): 9–12.

Haridas, V. V. *Zamorins and the Political Culture of Medieval Kerala*. Orient Blackswan, 2016.

Harikrishnan, S. *Social Spaces and the Public Sphere: A Spatial-History of Modernity in Kerala*. Routledge, 2023.

Hasnain, Nadeem, ed. *Islam and Muslim Communities in South Asia*. Serials Publications, 2006.

Haynes, Naomi, and Jason Hickel. "Introduction: Hierarchy, Value, and the Value of Hierarchy." *Social Analysis* 60, no. 4 (2016): 1–20.

Heesterman, J. C. *The Inner Conflict of Tradition: Essays in Indian Ritual, Kingship, and Society*. University of Chicago Press, 1985.

Heller, Patrick. *The Labour of Development: Workers and the Transformation of Capitalism in Kerala, India*. Cornell University Press, 1999.

Ho, Engseng. *The Graves of Tarim: Genealogy and Mobility Across the Indian Ocean*. University of California Press, 2006.

Hocart, A. M. *Caste: A Comparative Study*. Russell & Russell, (1950) 1968.

Hochschild, Arlie Russell. *The Managed Heart: Commercialization of Human Feeling*. University of California Press, 2012.

Hossain, Mozaffar. "The Story of Fatwa." *Interventions* 4, no. 2 (2002): 237–242.

Innes, C. A. *Madras District Gazetteer, Malabar*. Government Press, 1908.

Jairath, Vinod K., ed. *Frontiers of Embedded Muslim Communities in India*. Routledge, 2011.

Jeffrey, Craig, et al. *Degrees Without Freedom: Education, Masculinities, and Unemployment in North India*. Stanford University Press, 2008.

Jeffrey, Robin. *The Decline of Nayar Dominance: Society and Politics in Travancore, 1847–1908*. Sussex University Press, 1976.

———. "Matriliny, Marxism, and the Birth of the Communist Party in Kerala, 1930–1940." *Journal of Asian Studies* 38, no. 1 (1978): 77–92.

———. "'Destroy Capitalism!': Growing Solidarity of Alleppey's Coir Workers, 1930–40." *Economic and Political Weekly* 19, no. 29 (1984): 1159–1165.

———. *Politics, Women and Well Being: How Kerala Became "a Model."* Oxford University Press, 2001.

Jodhka, Surinder S. "Sikhism and the Caste Question: Dalits and Their Politics in Contemporary Punjab." *Contributions to Indian Sociology* 38, no. 1–2 (2004): 165–192.

———. "Dalits in Business: Self-Employed Scheduled Castes in North-West India." *Economic and Political Weekly* 45, no. 11 (2010): 41–48.

———. *Caste in Contemporary India*. Routledge, 2015.

———. *Caste: Oxford India Short Introductions*. Oxford University Press, 2012.

Jodhka, Surinder S., and Aseem Prakash. *The Indian Middle Class*. Oxford University Press, 2016.

Jones, Charlotte, et al. "Hospitality Work as Social Reproduction: Embodied and Emotional Labour During COVID-19." *Sociology* 58, no. 2 (2023): 471–488.

Kamir, Orit. "Honor and Dignity in the Film *Unforgiven*: Implications for Sociological Theory." *Law & Society Review* 40, no. 1 (2006): 193–234.

Kannan, K. P. "Rural Labour Relations and Development Dilemmas in Kerala: Reflections on the Dilemmas of a Socially Transforming Labour Force in a Slowly Growing Economy." *Journal of Peasant Studies* 26, no. 2–3 (1999): 140–181.

Kannan, K. P., and K. S. Hari. "Revisiting Kerala's Gulf Connection: Half a Century of Emigration, Remittances and Their Macroeconomic Impact, 1972–2020." *Indian Journal of Labour Economics* 63 (2020): 941–967.

Kareem, K.K. Muhomed Abdul. *Mampuram Thangal [Sayyid Mampuram]*. C. H. Muhammed and Sons, 1957.

Karinkurayil, Mohamed Shafeeq. "The Days of Plenty: Images of First Generation Malayali Migrants in the Arabian Gulf." *South Asian Diaspora* 13, no. 1 (2020): 51–64.

———. "A Strangeness One Can Occupy: Clothes and Their Codes in the Photographs of Gulf Migrants from Kerala." In *Migration in the Making of the Gulf Space: Social, Political, and Cultural Dimensions*, edited by Antia Mato Bouzas and Lorenzo Casini. Berghahn Books, 2022.

———. *The Gulf Migrant Archives in Kerala: Reading Borders and Belonging*. Oxford University Press, 2024.

Kasim, Muhammadali P. "Mappila Muslim Masculinities: A History of Contemporary Abjectification." *Men and Masculinities* 23, nos. 3–4 (2020): 542–557.

———. "Men, Capital and Hegemony: Male-Male Axis of Mappila Muslim Masculinities." *Journal of Men's Studies* 30, no. 2 (2022): 213–229.

———. "Mappila Muslim Men, Islamic Piety, and Reflexive Masculinities." *Contemporary Islam* (2025) Online first. https://doi.org/10.1007/s11562-025-00575-2

Kaviraj, Sudipta. "Filth and the Public Sphere: Concepts and Practices About Space in Calcutta." *Public Culture* 10, no. 1 (1997): 83–113.

Keeler, Ward. *The Traffic in Hierarchy: Masculinity and Its Others in Buddhist Burma*. University of Hawai'i Press, 2017.

Kerfoot, Deborah. "Body Work: Estrangement, Disembodiment and the Organizational Other." In *Body and Organization*, edited by John Hassard et al. Sage Publications, 2000.

Keyser-Verreault, Amélie. "The Continuum of Regaining One's Body: Childbirth and Reproductive Choice Under Beauty Pressure in Taiwan." *European Journal of Cultural Studies* 26, no. 2 (2022): 167–188.

Khan, C. G. Hussain. "Muslim Kinship in Dravidian Milieu." *Economic and Political Weekly* 38, no. 46 (2003): 4902–4904.

Khare, R. S. *The Untouchable as Himself: Ideology, Identity, and the Pragmatism Among Lucknow Chamars*. Cambridge University Press, 1984.

———, ed. *Caste, Hierarchy and Individualism: Indian Critiques of Louis Dumont's Contributions*. Oxford University Press, 2009.

Kiliyamannil, Thahir Jamal. "Neither Global nor Local: Reorienting the Study of Islam in South Asia." *Asian Journal of Social Science* 51, no. 4 (2023): 244–251.

Kooria, Mahmood. "Texts as Objects of Value and Veneration: Islamic Law Books in the Indian Ocean Littoral." *Sociology of Islam* 6, no. 1 (2018): 60–83.

Kottakkunnummal, Manaf. "Indigenous Customs and Colonial Law: Contestations in Religion, Gender and Family Among Matrilineal Mappila Muslims in Colonial Malabar, Kerala, c. 1910–1928." *SAGE Open* 4, no. 1 (2014): 1–12.

Koya, S. M. Muhammad. *Mappilas of Malabar: Studies in Social and Cultural History*. Sandhya Publications, 1983.

Ku, Kun-Hui, and Thomas Gibson. "Hierarchy and Egalitarianism in Austronesia." *Anthropological Forum* 29, no. 3 (2019): 205–215.

Kugle, Scott, and Roxani E. Margariti. "Narrating Community: The Qiṣṣat Shakarwatī Farmāḍ and Accounts of Origin in Kerala and Around the Indian Ocean." *Journal of the Economic and Social History of the Orient* 60, no. 4 (2017): 337–380.

Kugler, Adriana D., and Santosh Kumar. "Preference for Boys, Family Size, and Educational Attainment in India." *Demography* 54, no. 3 (2017): 835–859.

Kumar, Mukul. "Contemporary Relevance of Jajmani Relations in Rural India." *Journal of Rural Studies* 48 (2016): 1–10.

Kunju, A. P. Ibrahim. *Mappila Muslims of Kerala: Their History and Culture*. Sandhya Publications, 1989.

Lakshmi, L. R. S. *The Malabar Muslims: A Different Perspective*. Foundation Books, 2012.

Laws, Megan. "Egalitarianism". In *The Open Encyclopedia of Anthropology*, edited by Felix Stein, 2022. Online: http://doi.org/10.29164/22egalitarianism.

Leach, Edmund. *Political Systems of Highland Burma*. Athlone Press, 1970.

Lee, Joel. "Caste." In *Encyclopedia of Indian Religions: Islam, Judaism, and Zorastrianism*, edited by Z. R. Kassam et al. Springer, 2018a.

———. "Who Is the True Halalkhor? Genealogy and Ethics in Dalit Muslim Oral Traditions." *Contributions to Indian Sociology* 52, no. 1 (2018b): 1–27.

———. "Disgust and Untouchability: Towards an Affective Theory of Caste." *South Asian History and Culture* 12, no. 2–3 (2021a): 310–327.

———. *Deceptive Majority: Dalits, Hinduism, and Underground Religion*. Cambridge University Press, 2021b.

Lemons, Katherine. *Divorcing Traditions: Islamic Marriage Law and the Making of Indian Secularism*. Cornell University Press, 2019.

Levesque, Julien. "Debates on Muslim Caste in North India and Pakistan: From Colonial Ethnography to Pasmanda Mobilization." *CSH-IFP Working Paper* 15 (2020): 1–20.

———. "Does Caste Play a Political Role Among Muslims in India?" *GIS Asie*, April 2021. hal03196813.

Levesque, Julien, and Soheb Niazi. "Caste Politics, Minority Representation, and Social Mobility: The Associational Life of Muslim Caste in India." *Contemporary South Asia* 33, no. 3 (2023): 413–425.

Lévi-Strauss, Claude. *Myth and Meaning*. Routledge, 2001.

Lorenzen, David N. "Bhakti." In *The Hindu World*, edited by Sushil Mittal and Gene Thursby. Routledge, 2004.

Lukose, Ritty A. *Liberalization's Children: Gender, Youth, and Consumer Citizenship in Globalizing India*. Duke University Press, 2009.

Madan, T. N., ed. *Muslim Communities of South Asia: Culture, Society and Power*. Manohar, 2001.

Mahmood, Saba. *Politics of Piety: The Islamic Revival and the Feminist Subject*. Princeton University Press, 2005.

Makhdum, Sheikh Z. *Tuhfat-Al-Mujāhidīn*. Translated by S. Muhammad Husayn Nainar. University of Madras, 1942.

Malpas, Jeff, and Norelle Lickiss, eds. *Perspectives on Human Dignity: A Conversation*. Springer, 2007.

Manjule, Nagraj, dir. *Fandry*. E. V. Productions, 2013.

Manor, James. "Prologue: Caste and Politics in Recent Times." In *Caste in Indian Politics*, edited by Rajni Kothari. Orient Blackswan, (1970) 2010.

Marlow, Louis. *Hierarchy and Egalitarianism in Islamic Thought*. Cambridge University Press, 1997.

Marva M. "Traditional Maternity Carers of Malabar: Caste, Religion and Knowledge." *Ala: A Kerala Studies Blog* 4, December 14, 2018. https://alablog.in/issues/4/maternity-carers-of -malabar/.

Masquelier, Adeline. *Women and Islamic Revival in a West African Town*. Indiana University Press, 2009.

Mathur, P. R. G. *The Mappila Fisherfolk of Kerala*. Kerala Historical Society, 1978.

———. "Social Stratification Among Muslims in Kerala." In *Frontiers of Embedded Muslim Communities in India*, edited by Vinod K. Jairath. Routledge, 2011.

McGuire, Meredith. B. *Lived Religion: Faith and Practice in Everyday Life*. Oxford University Press, 2008.

Mehta, Deepak. *Work, Ritual, Biography: A Muslim Community in North India*. Oxford University Press, 1997.

Menon, Dilip M. "Becoming 'Hindu' and 'Muslim': Identity and Conflict in Malabar, 1900–1936." *CDS Working Paper* 225 (1994a): 1–27.

———. *Caste, Nationalism and Communism in South India, Malabar, 1900–1948*. Cambridge University Press, 1994b.

Metcalf, Barbara D., and Thomas R. Metcalf. *A Concise History of Modern India*. Cambridge University Press, 2001.

Miller, Daniel. "Exchange and Alienation in the "Jajmani" System." *Journal of Anthropological Research* 42, no. 4 (1986): 535–556.

Miller, E. J. "Caste and Territory in Malabar." *American Anthropologist* 56, no. 3 (1954): 410–420.

Miller, Roland E. *Mappila Muslims of Kerala: A Study in Islamic Trends*. Orient Longman, 1976.

Mines, Mattison. "Islamisation and Muslim Ethnicity in South India." *Man* 10, no. 3 (1975): 404–419.

Mittermaier, Amira. *Dreams That Matter: Egyptian Landscapes of the Imagination*. University of California Press, 2010.

Mohan, Sanal P. *Modernity of Slavery: Struggles Against Caste Inequality in Colonial Kerala*. Oxford University Press, 2015.

More, J. B. P. *Origin and Early History of the Muslims of Keralam, 700 AD–1600 AD*. Other Books, 2011.

Mosse, David. *The Saint in the Banyan Tree: Christianity and Caste Society in India*. University of California Press, 2012.

———. "Caste and Development." *World Development* 110 (2018): 422–436.

Narayan, Badri. "Inventing Caste History: Dalit Mobilisation and Nationalist Past." *Contributions to Indian Sociology* 38, no. 1–2 (2004): 193–220.

———. *The Making of the Dalit Public in North India: Uttar Pradesh, 1950–Present*. Oxford University Press, 2012.

Naseef, M. K., and Santhosh, R. "Waqf and Authority Dynamics: Reconfigurations of a Pious Institution in Colonial Malabar, South India." *Society and Culture in South Asia* 8, no. 1 (2022): 51–71.

Nasr, Seyyed H., et al. *The Study Quran: A New Translation and Commentary*. HarperOne, 2015.

Niazi, Soheb. "Sayyids and Social Stratification of Muslims in Colonial India: Genealogy and Narration of the Past in Amroha." *Journal of the Royal Asiatic Society* 30, no. 3 (2020): 467–487.

Obeyesekere, Gananath. *Karma and Rebirth: A Cross Cultural Study.* Motilal Banarasidass, 2005.

Omvedt, Gail. *Dalit Visions: The Anti-Caste Movement and the Construction of an Indian Identity.* Orient Longman, (1995) 2006.

Ortner, Sherry. *Anthropology and Social Theory: Culture, Power, and the Acting Subject.* Duke University Press, 2006.

Osella, Caroline. "Vital Exchanges: Land and Persons in Kerala." In *Territory, Soil and Society in South Asia*, edited by Daniele Berti and Gilles Tarabout. Manohar, 2009.

———. "Debating Shirk in Keralam, South India: Monotheism between Tradition, Text and Performance", *Open Library of Humanities* 1, no. 1 (2015): e7. Online: https://doi.org/10.16995/olh.22.

Osella, Filippo, and Benjamin Soares. "Religiosity and Its Others: Lived Islam in West Africa and South India." *Social Anthropology* 28, no. 2 (2020): 466–481.

Osella, Filippo, and Caroline Osella. "Migration, Money and Masculinity in Kerala." *Journal of the Royal Anthropological Institute* 6, no. 1 (2000a): 117–133.

———. *Social Mobility in Kerala: Modernity and Identity in Conflict.* Pluto Press, 2000b.

———. "Islamism and Social Reform in Kerala, South India." *Modern Asian Studies* 42, no. 2/3 (2008): 317–346.

———, eds. *Islamic Reform in South Asia.* Cambridge University Press, 2013.

Paik, Shailaja. *The Vulgarity of Caste: Dalits, Sexuality, and Humanity in Modern India.* Stanford University Press, 2022.

Panakkal, Abbas, and Nasr M. Arif, eds. *Matrilineal, Matriarchal, and Matrifocal Isal: The World of Women-Centric Islam.* Palgrave Macmillan, 2024.

Panakkal, Abbas, and K. M. Baharul Islam. "Cultural Integration in Muslim Communities: The Case of Malabar and Assam." In *South Asian Islam: A Spectrum of Integration and Indigenization*, edited by Nasr M. Arif and Abbas Panakkal. Routledge, 2024.

Pandey, Gyanendra. *The Construction of Communalism in Colonial North India.* Oxford University Press, 2006.

Pandian, Jacob. "The Hindu Caste System and Muslim Ethnicity: The Labbai of a Tamil Village in South India." *Ethnohistory* 25, no. 2 (1978): 141–157.

———. "Political Emblems of Caste Identity: An Interpretation of Tamil Caste Titles." *Anthropological Quarterly* 56, no. 4 (1983): 190–197.

Pandian, M. S. S. "One Step Outside Modernity: Caste, Identity Politics and Public Sphere." *Economic and Political Weekly* 37, no. 18 (2002): 1735–1741.

Panikkar, K. N. *Against the Lord and State: Religion and Peasant Uprisings in Malabar, 1836–1921.* Oxford University Press, 2001.

Parry, Jonathan. "Egalitarian Values in a Hierarchical Society." *South Asian Review* 7, no. 2 (1974): 95–119.

Parry, Jonathan, and Maurice Bloch, eds. *Money and the Morality of Exchange.* Cambridge University Press, 1989.

Patel, Kamna. "What Is in a Name? How Caste Names Affect the Production of Situated Knowledge." *Gender, Place & Culture* 24, no. 7 (2017): 1011–1030.

Pemberton, Kelly. "Women *Pirs*, Saintly Succession, and Spiritual Guidance in South Asian Sufism." *Muslim World* 96 (2006): 61–87.

Perumal, Shahdab. "Smell as a Marker of Social Boundary: Exploring the Role of Fish 'Stench.'" *South Asia: Journal of South Asian Studies*, 1–14. https://doi.org/10.1080/00856401.2024 .2440253

Piliavsky, Anastasia, ed. *Patronage as Politics in South Asia*. Cambridge University Press, 2014.

Piliavsky, Anastasia. *Nobody's People: Hierarchy as Hope in a Society of Thieves*. Stanford University Press, 2021.

Poyer, Lin. "Egalitarianism in the Face of Hierarchy." *Journal of Anthropological Research* 49, no. 2 (1993): 111–133.

Prakash, Aseem. "Dalits Enter the Indian Market as Owners of Capital: Adverse Inclusion, Social Networks, and Civil Society." *Economic and Political Weekly* 55, no. 5 (2015): 1044–1069.

Prakash, Gyan. "Reproducing Inequality: Spirit Cults and Labor Relations in Colonial Eastern India." *Modern Asian Studies* 20, no. 2 (1986): 209–230.

Prange, Sebastian. *Monsoon Islam: Trade and Faith on the Medieval Malabar Coast*. Cambridge University Press, 2018.

———. "Monsoon Landscape of Integrated Islam." In *South Asian Islam: A Spectrum of Integration and Indigenization*, edited by Nasr M Arif and Abbas Panakkal. Routledge, 2024.

Radhakrishnan, P. *Peasant Struggles, Land Reforms and Social Change: Malabar, 1836–1982*. Sage Publications, 1989.

Raheja, Gloria Goodwin. *The Poison in the Gift: Ritual, Prestation, and the Dominant Caste in a North Indian Village*. University of Chicago Press, 1988.

Rai, Santosh Kumar. "Social Histories of Exclusion and Moments of Resistance: The Case of Muslim Julaha Weavers in Colonial United Provinces." *Indian Economic and Social History Review* 55, no. 4 (2018): 549–574.

Rajan, S. Irudaya, and K. C. Zachariah. "Emigration and Remittances: New Evidences from the Kerala Migration Survey 2018." *CDS Working Paper* 483, (2019): 1–108.

Rathore, Gayatri J. S. "Asserting Caste? Bhishti Sanitation Workers and Muslim Caste Associations in Jaipur." *Contemporary South Asia* 31, no. 3 (2023): 469–482.

Ravindran, Gopinath. "Agrarian Production Processes, and Rural Inequality in Nineteenth-Century Malabar." *Studies in People's History* 3, no. 1 (2016): 29–44.

Rawat, Ramnarayan S. *Reconsidering Untouchability: Chamars and Dalit History in North India*. Indiana University Press, 2011.

Ricci, Ronit. *Islam Translated: Literature, Conversion, and the Arabic Cosmopolis of South and Southeast Asia*. University of Chicago Press, 2011.

Rio, Knut and Olaf H. Smedal., eds. *Hierarchy: Persistence and Transformation in Social Formations*. Berghahn Books, 2009.

Rio, Knut. "Melanesian Egalitarianism: The Containment of Hierarchy." *Anthropological Theory* 14, no. 2 (2014): 169–190.

Robbins, Joel. "Monism, Pluralism and the Structure of Value Relations: A Dumontian Contribution to the Contemporary Study of Value." *HAU: Journal of Ethnographic Theory* 3, no. 1 (2013): 99–115.

Robbins, Joel, and Jukka Siikala. "Hierarchy and Hybridity: Toward a Dumontian Approach to Contemporary Cultural Change." *Anthropological Theory* 14, no. 2 (2014): 121–132.

Robbins, Joel, and Julian Sommerschuh. "Values." In *The Open Encyclopedia of Anthropology*, edited by Felix Stein, 2016. Online: http://doi.org/10.29164/16values.

Robinson, Francis. "Islam and Muslim Society in South Asia." *Contributions to Indian Sociology* 17, no. 2 (1983): 185–203.

————. "Islamic Reform and Modernities in South Asia." *Modern Asian Studies* 42, no. 2–3 (2008): 259–281.

Robinson, Rowena, and Sathianathan Clarke, eds. *Religious Conversion in India: Modes, Motivations, and Meanings.* Oxford University Press, 2007.

Rousseau, Jean-Jacques. *The Discourse and Other Early Political Writings.* Cambridge University Press, (1755) 2018.

Roy, Asim. *Islamic Syncretic Tradition in Bengal.* Princeton University Press, 1983.

Safdar, Muhammad R., et al. "Socioeconomic Determinants of Caste-Based Endogamy: A Qualitative Study." *Journal of Ethnic and Cultural Studies* 8, no. 2 (2021): 39–54.

Saidalavi, P. C. "Muslim Social Organisation and Cultural Islamisation in Malabar." *South Asia Research* 37, no. 1 (2017): 19–36.

————. "Beyond the Normative: Ambiguity in the Making of a South Indian Sufi." *American Anthropologist* 124, no. 2 (2022): 319–332.

————. "Seeking *Antassu*: The Making of a Muslim Barber in South India." *HAU: Journal of Ethnographic Theory* 15, no. 1 (2025): 45–58.

————. "Ethical Listening Within a Culture of Difference." *Anthropology and Humanism* (forthcoming).

Samin, Navad. "Kafā'a fī l-Nasab in Saudi Arabia: Islamic Law, Tribal Custom, and Social Change." *Journal of Arabian Studies* 2, no. 2 (2012): 109–126.

Sarukkai, Sundar. "Experience and Theory: From Habermas to Gopal Guru." In *The Cracked Mirror: An Indian Debate on Experience and Theory*, Gopal Guru and Sundar Sarukkai. Oxford University Press, 2012.

Schielke, Samuli. "Being Good in Ramadan: Ambivalence, Fragmentation and the Moral Self in the Lives of Young Egyptians." *Journal of the Royal Anthropological Institute* 15, no. 1 (2009): S24-S40.

Schielke, Samuli, and Liza Debevec, eds. *Ordinary Lives and Grand Schemes: An Anthropology of Everyday Religion.* Berghahn, 2012.

Schneider, David M., and Gough, Kathleen, eds. *Matrilineal Kinship.* University of California Press, 1961.

Scott, James C. *Domination and the Arts of Resistance.* Yale University Press, 1990.

Shah, Alpa, et al. *Ground Down by Growth: Tribe, Caste, Class, and Inequality in Twenty-First-Century India.* Pluto Press, 2018.

Shah, A. M. *Exploring India's Rural Past: A Gujarat Village in the Early Nineteenth Century.* Oxford University Press, 2002.

Shah, Hafsa S. "Organising the Sheikh Sanitation Workers in Srinagar: From the Politics of Dignity to Pasmanda Activism." *Contemporary South Asia* 31, no. 3 (2023): 451–468.

Sharma, Arvind. "The Puruṣasūkta: Its Relation to the Caste System." *Journal of the Economic and Social History of the Orient* 21, no. 3 (1978): 294–303.

Shilling, Chris. *The Body and Social Theory.* Sage Publications, 1993.

Shultziner, Doron. "Human Dignity: Functions and Meanings." In *Perspectives on Human Dignity: A Conversation*, edited by Jeff Malpas and Norelle Lickiss. Springer, 2007.

Shultziner, Doron, and Itai Rabinovici. "Human Dignity, Self-Worth, and Humiliation: A Comparative Legal-Psychological Approach." *Psychology, Public Policy, and Law* 18, no. 1 (2012): 105–143.

Silva, Kalinga T. "Buddhism, Social Justice and Caste: Reflections on Buddhist Engagement with Caste in India and Sri Lanka." *History and Sociology of South Asia* 2 (2017): 220–232.

Simmel, Georg. *The Philosophy of Money*. Translated by Tom Bottomore and David Frisby. Routledge, 2004.

Smith-Hefner, Nancy J. *Islamizing Intimacies: Youth, Sexuality, and Gender in Contemporary Indonesia*. University of Hawaii Press, 2019.

Soloman, P. A., ed. *Travancore Coir Factory Workers Union Golden Jubilee Souvenir*. 1972.

Srinivas, M. N. "A Note on Sanskritization and Westernization." *Far Eastern Quarterly* 15, no. 4 (1956): 481–496.

———. *Social Change in Modern India*. Orient Blackswan, (1972) 2020.

Standing, Guy. "Understanding the Precariat Through Labour and Work." *Development and Change* 45, no. 5 (2014): 963–980.

Stewart, Tony K. "In Search of Equivalence: Conceiving Muslim-Hindu Encounter Through Translation Theory." *History of Religions* 40, no. 3 (2001): 260–287.

Strathern, Marilyn. *The Gender of the Gift: Problems with Women and Problems with Society in Melanesia*. University of California Press, 1988.

Stuart, H.A. *Census of India, 1891, Vol. XIII, Madras, Report*. The Superintendent Government Press, 1893.

Subramanian, Ajantha. *The Caste of Merit: Engineering Education in India*. Harvard University Press, 2019.

Suseendirarajah, S. "Caste and Language in Jaffna Society." *Anthropological Linguistics* 20, no. 7 (1978): 312–319.

Tarlo, Emma. *Entanglement: The Secret Lives of Hair*. Oneworld Publications, 2017.

Tharamangalam, Joseph. *Agrarian Class Conflict: The Political Mobilisation of Agricultural Labourers in Kuttanad, South India*. University of British Columbia Press, 1981.

Thiranagama, Sharika. "Respect Your Neighbor as Yourself: Neighborliness, Caste, and Community in South India." *Comparative Studies in Society and History* 61, no. 2 (2019): 269–300.

Thompson, E. P. "Time, Work-Discipline, and Industrial Capitalism." *Past and Present* 38, no. 1 (1967): 56–97.

Twigg, Julia, et al. "Conceptualising Body Work in Health and Social Care." *Sociology of Health & Illness* 33, no. 2 (2011): 171–188.

Uddin, Layli. "Casteist Demons and Working-Class Prophets: Subaltern Islam in Bengal, Circa 1872–1928." *Journal of Royal Asiatic Society* 33, no. 4 (2023): 1051–1075.

Varghese, George K. "Writing Family Histories: Identity Construction Among Syrian Christians." *Economic and Political Weekly* 39, no. 9 (2004): 897–900.

Varisco, Daniel M. "Metaphors and Sacred History: The Genealogy of Muhammad and the Arab 'Tribe.'" *Anthropological Quarterly* 68, no. 3 (2004): 139–156.

Vatuk, Sylvia. "Identity and Difference or Equality and Inequality in South Asian Muslim Society." In *Caste Today*, edited by C. J. Fuller. Oxford University Press, 1996.

Veer, Peter van der. *Religious Nationalism: Hindus and Muslims in India*. University of California Press, 1994.

Visakh, M. S., R. Santhosh, and C. K. Mohammed Roshan. "Islamic Traditionalism in a Globalizing World: Sunni Muslim Identity in Kerala, South India." *Modern Asian Studies* 55, no. 6 (2021): 2046–2087.

Viswanath, Rupa. *The Pariah Problem: Caste, Religion, and the Social in Modern India*. Columbia University Press, 2014.

Ward, Benjamin S., and Peter E. Conner. *Memoir of the Survey of the Travancore and Cochin States*. Travancore Sircar Press, 1863.

Werbner, Pnina. *Pilgrims of Love: The Anthropology of a Global Sufi Cult*. Hurst and Company, 2003.

Wiessner, Polly. "The Vines of Complexity." *Current Anthropology* 43, no. 2 (2002): 233–69.

Wiser, William H. *The Hindu Jajmani System*. Lucknow Publishing House, 1936.

Wolkowitz, Carol. "The Social Relations of Body Work." *Work, Employment and Society* 16, no. 3 (2002): 497–510.

———. *Bodies at Work*. Sage Publications, 2006.

Yanagisawa, Kiwamu and Shuji Funo. "How Mohallas were Formed: Typology of Mohallas from the Viewpoint of Spatial Formation and the Urbanization Process in Varanasi, India." *Japan Architectural Review* 1, no. 3 (2018): 385–395.

Ziadeh, Farhat J. "Equality (Kafā'ah) in the Muslim Law of Marriage." *American Journal of Comparative Law* 6, no. 4 (1957): 503–517.

Zigon, Jarrett. "Within a Range of Possibilities: Morality and Ethics in Social Life." *Ethnos* 74 no. 2 (2009): 251–276.

INDEX

abstract labor, 128, 134; capitalistic modulations of, 153
acculturation, idea of, 77
adultery, 2
adutthōn, 33, 141
aesthetic ecology, notion of, 122
agrarian relations, in colonial Malabar, 69–70
agrestic slaves, 8, 39
agricultural economy, 90
agricultural income, decline of, 132
agricultural labor, 18, 39, 47–48, 70, 71, 120, 128, 132, 134, 187–88
agricultural landless labor, in Kerala, 132
agricultural tenants and labor, demands of, 132
Ahmad, Imtiaz, 5
Ahmad, Zarin, 110
Ahmed, Shahab, 15, 21, 156
Ahmedian line of reasoning, 21
Ajlafs (commoners or Indian Muslims), 107
Alam, Arshad, 39
Al Fiqhul Islami, 76
Aligarh Muslim University, 95
Allah, 3, 21, 53, 90, 157, 158, 186
All India Pasmanda Muslim Mahaz (1998), 108
All India United Muslim Morcha (1993), 108
Ambedkar, B. R., 82, 94
Amir, Safwan, 81
Ammerman, Nancy, 14
Anchillath, Abdulla, 196n7
angādikkār (townspeople), 43
Ansari, Gaus, 5
Ansari, Khalid A., 108
antassu, 15, 23, 191; concept of, 128–32; construction of, 142; within the

household, 147–49; indexing of, 149–52; and institutionalizing of money, 142–45; value of, 152
anthropological scholarship, in South Asia, 8
anthropology of Islam, 13–14
anti-caste and self-respect movements, in India, 94
anti-caste mobilization, 83
anti-caste politics, in India, 187
Arabic (divine tongue of the Quran), 30
Arabic cosmopolis, 30
Arabic teaching (Afzalul Ulema), 169
Arabimalayalam writings, in the nineteenth century, 41
Arab missionary, 25, 191
Arab Muslims, 18, 25, 30, 33–34, 46, 160, 163, 190–91
Arab origin, theory of, 107
Arab traders, 38
artha, politico-economic domain of, 6
Arya Samajists, 111
Ashraf-Ajlaf-Arzal distinction, 111
Ashraf-Ajlaf distinction, 107
Ashrafs (nobles and foreigners), 107
assistant educational officer (AEO), 93
authenticity, notions of, 84
azān, 197n10

Babb, Lawrence, 51, 82
baradari, 107, 114
barber child, socialization of, 64
barber community (*ossān*/otthān/*ostha*), 1, 3, 18, 19, 22, 25, 32–37, 48, 97, 141; among Hindu castes, 59; awareness of social subordination, 135, 159; badge of honor, 144; behavior of Muslims toward, 81; bloodletting and circumcision work, 35, 58; collective strategies for livelihood,

ACKNOWLEDGMENTS

The idea of caste began to capture my imagination in 2013. So, this book ges-
tated for more than a decade until it assumed a rough form as my PhD thesis titled *Hierarchy, Values and Islam: Social Organisation of Muslims in South
India* at the Australian National University (ANU) in 2022. Over its course,
this project has amassed a pile of debts in gratitude, camaraderie, and compan-
ionship. First, I feel a deep sense of gratefulness to Vipin Kumar Chirakkara
who initially instilled in me the confidence and rigor to pursue an intellectual
life. I also thank Arshad Alam who supervised my MPhil dissertation titled
Caste, Religion and Politics: Muslims in Malabar at Jawaharlal Nehru University, New Delhi in 2015.

Without the continuing support, encouragement, and guidance offered
by my PhD supervisors, Assa Doron and Ronit Ricci, I would not have been
able to accomplish this feat. I thank them deeply and I feel quite fortunate
to have received their discipleship. This book is, ultimately, also a product of
that relationship, with deep appreciation. I am also deeply grateful to Robin
Jeffrey and Matt Tomlinson, my co-supervisors, for their advice and incisive
comments on various parts of this work. I must also thank my examiners
Filippo Osella, Ronie Parciack, and Stefan Schütte for reading the earlier iter-
ation of this book with patience and care and for offering fruitful comments
and suggestions for publication.

Some of the ideas in this book were initially formed, presented to, and cri-
tiqued by my friends and colleagues at the weekly Thesis Writing Group for
the Anthropology program at ANU. I have presented drafts of all the chapters
written here and received immensely helpful comments and feedback each
time. I thank Yasmine Musharbash and Assa Doron, the two faculty mentors
who have provided very constructive suggestions. I thank my fellow graduate
students Alex D'Aolaila, Anthea Snowsill, Dinith Adikari, Elvin Yifu, I-Chang
Kuo, Luke Corbin, Patrick Horton, Ruonan Chen, and Shaun Gessler for
reading and commenting on various drafts. I also thank Geoff Piggott and

Teena Saulo who were my office mates at ANU. Sitting across from each other in the two corners of the office, they patiently listened to my rants, brewed a cup of coffee together, and were ready to discuss the trials and tribulations of PhD whenever I wanted.

I have also benefited immensely from the kindness of fellow scholars, friends, and colleagues at various institutions across the world. I thank Saidali P. P., Milind Dongre, Jabir, P. K. Shaheen, Abdul Majeed O. P., Hani Naseef K. T., Abdulla Anchillath, Abbas Panakkal, Muhammed Haneefa, Nuaiman K. A., Safwan Amir, Muhammad Ali Jauhar, Muhammed Asaf, Abid Kakkeri, Vinil Baby Paul, Justin Lau, Helen Abbott, Kirsty Wissing, Umar Assegaf, and Justine Chambers.

I have been encouraged, challenged, and offered advice and company in several ways by innumerable colleagues and friends at ANU, Shiv Nadar University (SNU), and beyond. In particular, I thank Aditya Balasubramanian, Muhammad A. Kavesh, Daniel Andrew Birchok, Bharani Kollipara, Ravi Nandan Singh, Urmila Bhirdikar, Tuhina Ganguly, and Devika Bordia for reading different chapters of the book and providing very helpful and productive thoughts and suggestions. Coffee and tea have been an invariable part of intellectual life at SNU, and I thank Divya Kannan, Vasundhara Bhojvaid, Subhashim Goswami, Roma Chatterji, Hemanth Kadambi, and Iman Kumar Mitra for continuing camaraderie, stimulating conversations, support, and encouragement.

Most important, I owe it all to my interlocutors who narrated their stories with laughter, pain, and sadness. I hope to have done justice to their narratives and sentiments. I particularly thank Hassankutty N. K., M. K. Muhammad Valanchery, P. K. Abu Nilambur, M. Ummar Alathiyur, Assain N. K. Mannur, Ummer Unniyalungal, and Ayisha Pathiriyal. I am deeply indebted to Saidalavi N. K. for his persisting interest in the project and constant queries and information regarding various aspects of Muslim social life in Malabar. I dedicate this book to the spirit and enthusiasm all my interlocutors showed for the project.

I have been to various libraries and archives across Kerala to look up old documents or read some magazines or books. The staff at the Calicut Regional Archives, particularly Varghese Samuel; the staff at the Appan Thampuran Library; and the staff at the C. H. Library, Calicut, have been immensely helpful.

Umma and Uppa, you have always been supportive of whatever I have ventured to do academically, even though you did not often understand the content or the purpose of what I have been doing. Your kindness and generosity have been kept alive to this day. I am fortunate to be your son, Alhamdulillah! I also thank my two siblings, Shameem and Mubashira for caring, supporting, and motivating throughout the writing process.

My wife Noora and our children Ilhan and Ishaal have been the force that kept me going through the hard times and helped me persist at reading, writing, and editing. It is all here now; thank you for being patient, accommodating, and supportive throughout this process. I love you.

Oh Allah! Everything is created by you, and everything is dependent on you. Alhamdulillah! Off this goes.

A version of Chapter 6 appeared as the article "Seeking Antassu: The Making of a Muslim Barber in South India," *HAU: Journal of Ethnographic Theory* 15, no. 1 (2025): 45–58.

www.ingramcontent.com/pod-product-compliance
Lightning Source LLC
Chambersburg PA
CBHW022307280326
41932CB00010B/1010